"I read *Gospel of Glory* with great pleasure and with my own commentary on John within reach. I found frequent agreement, occasional disagreement, and, on every page, enrichment. The first chapter alone ('individualism' in John's Gospel) is worth the price of the book. The chapter on the Gospel's first week offers a fascinating glimpse of what Bauckham's forthcoming commentary on John may look like, and yet *Gospel of Glory* is no mere appetizer but a meal in itself."

—**J. Ramsey Michaels**, Missouri State University, Springfield

"From individual to community, from glory to the cross, from sacraments to dualism, from the call of the disciples to their later witness, *Gospel of Glory* breaks new ground. Not only is John's narrative now welcomed to be read alongside the Synoptics in discerning the Jesus of history, but the Synoptics can now be read side by side fruitfully as informing the Christ of faith. Readers of John's Gospel—and of the others—will want to read this book!"

—**Paul N. Anderson**, George Fox University

GOSPEL OF GLORY

MAJOR THEMES IN JOHANNINE THEOLOGY

RICHARD BAUCKHAM

BakerAcademic

a division of Baker Publishing Group
Grand Rapids, Michigan

© 2015 by Richard Bauckham

Published by Baker Academic
a division of Baker Publishing Group
PO Box 6287, Grand Rapids, MI 49516-6287
www.bakeracademic.com

Printed in the United States of America

Library of Congress Cataloging-in-Publication Data
Bauckham, Richard.
    Gospel of glory : major themes in Johannine theology / Richard Bauckham.
        pages cm
    Includes bibliographical references and index.
    ISBN 978-0-8010-9612-9 (pbk.)
    1. Bible. John—Theology. I. Title.
BS2615.52.B379 2015
226.5′06—dc23   2015003289

15   16   17   18   19   20   21   7   6   5   4   3   2   1

In keeping with biblical principles of creation stewardship, Baker Publishing Group advocates the responsible use of our natural resources. As a member of the Green Press Initiative, our company uses recycled paper when possible. The text paper of this book is composed in part of post-consumer waste.

Dedicated to the memory of the great
British Johannine scholars:

Brooke Foss Westcott

Edwyn Clement Hoskyns

Charles Harold Dodd

John Arthur Thomas Robinson

Barnabas Lindars

Charles Kingsley Barrett

Contents

Preface

In this volume, I do not attempt a comprehensive coverage of the theology of John's Gospel but focus on some major themes, including some that have been much neglected and others that have been very much debated during the last century of New Testament scholarship. The most neglected of the topics I tackle is what in chapter 1 I call the "individualism" of the Gospel of John. (I put the term in quotes to indicate that it does not refer to the kind of individualism that characterizes contemporary Western culture.) This is a prominent aspect of the Gospel that most recent scholars have managed to ignore, probably because it is the last thing they would expect to find in John. Working on this topic, I became aware that in order to do justice to the Gospel, we must recognize that it lays emphasis both on the individual believer and on the community of believers. We should not allow either to cancel out the other. But the theme of community in John has the added dimension of characterizing John's understanding of God as well as his understanding of believers, and so chapter 2 explores the relationship of divine and human community.

Most Johannine scholars recognize that "glory" is a key term in the Gospel of John, but there are few extended treatments of it. Chapter 3 therefore offers an analytical overview of this theme. The cross of Christ, on the other hand, along with his resurrection and exaltation, has received a great deal of attention, not least in the commentaries. But in chapter 4 I have adopted a fresh approach by viewing the cross and the resurrection/exaltation of Jesus in relation to four key themes of the Gospel: love, life, glory, and truth. I believe this approach throws fresh light on John's understanding of the key events in his christological story. Chapters 5 ("Sacraments?") and 6 ("Dualisms") treat aspects of John's theology that have proved highly problematic and debatable in Johannine scholarship. There is nothing approaching a scholarly consensus on sacraments in John, not even on whether there is a sacramental aspect to his theology at all. This topic requires some methodological rigor if it is to be significantly clarified. In the title of chapter 6, I have used the plural noun in contrast to the usual talk of Johannine dualism. Discussion of this topic has suffered from oversimplification. By making distinctions between different kinds of duality in John, I hope to clarify the roles they play in his theology.

Chapter 7 adopts a quite different approach, focusing not on a theme but on a key section of the Gospel's narrative (1:19–2:11). The aim is to illuminate the way theological meaning is conveyed by narrative in this Gospel, one very remarkable feature of which is the wide range of additional dimensions of meaning beyond the literal meaning that the narratives are constructed to evoke. Finally, chapter 8 takes up the issue of the differences between the Johannine Jesus and the Jesus(es) of the Synoptic Gospels, not as an issue about the historical Jesus but as an issue about how Christian readers of the Gospels can read the four different Gospels as providing complementary angles on the ultimately one Christ of faith. It is a serious failure of Gospels scholarship in the service of the church and Christian faith that scholars seem commonly quite content to emphasize the distinctive portrayal of Jesus in each Gospel without facing the subsequent question: what are Christian believers to do with this diversity? This chapter is a first approach to reflection on how the diversity within the fourfold Gospel canon can function for Christian faith and theology that takes that fourfold canon seriously as its means of access to the one Jesus Christ who is the same yesterday, today, and forever.

Each chapter of this book is a self-contained essay, and so the chapters can be read in any order. Readers who are interested in my approach to such questions as the historical origins and context of the Gospel can turn to my earlier collection of essays[1] and in particular its introduction. In the present volume, I have left aside all such questions in order to focus entirely on the theological content of the Gospel.

Most of the chapters have a prehistory. The origins of chapter 1 lie in the third C. F. D. Moule Memorial Lecture, entitled "John: A Gospel for Individualists?," which I gave in June 2010 at Ridley Hall, Cambridge. (It was inspired by a significant but neglected article by Moule.) In a later incarnation, this lecture became the Graham Stanton Memorial Lecture, given in September 2010 in Bangor, Wales, at the British New Testament Conference of that year. I was delighted to be able to honor these two great New Testament scholars,

---

1. *The Testimony of the Beloved Disciple: Narrative, History, and Theology in the Gospel of John* (Grand Rapids: Baker Academic, 2007).

the latter a pupil of the former. Chapter 2 was designed as a companion to chapter 1, and I gave the two lectures at Western Theological Seminary, Holland, Michigan, in January 2012, when I also gave the lecture on which chapter 2 is based at the University of Notre Dame, South Bend, Indiana. This lecture made another appearance in the New Testament seminar at the University of Durham in February 2012. In 2013 I gave the Trinity Lectures at Trinity College, Singapore, under the title "Aspects of the Theology of John's Gospel." The four lectures in the series were those on which chapters 1, 2, 3, and 8 of this book are based. Chapter 8 also formed the Henton Davies Lecture for 2014, given at Regent's Park College, Oxford. I am very grateful to my hosts and my audiences on these various occasions, for making them enjoyable events and for the stimulating comments and questions I received. Finally, chapter 4 originated as a paper for a small symposium on the Gospel of John that took place at Madingley Hall, Cambridge, in January 2014. The highly interdisciplinary discussions of the small group of people chosen and gathered by David Ford for that occasion went beyond the confines of the discussions New Testament scholars usually have among themselves and proved very rewarding.

Two of the chapters are also published elsewhere. Chapter 5 is a longer version of "Sacraments and the Gospel of John," in *The Oxford Handbook of Sacramental Theology*, edited by Hans Boersma and Matthew Levering (Oxford: Oxford University Press, 2015), and is used here by permission of Oxford University Press. Chapter 6 was first published under the title "Dualism and Soteriology in Johannine Theology," in *Beyond Bultmann: Reckoning a New Testament Theology*, edited by Bruce W. Longenecker and Mikeal C. Parsons (Waco: Baylor University Press, 2014), 133–53, and appears here by permission of Baylor University Press.

Abbreviations

General and Bibliographic

AB	Anchor Bible
ABD	*Anchor Bible Dictionary*. Edited by D. N. Freedman. 6 vols. New York: Doubleday, 1992.
ACCS	Ancient Christian Commentary on Scripture
ACW	Ancient Christian Writers
AnBib	Analecta biblica
ANTC	Abingdon New Testament Commentaries
ASBF	Analecta Studium Biblicum Franciscanum
BECNT	Baker Exegetical Commentary on the New Testament
Bib	*Biblica*
BibInt	*Biblical Interpretation*
BIS	Biblical Interpretation Series
BNTC	Black's New Testament Commentaries
BRBS	Brill's Readers in Biblical Studies
BTB	*Biblical Theology Bulletin*
CBQ	*Catholic Biblical Quarterly*
ConBNT	Coniectanea biblica: New Testament Series
ConC	Concordia Commentary
DCH	*Dictionary of Classical Hebrew*. Edited by David J. A. Clines. 8 vols. Sheffield: Sheffield Phoenix Press, 1993–2011.
DRev	*Downside Review*
DSD	*Dead Sea Discoveries*
ECC	Eerdmans Critical Commentary
ExpTim	*Expository Times*

FCB	Feminist Companion to the Bible
ICC	International Critical Commentary
JAJS	Journal of Ancient Judaism Supplements
JBL	*Journal of Biblical Literature*
JSNT	*Journal for the Study of the New Testament*
JSNTSup	Journal for the Study of the New Testament: Supplement Series
JSPSup	Journal for the Study of the Pseudepigrapha: Supplement Series
LD	Lectio divina
LNTS	Library of New Testament Studies
LQ	*Lutheran Quarterly*
LSTS	Library of Second Temple Studies
LTP	*Laval théologique et philosophique*
LTPM	Louvain Theological and Pastoral Monographs
LXX	Septuagint, Greek Old Testament
NBf	*New Blackfriars*
NCB	New Century Bible
Neot	*Neotestamentica*
NETS	*A New English Translation of the Septuagint.* Edited by Albert Pietersma and Benjamin G. Wright. New York: Oxford University Press, 2007.
NICNT	New International Commentary on the New Testament
NIGTC	New International Greek Testament Commentary
NovT	*Novum Testamentum*
NovTSup	Supplements to Novum Testamentum
NSBT	New Studies in Biblical Theology
NTL	New Testament Library
NTS	*New Testament Studies*
NTT	New Testament Theology
OTP	*Old Testament Pseudepigrapha.* Edited by J. H. Charlesworth. 2 vols. New York: Doubleday, 1983–85.
RB	*Revue biblique*
RevScRel	*Revue de sciences religieuses*
RSR	*Recherches de science religieuse*
SBAZ	Studien zur biblischen Archäologie und Zeitgeschichte
SBLAB	Society of Biblical Literature Academia Biblica
SBLECL	Society of Biblical Literature Early Christianity and Its Literature
SBLEJL	Society of Biblical Literature Early Judaism and Its Literature
SBLMS	Society of Biblical Literature Monograph Series
SBLSymS	Society of Biblical Literature Symposium Series
SBT	Studies in Biblical Theology

SC	Sources chrétiennes
SHS	Scripture and Hermeneutics Series
SJLA	Studies in Judaism in Late Antiquity
SNTA	Studiorum Novi Testamenti auxilia
SNTSMS	Society for New Testament Studies Monograph Series
SP	Sacra Pagina
STDJ	Studies on the Texts of the Desert of Judah
SVTQ	*St. Vladimir's Theological Quarterly*
TDOT	*Theological Dictionary of the Old Testament*. Edited by G. J. Botterweck and H. Ringgren. Translated by J. T. Willis, G. W. Bromiley, and D. E. Green. Grand Rapids: Eerdmans, 1974–.
ThTo	*Theology Today*
TJ	*Theological Journal*
TNTC	Tyndale New Testament Commentaries
TS	*Theological Studies*
TynBul	*Tyndale Bulletin*
WBC	Word Biblical Commentary
WUNT	Wissenschaftliche Untersuchungen zum Neuen Testament

Old Testament

Gen.	Genesis	Song	Song of Songs
Exod.	Exodus	Isa.	Isaiah
Lev.	Leviticus	Jer.	Jeremiah
Num.	Numbers	Lam.	Lamentations
Deut.	Deuteronomy	Ezek.	Ezekiel
Josh.	Joshua	Dan.	Daniel
Judg.	Judges	Hosea	Hosea
Ruth	Ruth	Joel	Joel
1–2 Sam.	1–2 Samuel	Amos	Amos
1–2 Kings	1–2 Kings	Obad.	Obadiah
1–2 Chron.	1–2 Chronicles	Jon.	Jonah
Ezra	Ezra	Mic.	Micah
Neh.	Nehemiah	Nah.	Nahum
Esther	Esther	Hab.	Habakkuk
Job	Job	Zeph.	Zephaniah
Ps(s).	Psalm(s)	Hag.	Haggai
Prov.	Proverbs	Zech.	Zechariah
Eccles.	Ecclesiastes	Mal.	Malachi

New Testament

Matt.	Matthew	1–2 Thess.	1–2 Thessalonians
Mark	Mark	1–2 Tim.	1–2 Timothy
Luke	Luke	Titus	Titus
John	John	Philem.	Philemon
Acts	Acts	Heb.	Hebrews
Rom.	Romans	James	James
1–2 Cor.	1–2 Corinthians	1–2 Pet.	1–2 Peter
Gal.	Galatians	1–3 John	1–3 John
Eph.	Ephesians	Jude	Jude
Phil.	Philippians	Rev.	Revelation
Col.	Colossians		

Other Jewish and Christian Writings

Ag. Ap.	Josephus, *Against Apion*
Ant.	Josephus, *Jewish Antiquities*
1 Apol.	Justin, *Apologia I (First Apology)*
2 Bar.	*2 Baruch (Syriac Apocalypse)*
Barn.	*Barnabas*
b. Yebam.	Babylonian Talmud, *Yebamot*
CD	Cairo Genizah copy of the *Damascus Document*
Conf.	Philo, *On the Confusion of Tongues*
1 En.	*1 Enoch (Ethiopic Apocalypse)*
Jub.	*Jubilees*
J.W.	Josephus, *Jewish War*
Let. Aris.	*Letter of Aristeas*
Life	Josephus, *The Life*
m. 'Abot	Mishnah, *'Abot*
1–4 Macc.	1–4 Maccabees
m. Ketub.	Mishnah, *Ketubbot*
MT	Masoretic Text
Phld.	Ignatius, *To the Philadelphians*
1QH	*Thanksgiving Hymns*
1QM	*War Scroll*
1QpMic	*Pesher to Micah*
1QS	*Community Rule*
4Q177	*4QCatena A*

11QT	*Temple Scroll*
Rom.	Ignatius, *To the Romans*
Sir.	Sirach
Smyrn.	Ignatius, *To the Smyrnaeans*
Spec.	Philo, *On the Special Laws*
Strom.	Clement of Alexandria, *Stromata (Miscellanies)*
T. Jos.	*Testament of Joseph*
Tob.	Tobit
Trall.	Ignatius, *To the Trallians*
Virt.	Philo, *On the Virtues*
Wis.	Wisdom of Solomon

1

"Individualism"

The title of this chapter echoes that of an article that Charles F. D. Moule published in 1962: "The Individualism of the Fourth Gospel."[1] But, unlike Moule, I have put the word "individualism" in quotation marks. It has become quite a slippery word, and the issues it might evoke for New Testament scholars today are not necessarily those that Moule had in mind. He was not thinking of the contrast between individualist and collectivist cultures that may well occur to us, either because we have become aware of how exceptional the extremely individualistic culture of the modern West is, or because we have been warned not to read modern Western individualism, anachronistically or ethnocentrically, into the New Testament. When Moule referred to the individualism of the Fourth Gospel, he meant that this Gospel lays considerable emphasis on the relationship of the individual believer to Jesus Christ,[2] by contrast with

1. Charles F. D. Moule, "The Individualism of the Fourth Gospel," *NovT* 5 (1962): 171–90; reprinted in Charles F. D. Moule, *Essays in New Testament Interpretation* (Cambridge: Cambridge University Press, 1982), 91–109; and in *The Composition of John's Gospel: Selected Studies from Novum Testamentum*, ed. David E. Orton, BRBS 2 (Leiden: Brill, 1999), 21–40. See also Charles F. D. Moule, "A Neglected Factor in the Interpretation of Johannine Eschatology," in *Studies in John: Presented to Professor Dr. J. N. Sevenster on the Occasion of His Seventieth Birthday*, ed. M. C. Rientsma, NovTSup 24 (Leiden: Brill, 1970), 155–60, where he extends his argument to 1 John.
2. This is also what John F. O'Grady means by the "individualism" of the Gospel ("Individualism and the Johannine Ecclesiology," *BTB* 5 [1975]: 235–45).

the more corporate understanding of the Christian community to be found in the Pauline literature.[3] As we shall see, Moule was quite correct in claiming that, even though he presented only a small part of the evidence for it. It is remarkable how few scholars writing since Moule have noticed this feature of the Gospel at all,[4] perhaps because the imaginary Johannine community has cast such a spell over Johannine scholarship.[5]

Clarifications and Definitions

Daniel Shanahan remarks that "the term 'individualism' opens up a labyrinth of meaning."[6] There is a large literature—in anthropology, classical studies, medieval and modern history, political philosophy, postmodern philosophy, social psychology, and other disciplines. There is also considerable debate over whether the individualism of the modern West should be evaluated positively or negatively. It is not surprising that the meaning of the term is not entirely stable, and so I want to begin with some clarifications and definitions.

First, I would distinguish between individualism, on the one hand, and individuation or individuality, on the other.[7] Individualism is a cultural variable, but individuality is a feature of all human experience. At least, if ever there was human experience without individuation, it predated the historical

3. Moule, "Individualism," 104.

4. Those who have noted it include O'Grady, "Individualism"; James D. G. Dunn, *Jesus and the Spirit: A Study of the Religious and Charismatic Experience of the First Christians as Reflected in the New Testament* (London: SCM, 1975), 354–55; Raymond E. Brown, *The Churches the Apostles Left Behind* (London: Chapman, 1984), 84–101; Jerome H. Neyrey, *An Ideology of Revolt: John's Christology in Social-Science Perspective* (Philadelphia: Fortress, 1988), 145; Thomas L. Brodie, *The Gospel according to John: A Literary and Theological Commentary* (New York: Oxford University Press, 1993), 31–39; George B. Caird, *New Testament Theology*, ed. L. D. Hurst (Oxford: Clarendon, 1994), 221; D. Moody Smith, *The Theology of the Gospel of John*, NTT (Cambridge: Cambridge University Press, 1995), 145; Ruth Edwards, *Discovering John* (London: SPCK, 1993), 140–41; Raymond E. Brown, *An Introduction to the Gospel of John*, ed. Francis J. Moloney (New York: Doubleday, 2003), 226–27.

5. For my view that the Gospel of John was not written for any specific Christian community and that the quest for the "Johannine community" has been fruitless, see Richard Bauckham, "For Whom Were Gospels Written?," in *The Gospels for All Christians: Rethinking the Gospel Audiences*, ed. Richard Bauckham (Grand Rapids: Eerdmans/Edinburgh: T&T Clark, 1997), 9–48; Bauckham, *The Testimony of the Beloved Disciple: Narrative, History, and Theology in the Gospel of John* (Grand Rapids: Baker Academic, 2007), 21–22, 113–23.

6. Daniel Shanahan, *Toward a Genealogy of Individualism* (Amherst: University of Massachusetts Press, 1992), 13.

7. For the distinction, see Nigel Rapport, *Transcendent Individual: Towards a Literary and Liberal Anthropology* (London: Routledge, 1997), 6; Anthony P. Cohen, *Self Consciousness: An Alternative Anthropology of Identity* (London: Routledge, 1994), 168–69; Gary W. Burnett, *Paul and the Salvation of the Individual*, BIS 57 (Leiden: Brill, 2001), 46.

record. By individuality, I mean self-awareness, the individual's awareness of self as a distinguishable entity, not merely in a physical sense but in terms of subjectivity. Human beings in all cultures throughout history have been aware of themselves as distinct subjects of feeling, thinking, decision, and action. After all, it is demonstrable that even nonhuman primates have a degree of self-awareness, evidenced by their ability to recognize themselves in a mirror. There is no doubt that first-century people could recognize themselves in mirrors. Perhaps somewhat more controversially, I would say that the self-awareness that is universally characteristic of humans makes introspection and inner dialogue possible.[8]

This universal self-awareness need not imply the strong sense of unique personality that modern individualism entails, nor does it make the individual the sovereign arbiter of his or her destiny in the modern, "I did it my way" sense. Doubtless for many ancient people their personal narrative was more about what happened to them and what God or the gods did to them and for them than it was about personal achievement. It was closely entwined with the narrative of the group to which they belonged, and it distinguished the unique individual more in terms of roles, types, and relationships than in terms of complex personality.[9]

Debates about individualism in ancient Mediterranean societies are sometimes clouded by the mistaken perception that what I have called individuation or individuality is at stake. Usually it is not. On the contrary, individuality is presupposed. The "dyadic personality" that Mediterranean anthropology reveals, according to Bruce Malina,[10] is a case in point. To say that an individual's self-perception is dependent on, even determined by others' perception of him or her, presupposes that the individual does have self-perception. Similarly and importantly, to claim that ancient people perceived the self in relational terms, as essentially related to others or to the group, rather than as the autonomous and atomized individuals that modern individualism envisages, presupposes selves that were distinguishable, however closely related. Without individuation there would be, not relationality, but sheer undifferentiated mass.

8. For the Greco-Roman world, see F. Gerald Downing, "Persons in Relation," in *Making Sense in (and of) the First Christian Century*, JSNTSup 197 (Sheffield: Sheffield Academic Press, 2000), 43–61, here 57–60.

9. But portraiture (e.g., at Palmyra and in Roman Egypt) deserves study as evidence of a strong sense of individuality.

10. Bruce J. Malina, *The New Testament World: Insights from Cultural Anthropology*, 2nd ed. (Louisville: Westminster John Knox, 1993), 67. For an argument that modern Western people are more "dyadic" than their individualist ideology admits, see Downing, "Persons in Relation," 45–46.

Individualism is usefully understood by contrast with its opposite: collectivism. A minimal definition is that in an individualist society the goals of the individual take precedence over the goals of the group, whereas in a collectivist society the goals of the society take precedence over the goals of the individual.[11] But it is very important to note that societies are not simply individualistic or collectivist; rather, they are located on a spectrum, making them more or less individualistic, more or less collectivist. Moreover, within any society there will be some people who are more individualistic, some more collectivist. These variables mean that the mix and the pattern of individualism and collectivism in any historical society cannot be predicted through the dogmatic imposition of a model but must be allowed to emerge from detailed study of the historical evidence.

With regard to first-century Greco-Roman society, including Jewish Palestine—although ideally one would want to be more specific than that—I work with a very general hypothesis: as societies go, it was a relatively collectivist one, certainly much more so than our own; but, whereas social goals and norms were powerful, they were not irresistible by the individual. We can observe them being resisted especially in two kinds of ways. First, there is the selfish individual who breaks with the conventions and expectations of the group in order to pursue personal gain.[12] Such behavior was strongly disapproved but certainly occurred, as in the case of the prodigal son in the parable. But, second, individuals could break with group norms and responsibilities for reasons of religious or philosophical conviction. It seems to me that it is with figures such as the Cynics or the desert fathers that Malina's model is insufficiently flexible to deal adequately.

The Johannine Evidence

Aphoristic Sayings about the Individual's Relationship with Jesus

As far as I know, the evidence in the Gospel of John for a strong emphasis on the individual's relationship with Jesus has never been adequately assembled or assessed. I offer two main types of evidence, of which the first is *aphoristic sayings about the individual's relationship with Jesus*. I have analyzed this material in table 1.1, where I list sixty-seven sayings in five different grammatical forms. I call them aphoristic sayings because they conform to these fixed literary forms and because the majority of them, though they suit their

---

11. Bruce J. Malina, *The Social World of Jesus and the Gospels* (London: Routledge, 1996), 74; Burnett, *Paul*, 46–50, both following cross-cultural psychologist Harry C. Triandis.
12. See Burnett, *Paul*, 33.

context, could also be lifted out of their contexts and would make sense as stand-alone aphorisms. In the case of double sayings like the first example in table 1.1 ("The one who believes in the Son has eternal life, but the one who refuses to believe in the Son will not see life"), I have counted such a double saying as two sayings. If one counted only one saying in such cases, then the total number of sayings would fall, but would still be more than fifty. For the sake of comparison I have also listed the quite numerous examples in the Johannine letters.

In most cases these sayings are quite explicitly about the individual's relationship with Jesus, but in a few cases the relationship with Jesus is only implicit. Nevertheless, we clearly have here a type of saying, prolific in the Gospel, whose specific function is to speak of the individual's relationship with Jesus. (It is unfortunate that some recent translations, such as the NRSV, turn many of these sayings into plural form. This has the laudable purpose of avoiding gendered language, but it obscures a notable feature of the Gospel.)

To appreciate the significance of these sayings, consider, for example, the justly famous 3:16 (justly famous because it admirably summarizes this Gospel's narrative of salvation): "God so loved the world that he gave his only Son, so that everyone who believes in him should not perish but have eternal life." John could have said "so that all who believe in him should not perish. . . ." Indeed, following the reference to the world ("God so loved the world") and preceding further references to the world in the following verse (God sent the Son "so that the world may be saved by him"), one might expect the plural rather than the singular form. But instead, even in this rather universalistic context, John's choice of the singular highlights believing in Jesus as the act of each individual. It is as though every individual stands alone before Jesus and must make his or her own act of faith—or of disbelief, as the case may be.

Many of these sayings are about "the one who believes" in Jesus, or use expressions broadly equivalent, such as "to come to" Jesus, "to drink from the water" Jesus gives, "to eat" the bread of life or the flesh of Jesus, "to look" to Jesus, "to accept" Jesus's testimony, "to enter the sheepfold through" Jesus the gate. Most of these sayings refer to eternal life as the consequence of believing in Jesus. Such sayings function to invite unbelievers to put faith in Jesus, and it is therefore not surprising that there are concentrations of them in Jesus's conversation with Nicodemus in chapter 3, in the Bread of Life Discourse in chapter 6, and in the summary of Jesus's message in the closing verses of chapter 12. In chapters 14–15, on the other hand, where Jesus addresses the disciples, the aphoristic sayings lay more emphasis on loving Jesus and keeping his commandments.

Of course, statements in the Gospel about people's relationship to Jesus are not limited to these aphoristic sayings. We find, for example, statements in the second person plural, addressed by Jesus to the crowds or the Jewish authorities or the disciples, the last especially in chapters 13–16. Jesus also talks about his disciples and future believers, in the third person plural, in his prayer to the Father in chapter 17. He pronounces a blessing on those who do not see and yet believe (20:29). This material is not insignificant, but in formal terms it is quite varied. Nothing like a standard aphoristic form is employed. Beside the second person plural and third person plural statements of many kinds, the third person singular aphoristic sayings stand out as dominant.

Table 1.1 Sixty-Seven Aphoristic Sayings about the Individual's Relationship with Jesus

Type 1. "**The one who . . .**" (*ho* + participle) (37 sayings)

Examples:

The one who believes in the Son has eternal life, but the one who refuses to believe in the Son will not see life, but must endure God's wrath. (3:36)

The one who loves me will be loved by my Father, and I will love him/her, and reveal myself to him/her. (14:21b)

John 3:18a; 3:18b; 3:21; 3:33; 3:36a; 3:36b; 5:23b; 5:24; 6:35a; 6:35b; 6:37b; 6:45; 6:47; 6:54; 6:56; 6:57; 6:58; 7:37–38; 8:12; 8:47; 11:25; 12:25a; 12:25b; 12:35; 12:44; 12:45; 12:48; 13:10; 13:20a; 13:20b; 14:9; 14:12; 14:21a; 14:21b; 14:24; 15:5; 15:23

(1 John 2:4; 2:6; 2:9; 2:10; 2:11; 3:7; 3:10c; 3:14b; 3:24; 4:6a; 4:8; 4:16c; 4:18b; 4:21b; 5:10a; 5:10b; 5:12a; 5:12b; 2 John 9b; 3 John 11a; 11b)

Type 2. "**If anyone . . .**" (*ean tis . . .*) (14 sayings)

Examples:

If anyone keeps my word, he/she will never see death. (8:51)

If anyone hears my words and does not keep them, I do not judge him/her. (12:47)

Readers or hearers are simply not allowed to forget that response to Jesus has to be individual to be real.

John could have created similar aphoristic sayings in the third person plural—"those who believe in me . . ."; "all those who keep my words . . ."—but he actually does so only once. This exception is a prominent as well as singular one because it occurs in the prologue: "To as many as [*hosoi*] received him, he gave power to become children of God, to those who believe in his name" (1:12). The explanation for this exception lies most likely in the fact that the aphoristic sayings in the rest of the Gospel have a paraenetic function: they invite belief or love or obedience. The prologue, on the other hand, is not

---

John 3:3; 3:5; 6:51; 7:17; 7:37; 8:51–52; 10:9; 11:9; 11:10; 12:26a; 12:26b; 12:47; 14:23; 15:6

(1 John 2:11)

Type 3. **"Everyone who . . ."** (*pas ho* + participle) (12 sayings)

Examples:

Everyone who looks to the Son and believes in him will have eternal life, and I shall raise him/her up at the last day. (6:40)

Everyone who is of the truth hears my voice. (18:37)

John 3:15; 3:16; 3:20; 4:13; 6:37a; 6:40; 8:34; 11:26; 12:46; 15:2a; 15:2b; 18:37

(1 John 3:4; 3:6a; 3:6b; 3:8; 3:9; 3:10b; 3:15; 4:7; 5:1a; 5:1b; 5:4; 2 John 9a)

Type 4. **"Whoever . . ."** (*hos an . . .*) (1 saying)

John 4:14

(1 John 3:17; 4:15; cf. 1 John 4:6b: *hos*)

Type 5. **"No one . . ."** (*oudeis . . .*) (3 sayings)

John 6:44; 6:65; 14:6

inviting but narrating. It tells the story of the Word's procurement of salvation and views the faith of believers in Jesus as a historic fact, not as possibility for the present or the future. The plural is therefore more appropriate.

There are some aphoristic sayings about the individual's relationship to Jesus in the Synoptic Gospels. Here are three examples from Mark: "Whoever does the will of God, that one is my brother and sister and mother" (3:35); "If anyone wishes to follow me, let him deny himself and take up his cross and follow me" (8:34); "Whoever is ashamed of me and my words . . . , the Son of Man will be ashamed of him/her when he comes in the glory of his Father" (8:38). There are not many of these, and they do not use the characteristic Johannine language of believing in Jesus, loving Jesus, having eternal life, and so forth, but they show perhaps that, as in other cases, something characteristic of the words of Jesus in John has a starting point in the traditional sayings of Jesus.

We may now consider the significance of these sayings in the context of a relatively collectivist society. They do not, of course, preclude groups of people becoming believers in Jesus (e.g., the siblings Lazarus, Martha, and Mary), but they do seem to insist that each individual must make a personal response in faith to Jesus, and they allow the possibility of an individual making that step of faith alone (e.g., the formerly blind man in chap. 9).

Bruce Malina discusses conversion in the case of people becoming disciples of Jesus in the Synoptic Gospels. Since the Synoptics lay considerable emphasis on the fact that conversion may mean breaking completely with the extended family in-group, Malina needs to explain how making such a break is possible for persons whose self-awareness is entirely dependent on the group. He makes two points. One is that conversion must be from one in-group to another, in this case to the fictive kin group of Jesus and his disciples.[13] In the context of the Synoptic Gospels, this point has something to be said for it. The second point is that the step of conversion cannot be taken without the support of at least one other member of the person's group. Malina cites the pairs of brothers, Peter and Andrew, James and John, and the fact that disciples come from the same locality, such as Capernaum.[14] But it is easy to cite contrary examples, such as Bartimaeus or Zacchaeus, while the three would-be followers of Jesus in Luke 9:57–62 surely present as typical Jesus's invitation to lone individuals to become his disciples.

In the case of the Johannine sayings that speak of the individual's conversion to belief in Jesus, the absence of any hint of joining a new group, the

13. Malina, *Social World*, 86–87.
14. Malina, *Social World*, 90.

community of Jesus's disciples, is striking. Of course, there is such a group, but it is apparently irrelevant to these sayings, which represent believing in Jesus as a matter between Jesus and the believer and no one else. Like the blind man healed by Jesus who stubbornly maintains his loyalty to Jesus when even his parents fail to support him (9:1–31), the individual of the aphoristic sayings finds it sufficient to belong to Jesus. This person is not, of course, the modern individualist who takes his or her own chosen path in complete independence of anyone else, free from all commitments to others. The prodigal in the parable is more like that; but the individual who comes to Jesus in these Johannine sayings finds a new relational focus for life. Jesus himself is all the in-group such a person needs. Their identity and self-awareness are now entirely dependent on him.[15]

There are just two passages in the Gospel in which aphoristic sayings occur in relation to the Christian community, but in both cases it is notable how the stress is still on the individual's relation to Jesus. First, there is the Good Shepherd Discourse, in which the sheep certainly belong to a flock, but the remarkable feature is that the shepherd calls each of the sheep by name (10:3).[16] The second passage is the parable of the vine, in which it is each branch's relationship to Jesus that determines whether it remains in the vine or is removed (15:1–6). But in this case the stress on the individual also serves to ground the community, since it is only by keeping Jesus's commandments that the individual remains in relation to him (15:10). As the Gospel goes on to explain, Jesus's commandments really amount to the single new commandment: the disciples must love one another (15:12). Thus the life of the community, the disciples' mutual love, stems from the relationship between each individual and Jesus. The latter entails the former, but individual relationship to Jesus has priority.[17] The community is constituted by individual relationship with Jesus and subsists only through individual relationship with Jesus.

"In-One-Anotherness" (Personal Coinherence)

The aphoristic sayings about the individual's relationship with Jesus concern not only the individual's initial coming to faith in Jesus, but also the continuing Christian life, envisaged as an intimate and abiding relationship between

15. Note also the story of Mary's extravagant act of anointing Jesus in John 12:1–18. Here Judas expresses the social norm (12:5) to which Mary shockingly fails to conform. What justifies Mary's break with social expectations is that her action recognizes Jesus as the one who inspires it.

16. This feature of the parable is surely echoed in John 20:16; 21:15.

17. Evidently this point is compatible with "Mediterranean anthropology," because it is made by Bruce J. Malina and Richard L. Rohrbaugh, *Social-Science Commentary on the Gospel of John* (Minneapolis: Fortress, 1998), 234.

the individual and Jesus. In order to investigate the nature of this relationship further, I shall begin with one of the many aphoristic sayings in the Bread of Life Discourse of chapter 6. This is the saying that makes the last fresh point before the discourse recapitulates its dominant theme in closing. It is the saying "The one who eats my flesh and drinks my blood abides in me, and I in him/her" (6:56). This is the first occurrence in the Gospel of the theme I call "in-one-anotherness"; it could also be called "personal coinherence" (see table 1.2).[18]

We should notice, first, the individualizing use of eucharistic language (also in 6:54). The *language* cannot but be eucharistic in origin, whether or not (the point is disputed) it is used here with reference to the Eucharist.[19] Certainly the rather shocking image of drinking blood as well as eating flesh indicates the individual's participation in the life of Jesus, the divine life that he shares with the Father. Paul, when he uses eucharistic language, envisages the corporate body of Christ, united by the one loaf we all share and the one cup we all drink (1 Cor. 10:16–17), but here in John's only use of such language only the individual believer is in view.

On the words "abides in me and I in him/her" Barnabas Lindars makes a perceptive comment:

> This is the climax of the discourse. All the metaphors are dropped, and the whole thing is put into terms of personal relationship. . . . John's thought never moves in ontological or quasi-magical categories. As the mode of receiving Jesus is to "come to" him and to "believe in" him, so the effect must be put into terms of personal, ethical, relationship. It is this relationship which persists beyond the present age to the time of the general resurrection.[20]

In other words, what it means to have eternal life and live forever is here spelled out in terms of intimate relationship with Jesus, whose life is the life of God. Of course, the language of "in-one-anotherness," despite Lindars's comment, is still metaphorical. It uses a spatial image (being "in" one another) to suggest the most intimate form of personal relationship.[21] The use of this language here anticipates the rather frequent use of it in chapters 14–17.

John's use of this image of relationship should not be assimilated to Paul's talk of being "in Christ," because although Paul can use this language

---

18. On the closely related image of "abiding" in John, see Dorothy A. Lee, *Flesh and Glory: Symbol, Gender, and Theology in the Gospel of John* (New York: Crossroad, 2002), 88–99.

19. This issue is fully discussed in chapter 5, "Sacraments?"

20. Barnabas Lindars, *The Gospel of John*, NCB (London: Marshall, Morgan & Scott, 1972), 269.

21. This point is made by Charles H. Talbert, *Reading John: A Literary and Theological Commentary on the Fourth Gospel and the Johannine Epistles* (London: SPCK, 1992), 139.

Table 1.2 "In-One-Anotherness" (Personal Coinherence)

The one who eats my flesh and drinks my blood abides in me, and I in him/her. (6:56)

I know my own and my own know me, just as the Father knows me and I know the Father. (10:14–15)

The Father is in me and I am in the Father. (10:38)

I am in the Father and the Father is in me. (14:10)

The Spirit of truth . . . abides with you, and he will be in you. (14:17)

I am in my Father, and you in me, and I in you. (14:20)

[My Father and I] will come to him/her and make our home with him/her. (14:23)

Parable of the Vine

I am the true vine, and my Father is the vine grower. ^{2}Every branch in me that bears no fruit he removes. Every branch that bears fruit he prunes to make it bear more fruit. . . . ^{4}*Abide in me and I will abide in you.* Just as the branch cannot bear fruit by itself unless it abides in the vine, neither can you unless you *abide in me.* ^{5}I am the vine, you are the branches. The one who *abides in me and I in him/her* bears much fruit, because apart from me you can do nothing. ^{6}If anyone *does not abide in me*, he/she is like a branch that is thrown away and withers; such branches are gathered, thrown into the fire, and burned. ^{7}If you *abide in me, and my words abide in you*, ask for whatever you wish, and it will be done for you. . . . ^{9}As the Father has loved me, so I have loved you; abide in my love. ^{10}If you keep my commandments, you will abide in my love, just as I have kept my Father's commandments and abide in his love. (15:1–2, 4–7, 9–10)

Jesus's Prayer to the Father

[I ask] that they may all be one. As *you, Father, are in me and I in you*, may they also be *in us*, so that the world may believe that you have sent me. ^{22}The glory that you have given me I have given them, so that they may be one, as we are one, ^{23}*I in them and you in me*, that they may become completely one, so that the world may know that you have sent me. . . . ^{26}I made your name known to them, and I will make it known, so that *the love with which you have loved me may be in them, and I in them.* (17:21–23, 26)

individually (e.g., 2 Cor. 5:17), and although he occasionally also speaks of Christ being "in" Christians (Rom. 8:10) or even in the individual believer (Gal. 2:20), he does not put these things together in a phrase like "Christ in me and I in Christ." By contrast, John's usage is characteristically reciprocal. Usually the form is "A in B and B in A," though there are variations. Moreover, John also applies the same formula to the relationship between Jesus and the Father, for which there is no sort of parallel in Paul. The difference between John and Paul exempts us from any need to enter the discussion of the meaning of the Pauline language.

Perhaps under the influence of the Pauline language, commentators on John tend to be anxious to make the point that the relationship that John envisages is not symmetrical.[22] The way in which the believer relates to Jesus cannot be just the same as the way Jesus relates to the believer. The immediate context in John itself makes this point: the believer receives eternal life from Jesus but does not give Jesus eternal life. But to make this point only is to miss the fact that what the "in-one-anotherness" language itself *expresses* is precisely reciprocity.

Attempts to find precedents for or parallels to this Johannine language in Philo, the Hermetica, or even Ignatius[23] fail because these, like Paul, lack the distinctive and simple reciprocity of the Johannine formula. Old Testament formulae—"I will be your God, and you shall be my people" (e.g., Lev. 26:12); "I will be his father, and he shall be my son" (2 Sam. 7:14)[24]—offer an emphatically asymmetrical sort of reciprocity rather than the simple reciprocity of the Johannine formula. Rather than seeking the background to John's usage in any language, Old Testament or Hellenistic, about the relationship of humans to the divine, I think we should regard the Johannine formula of reciprocity as most likely an original coinage, invented by John to express the personal coinherence that mutual love involves. This alone explains the simple, rather than asymmetrical, reciprocity.[25]

This Johannine image of in-one-anotherness is of considerable significance for our understanding of the Johannine stress on the individual's relationship with Jesus. One ingredient of modern Western individualism is an

---

22. For example, Donald A. Carson, *The Gospel according to John* (Leicester: Inter-Varsity; Grand Rapids: Eerdmans, 1991), 298.

23. Charles H. Dodd, *The Interpretation of the Fourth Gospel* (Cambridge: Cambridge University Press, 1953), 187–92; David L. Mealand, "The Language of Mystical Union in the Johannine Writings," *DRev* 95 (1977): 19–34.

24. These are cited by Mealand, "Language," 28–29.

25. Compare Song 6:3: "I am my beloved's and my beloved is mine." This is unlikely to lie behind John's usage, since it does not employ the spatial metaphor ("in"), but it does illustrate how a love relationship is naturally expressed in simple reciprocity.

understanding of the self as an independent and firmly bounded unit,[26] averse to compromising its independence through committed involvement with others. This probably owes something to a spatial image of the body as a physical boundary that encloses the person and marks it out as an independent unit. One thinks of the notion of personal space. For individuals for whom personal space is essential, the Johannine spatial image of two individuals occupying the same space, somehow coinciding or overlapping, may not easily appeal. But even modern Western individualists experience some degree of dissolution of personal space in intimate relationships. When the body is understood more as the medium of transcending the bounded self in relationship with other reality (one need only think of the experience of hugging), then the Johannine spatial image becomes more accessible. Bodies do not isolate us from each other but rather make openness to others possible. The Johannine image posits centered selves with open boundaries, persons who can be part of each other without losing their self-identity. It is an image that breaks open the self-enclosed independence of the bounded self.

John's "in-one-another" language is used of the individual's relationship with Jesus, of the relationship of the group of disciples with Jesus, and also of the relationship between Jesus and his Father. This last is the relationship from which the Gospel's whole narrative of salvation derives. It is the source of the eternal life that Jesus brings into the world and also of the life of loving relationship that is the inner nature of eternal life. As the love between the Father and the Son overflows into the world, the in-one-anotherness of the Father and the Son becomes the source of the in-one-anotherness of Jesus and the believer.[27] It may therefore be worth considering whether the fact that the Gospel portrays the divine life itself as the closest conceivable relationship between two individual persons, the Father and the Son, may in part account for the Gospel's emphasis on the one-to-one relationship of the believer to Jesus.

Jesus in Dialogue with Individual Gospel Characters

A prominent feature of John's narrative is the series of extended conversations that Jesus has with individuals. The most extensive are these seven:

Nathanael (1:47–51)

Nicodemus (3:1–21)

Samaritan woman (4:7–26)

---

26. On the bounded self, see Kenneth J. Gergen, *Relational Being: Beyond Self and Community* (Oxford: Oxford University Press, 2009), 3–28.

27. This point is developed further in chap. 2, "Divine and Human Community."

Martha (11:20–27)
Pilate (18:33–19:12)
Mary Magdalene (20:14–17)
Peter (21:15–22)

There are other, shorter dialogues (such as with the royal official, the man born blind, Peter at the supper, Thomas after the resurrection). However, the seven I have listed are significant not only for their relative length but also because, with the possible exception of the dialogue with Nathanael, they take place in private. In most of these cases it is made abundantly clear that no one else is present. Of course, the Synoptic Gospels also feature many encounters between Jesus and individuals, but the conversations are usually much briefer, and they are almost never in private. (The only exception may be Matthew's version of Peter's rebuke of Jesus [Matt. 16:22–23]. In Mark's version it is clear that the other disciples are within earshot [Mark 8:32–33], but not in Matthew.) The extended private conversations are a distinctive feature of John's Gospel, one of its many differences from the Synoptics.

Moreover, John has exercised his considerable storytelling skills to very good effect in these conversations. They are full of memorable moments: the Samaritan woman's evasive answer when Jesus refers to her husband (4:17); Pilate's cynical question, "What is truth?" (18:38); Mary Magdalene's delayed recognition of Jesus when he speaks her name (20:14–16); Peter's hurt at being asked three times whether he loves Jesus (21:17). Some of Jesus's most important theological claims occur in these dialogues: "You must be born from above" (3:7); "I am the resurrection and the life" (11:25); "My kingdom is not from this world" (18:36); and others. Unlike Jesus's debates with the Jewish authorities, these dialogues are never repetitive. Each has its own theme. In most cases the dialogue is a journey for Jesus's interlocutor. These individuals end it in a different place from where they began it. Their lives are significantly changed.

A story of an individual is generally more engaging than that of an undifferentiated group, as John's story of Mary Magdalene is by comparison with those of the women at the tomb in the other Gospels. An individual attracts greater empathy or identification. Is this just because we are modern individualists or would it have been the case for early hearers or readers of John? That it was the case for them I take it the very existence of these stories in John, as well as many similar in ancient literature, is sufficient evidence. Of course, these individuals are embedded in groups—the Samaritan woman in her village, Martha in her family, Mary Magdalene in the group of disciples—but they are far from merely typical of their group.

The characters in John's Gospel have usually been judged to be flat rather than round characters, one-dimensional in exhibiting only single character traits, static rather than developing through experiences, types rather than personalities. The work of Cornelis Bennema has recently challenged this view.[28] He rightly cites studies that have shown that ancient literature can deliver more complex and subtle characterizations than has often been thought, and that round personalities are portrayed, not merely one-dimensional types.[29] (The best studies have been of Greek tragedy; more work needs to be done, for example, on the Greek novels, Greco-Roman biography, or the portrayal of biblical characters in Josephus or the Pseudepigrapha.) Bennema adopts a theory of characterization that enables him to analyze the portrayal of characters in John's Gospel, assessing them for complexity, development, and penetration of inner life, and then to plot the characters along a continuum that shows degrees of characterization. The continuum runs from agent (a mere walk-on part) through type (a stock or flat character) and personality (showing a degree of complexity and development) to, finally, individual or person (the most developed or complex characters). (It is unfortunate that he uses the term "individual" very differently from how I have used it earlier in this chapter.)

The results for the seven characters in the extended one-to-one dialogues with Jesus are of interest.[30] Only one of them (Nathanael) emerges as merely a type, one other (Martha) Bennema places on the borderline between type and personality, three count as personalities (Mary Magdalene, Nicodemus, the Samaritan woman), one (Pontius Pilate) Bennema places on the borderline between personality and individual, while Peter emerges fully as an individual (though through a series of narratives, not only his private dialogue with Jesus). Thus, generally, the characters in the extended private dialogues with Jesus are among the most developed in the Gospel.

However, I think that characterization is only one aspect of the way these dialogues work. At least as important is that each of the characters has a unique story. They encounter Jesus in quite different and particular circumstances. It is not only, as has often been noticed, that they respond differently to Jesus, but that Jesus deals with each of them differently, according to their individual

28. Cornelis Bennema, "A Theory of Character in the Fourth Gospel with Reference to Ancient and Modern Literature," *BibInt* 17 (2009): 375–421; Bennema, *Encountering Jesus: Character Studies in the Gospel of John* (Milton Keynes: Paternoster, 2009).

29. Bennema, "Theory," 379–89.

30. Bennema, *Encountering*, 203–4.

circumstances.[31] Sometimes he initiates the dialogue, as, for example, rather shockingly in the case of the Samaritan woman, or tenderly, as a familiar friend, in the case of Mary Magdalene. Sometimes he responds to an approach, as with Nicodemus or Pilate. He does not deal with them according to some standard formula, but rather he engages the particular point in their lives at which he encounters them: Martha mourning for her brother, Peter in his awareness of having failed. With Nicodemus he starts quite bluntly with the point that this religious expert does not understand and especially needs to understand. The particularities of each encounter determine the themes of the dialogues, different in each case.

The view that the characters in John function to typify a range of different responses to Jesus (a view that Bennema endorses) neglects the particularities of the circumstances and the uniqueness of each character's story. It is not just that they respond differently, in ways the narrator leads hearers or readers to approve or disapprove, but also Jesus approaches them differently at unique moments or distinct circumstances in their lives. To classify the characters only in terms of characterization and type of response to Jesus, as Bennema does, reduces the particularities of the stories. What the stories do is to draw the hearers or readers into imaginative empathy with each character encountering Jesus in his or her particular circumstances. The stories surely do draw hearers or readers into their own encounters with Jesus, but the idea that the hearer or reader must run through a range of characters and responses until finding the one that fits for him or her is much too schematic and artificial. These characters are not models of faith so much as illustrations of the wide variety of ways in which different people in different circumstances may encounter Jesus.

Finally, we need to bring these stories of individuals in one-to-one dialogue with Jesus into relationship with the aphoristic sayings about the individual's relationship with Jesus that were our first area of Johannine evidence. The characters act out the contents of the aphoristic sayings. They come to faith in Jesus or renew and deepen their faith after the interruption of Jesus's death. Pilate exemplifies the negative sayings about the individual who resists Jesus's message and appeal. Peter exemplifies the believer's love for Jesus and obedience to Jesus. The emphasis of the sayings on the individual is replicated in these stories that portray actual individuals in relationship with Jesus. But the stories also do something that the sayings cannot. Their particularity enables

---

31. This aspect is explored in Jason Sturdevant, "The Pedagogy of the Logos: Adaptability and the Johannine Jesus" (PhD diss., Princeton Theological Seminary, 2013), which I have not seen. The author tells me that it will be published.

them to evoke the diversity of circumstances in which Jesus can be expected to call a variety of different individuals to faith or discipleship. Not only do they confront the hearers or readers with different possibilities of response (the sayings also do that); they surely also encourage hearers or readers to expect Jesus to meet them and direct them in the particularity of their individual lives and circumstances.

Conclusion

In the next chapter we shall see that John also has a central place for community in his theology, but it is important to appreciate the prominence of "individualism" and not allow it to be canceled or obscured by the material on community. The emphasis on the faith and discipleship of the individual is a distinctive feature of this Gospel that has not been given its due. Despite the fact that Johannine scholars work in the context of a highly individualistic culture and some of them within a context of rather individualistic piety, the strong emphasis on community in late twentieth-century theology, in the form-critical heritage of modern Gospels studies, and in the currents of social-scientific ideas that have influenced New Testament scholars in recent decades seems to have prevailed in Johannine scholarship.[32]

But what accounts for this unusual emphasis on the individual in John's Gospel? This question is not easy to answer. There may well be more than one factor. John may have been particularly aware that in a relatively collectivist society individuals needed strong encouragement to step outside the social norms and expectations of their group. It may be significant that in chapter 6, where we have noted the strikingly individualizing use of eucharistic language, the "people" and the "Jews" speak with one voice, as though speaking for collective opinion. To eat of the bread that Jesus gives, individuals must opt out of the customary reactions of the group. It is also notable that the language of the aphoristic sayings climaxes in truly shocking and offensive language: the only way for the individual to receive eternal life is to eat Jesus's flesh and to drink his blood (6:55–57). Even many of Jesus's disciples find these claims

---

32. David Rensberger's *Overcoming the World: Politics and Community in the Gospel of John* (London: SPCK, 1989) is a good example of an interest in community simply overriding the role of the individual in John. For example, Nicodemus is said to function as a "*communal symbolic figure*" (p. 38). It is true that, in the perspective of the whole Gospel, "birth from above" makes one a member of the new community of Jesus's disciples, but there is nothing about that in John 3, and reading group conflicts within the "Johannine community" into that chapter runs counter to the clear concern of the chapter, which is with how individuals may receive the eternal life that Jesus brings.

unacceptable (6:60–61) and so desert him (6:66). The radical clash between Jesus's requirement and the accepted norms of the society is dramatized, so that the need for the individual who adheres to Jesus to break with such social expectations stands out the more starkly. This is also the effect of Jesus's repeated statement that no one can come to him unless drawn by the Father (6:44, 65). The social solidarity is too strong for anyone on personal initiative to break out of it.

All this, however, could conceivably have been presented in terms of the difficult exercise of forsaking one in-group in order to join another (which is how "Johannine community" readings of the Gospel are inclined to read it). But instead, the aphorisms focus exclusively on Jesus. It is to Jesus—not into a new community—that the individual must come. Eating his flesh and drinking his blood are not participation in a common meal but rather eating Jesus (6:57) so that the individual may abide in Jesus and Jesus in the individual (6:56). Nothing permits us to import ideas of eucharistic fellowship into this passage. Instead, we have an example of this Gospel's remarkable concentration on the person of Jesus. The focus of the aphoristic sayings, like that of the narratives of individual dialogues, on the individual believer or disciple is matched by their focus on Jesus. Consequently, as we have noticed, when there is a movement from individual to community, it is a movement from individual to Jesus and thence to the community of those who believe in and love Jesus. The parable of the vine (15:1–11) takes up the Hebrew Bible's use of the vine as a symbol for the people of God (Ps. 80:8–16), but it is Jesus who is the vine and the disciples his branches. Each must abide in him. This is the closest John gets to the "in Christ" language of the Pauline Epistles, but John has nothing like the Pauline image of the body of Christ in which the different members function in reciprocal interaction.

The Gospel's focus on the individual and Jesus has a further dimension that will help to explain its "individualism." This Gospel values the relationship of personal intimacy between the individual believer and Jesus. We see this in the Beloved Disciple's own special closeness to Jesus (13:23; 21:20), which plausibly depicts this disciple's actual friendship with Jesus during Jesus's earthly life, a friendship that lay at the root of the Gospel's spirituality. We see it also in the Gospel's moving depiction of Jesus's reunion with Mary Magdalene, in which he evokes her recognition by the familiar way he speaks to her (20:16), but in which there is also a recognition that the intimacy between them can continue only in another mode (20:17).[33] In the next chapter we shall explore further the "in-one-another" language that the Gospel uses

33. See Sjef van Tilborg, *Imaginative Love in John*, BIS 2 (Leiden: Brill, 1993), 200–206.

to suggest the special intimacy of relationship between Jesus and the disciples and between Jesus and the Father. But we have already observed that it can be used of the risen and exalted Jesus's relationship both with the disciples as a group and with individuals. It is not used of the earthly Jesus's relationship with anyone, and it is not used of the disciples' relationship with one another, suggesting that it designates a relationship whose intimacy goes beyond the closeness that human persons may experience with one another in this world. Perhaps the word "mysticism" may be cautiously used in this connection.[34] In any case, in the perspective of Christian history, there is nothing strange about a focus on the individual's intimacy with the living Jesus. This need not be "individualistic" if that means excluding an important role for the corporate life and worship of the community, but it does mean that there is individual experience that is not reducible to the corporate. Among the New Testament documents, it is in John's Gospel that this individual experience of relationship with Jesus is most clearly and frequently evoked, and we should not be tempted, either for theological or for sociological reasons, to flatten the contours of the canon to the detriment of this specially Johannine emphasis.

It has often been noticed that there is a resemblance between what is said of the Beloved Disciple's closeness to Jesus (he reclined "on the breast" [en tō kolpō] of Jesus [13:23]) and what is said of the Son's closeness to the Father (he is "on the breast" [eis ton kolpon] of the Father [1:18]).[35] This resemblance is matched by the parallel use of "in-one-another" language: Jesus is in the believer and the believer is in Jesus (6:56; 15:5), while Jesus is in the Father and the Father is in him (10:38; 14:10; 17:21). As I have already suggested, there may be a connection here with the "individualism" of the Gospel. The love between the Father and the Son, their unsurpassable intimacy, is the source from which relationship between God and humans derives. The one-to-one relationship in the divine life is reflected especially in the Beloved Disciple's closeness to Jesus and in every believer's "personal coinherence" with Jesus. In neither case does the one-to-one relationship exclude others: the kind of love this Gospel describes cannot be confined to any one relationship but always overflows. Yet in both cases the one-to-one relationship is special and irreplaceable.

34. It used to be a topic of discussion "whether the type of religion represented by the Fourth Gospel can or cannot properly be described as 'mysticism'" (Dodd, *Interpretation*, 197), a discussion that involved the relationship between John and so-called Hellenistic mysticism. See also André Feuillet, *Johannine Studies*, trans. Thomas E. Crane (Staten Island, NY: Alba House, 1964), 169–80. The trend away from a "Hellenistic" background to John may account for the rarity with which the topic is raised in more recent Johannine scholarship.

35. For example, van Tilborg, *Imaginative Love*, 89.

2

Divine and Human Community

The Word "One"

In the previous chapter I explored the significance of certain ways of speaking that occur frequently in the Gospel of John. In the present chapter I shall focus on the significance of one particular word in a limited number of texts. The word is "one" (Greek *heis*, *mia*, *hen*), which, of course, occurs many times in John's Gospel, as it does in the rest of the New Testament and throughout Greek literature. But in a limited number of texts in John's Gospel—twelve instances of the word in eight texts (see table 2.1)—this little word "one" becomes a theologically very potent term.

We shall begin with some thoughts about the meaning of the word "one" that are true of the Hebrew *'eḥād*, of the Greek *heis*, and also of the English "one." It is, of course, the first of the cardinal numbers (1, 2, 3, 4, etc.), but is far from being merely one of the cardinal numbers. It is used in a much wider variety of ways and with a far wider significance than "two," "three," or any of the other numerals. "One" is much more than a number.

For present purposes we may ignore many of the complexities of the use of this word "one" in Hebrew, Greek, or English and simply focus our attention on two different kinds of significance that statements that persons or things are "one" can have in all three of those languages. On the one hand, the word "one" can signify uniqueness or singularity: that there is only one of the person or thing in question. In English we tend to say "only one" when this is our meaning, but not always (e.g., "there is one person I wish to speak to"). On the other hand, the word "one" can signify unity: being united or unified. Whereas in the first case, uniqueness, we are thinking of one as opposed to

---

Table 2.1 Significant Occurrences of "One"

The Eight Key Texts

we have one father, God (8:41)

so there will be one flock, one shepherd (10:16b)

the Father and I are one (10:30)

to have one man die for the people (11:50 [= 18:14])

to gather into one [*eis hen*] the dispersed children of God (11:52b)

so that they may be one, as we are one (17:11)

that they may all be one (17:21a)

so that they may be one, as we are one, I in them and you in me, that they may become completely one [*teteleiōmenoi eis hen*] (17:22b–23b)

"One" + "In-One-Another"

the Father and I are one (10:30) [in parallel with]
the Father is in me and I am in the Father (10:38)

I ask not only on behalf of these, but also on behalf of those who will believe in me through their word, [21]that they may all be *one*. As *you, Father, are in me and I in you*, may they also be *in us*, so that the world may believe that you have sent me. [22]The glory that you have given me I have given them, so that they may be *one*, as we are *one*, [23]*I in them and you in me,* that they may become *completely one*, so that the world may know that you have sent me. . . . [26]I made your name known to them, and I will make it known, so that *the love with which you have loved me may be in them, and I in them.* (17:20–23, 26)

---

many, in the second case, unity, we are thinking of unity as opposed to division. A group of people may be united, and in English we might sometimes say of such a group that they are "one" or perhaps "as one," though we would more often use the word "united." A nice example of "one" itself having the sense of "united" is the phrase "one nation under God" in the United States Pledge of Allegiance. The point is not to claim that there is only one nation, but to regard the nation as united.

So, as we look for theologically significant uses of this word "one," we need to bear in mind these two different dimensions of meaning. The word can point to the uniqueness of a single person or thing: there is only one of them. Or the same word can point to the unity of a group of persons or things: the group is united rather than divided.

Early Jewish Background

The very ordinary little word "one" was a theologically very potent word for Jews of the Second Temple period because of its occurrence in the Shema.[1] The Shema was the nearest thing to a Jewish creed, recited by observant Jews every morning and evening,[2] and so probably more familiar than any other scriptural text. It is the passage of Deuteronomy that begins thus:

> Hear, O Israel, the LORD our God, the LORD is one. You shall love the LORD your God with all your heart, and with all your soul, and with all your might. (Deut. 6:4–5)[3]

The grammar of the first sentence can be construed in more than one way (some modern translations have "the LORD our God is one LORD"), but there is good evidence that the usual way in which Jews of the Second Temple period read it was "the LORD our God, the LORD is one." Any passage in Jewish literature that says that "God is one" or that there is "one God" (meaning "only one God") can be confidently regarded an echo of the Shema. There are many such echoes in the literature of the late Second Temple period, because the belief that there was only one God was the central distinctive of Jewish

---

1. See now especially Erik Waaler, *The Shema and The First Commandment in First Corinthians: An Intertextual Approach to Paul's Re-reading of Deuteronomy*, WUNT 2/253 (Tübingen: Mohr Siebeck, 2008), chap. 4.

2. This was in literal obedience to Deut. 6:7b; cf. Josephus, *Ant.* 4.212; *Let. Aris.* 160; 1QS 10.10.

3. The extent of the passages recited probably varied at this time but probably would have included at least Deut. 6:4–9; 11:13–21.

faith in the religiously pluralistic world of the time. Jews were exceptional and widely known to be so because they acknowledged and worshiped only one God. Moreover, this one God was not just an article of faith. According to the Shema, God's people were to love him with their whole being, not only worshiping this one God alone, but also practicing their exclusive devotion to him through obedience to his law, the Torah.

Of the two dimensions of the meaning of "one," this usage is clearly a case of uniqueness: there is only one God, not many. In Jewish literature of this period there is never any implication of the other meaning: God is unified rather than divided. Jewish writers evidently were not concerned with that issue. The idea that divine nature, by contrast with finite creatures, is indivisible or noncomposite occupied the Greek philosophical tradition and became an issue for the fathers of the early church, but it is not apparent in Jewish literature of this period, not even in Philo of Alexandria, the Jewish thinker who appropriates Greek philosophical ideas in many respects.

So for late Second Temple Judaism, "God is one" means that there is only one God. However, we also need to consider the use of the word "one" in Jewish literature with reference to God's people Israel. There are a series of passages in the biblical prophets that are key texts for understanding John's usage of the word "one": Ezek. 34:23; 37:15–24; Mic. 2:12; Hosea 1:11a (2:2a MT); Isa. 45:20a (see table 2.2).[4] These passages reflect the biblical narrative that tells how, following the glorious days of Solomon's united kingdom, Israel was tragically divided into the two kingdoms of Israel and Judah, the northern and the southern tribes. People from both kingdoms were taken into exile, first northern Israel by the Assyrians, then the people of Judah by the Babylonians. The result was that the hope for the future of God's people in the prophets includes the expectation that God will regather his people, whom he has scattered among the nations, returning them to the land of Israel. This is a reuniting of God's people, in the general sense that Israelites from all over the world will be regathered in the holy land, but also more specifically in the sense that the northern and southern tribes will be reunited as a single people under the rule of the new David, the Messiah, who will rule God's one people on behalf of the one God.

These passages use both the ordinary word "one" (*'eḥād*) and the word *yaḥad*, with related words, which have the sense of "together," "coming together into one." Whether *'eḥād* and *yaḥad* are etymologically connected is

4. In most of these passages the Old Greek version (LXX) is significantly different from the Hebrew, not always reproducing the terms "one" or "together." But in my view, John studied the Scriptures primarily in Hebrew and quotes the LXX when it is convenient to do so.

Table 2.2 "Oneness": Biblical Sources and Jewish Parallels

Hebrew Bible

YHWH our God, YHWH is one. (Deut. 6:4)

I will set up over them *one shepherd*, my servant David, and he shall feed them: he shall feed them and be their shepherd. (Ezek. 34:23)

The word of the LORD came to me: [16]Mortal, take a stick and write on it, "For Judah, and the Israelites associated with it"; then take another stick and write on it, "For Joseph (the stick of Ephraim) and all the house of Israel associated with it"; [17]and join them *together* [*'el-'eḥād*] into *one stick*, so that they may become *one* [*la'ăḥādîm*] in your hand. [18]And when your people say to you, "Will you not show us what you mean by these?" [19]say to them, Thus says the Lord GOD: I am about to take the stick of Joseph (which is in the hand of Ephraim) and the tribes of Israel associated with it; and I will put the stick of Judah upon it, and make them *one stick*, in order that they may be *one* in my hand. [20]When the sticks on which you write are in your hand before their eyes, [21]then say to them, Thus says the Lord GOD: I will take the people of Israel from the nations among which they have gone, and will gather them from every quarter, and bring them to their own land. [22]I will make them *one nation* in the land, on the mountains of Israel; and *one king* shall be king over them all. Never again shall they be two nations, and never again shall they be divided into two kingdoms. . . . [24a]My servant David shall be king over them; and they shall all have *one shepherd*. (Ezek. 37:15–22, 24a)

> I will surely gather all of you, O Jacob,
> I will gather the survivors of Israel *together* [*yaḥad*] (or *as a community* [?]).
> I will set them like sheep in a fold,
> like a flock in its pasture:
> it will resound with people. (Mic. 2:12 NRSV altered)

The people of Judah and the people of Israel shall be gathered *together* [*yaḥdāw*], and they shall appoint for themselves *one head*. (Hosea 1:11a [2:2a MT])

> Assemble yourselves and come together [*yaḥdāw*],
> draw near, you survivors of the nations! (Isa. 45:20a)

Amidah: Blessing 10 (The Gathering of the Exiles)

> Sound the great horn for our freedom
> and lift a banner to gather in our exiles.
> You are praised, Lord, who gathers in the outcasts of his people
> Israel.
>
> (Genizah Palestinian version)[a]

> Sound the great horn for our freedom;
> lift up a banner to gather in our exiles;
> and gather us together [*yaḥad*] from the four corners of the earth.
> You are praised, Lord, who gathers in the outcasts of his people
> Israel.
>
> (current Ashkenazi version, Babylonian origin)[b]

"One God, One People" in First-Century CE Sources

[Moses commanded:] Let there be one holy city in that place in the land of Canaan that is fairest and most famous for its excellence, a city which God shall choose for himself by prophetic oracle. And let there be one temple therein, and one altar of stones. . . . In no other city let there be either altar or temple; for God is one and the Hebrew race is one. (Josephus, *Ant.* 4.200–201)

For we are all a people of the Name, we, who have received one Law from the One. (*2 Bar.* 48.23–24)

. . . the highest kinship, the kinship of having one citizenship and the same law and one God who has taken all members of the nation for his portion. (Philo, *Spec.* 4.159)

For the most effectual love-charm, the chain which binds indissolubly the goodwill which makes us one [*eunoias henōtikēs*] is to honor the one God. (Philo, *Spec.* 1.52)

. . . the highest and greatest source of this unanimity [of the Hebrews] is their creed [*doxa*] of a single God [*tou henos theou*], through which, as from a fountain, they feel a love [*philia*] for each other, uniting them in an indissoluble bond [*henōtikē kai adialytō*]. (Philo, *Virt.* 35)

There is one body and one Spirit, just as you were called to the one hope of your calling, one Lord, one faith, one baptism, one God and Father of all. (Eph. 4:4–6)

---

a. Translation by Jakob J. Petuchowski, in *The Lord's Prayer and Jewish Liturgy*, ed. Jakob J. Petuchowski and Michael Brocke (London: Burns & Oates, 1978), 29.

b. Translation by Petuchowski, in *Lord's Prayer*, 32.

debated (*TDOT* 6:41–42), but there is no doubt that ancient Jewish readers would have connected them closely. Both concern oneness. The term *yaḥad* is especially interesting because it was adopted by the members of the Qumran community as their technical term for their own community. They made it a noun with the sense of "comm-unity," a group of people who are united.[5] No one else seems to have used the word *yaḥad* in that way, but, since the Qumran community were in the habit of reading biblical prophecies with reference to themselves and their contemporaries, it seems likely that they took the term from Mic. 2:12, where God promises to gather the exiles of Israel "together" (*yaḥad*).[6] Modern translations take *yaḥad* there as an adverb, meaning "together," but the Qumran community may well have read it as a noun: God will gather the exiles "as a community." They thought of themselves as the beginning of that regathering of Israel that was expected to take place in the last days.

Some scholars think that the ideas of the Qumran community lie somewhere in the background to the Gospel of John, and in that case the Qumran use of *yaḥad* would be especially significant for reading the Gospel.[7] However, in my view, there is no special connection between Qumran and John.[8] So I mention the Qumran usage merely as an illustration of how Jews in this period might think of the promised reuniting of the people.

If we refer again to the two dimensions of the meaning of "one," it is clear that, when these passages in the prophets speak of Israel in the future becoming one, the meaning is unitedness, the overcoming of division and separation in the reuniting of all Israelites into a unified people once again. Although Israel as the people of God is unique (God's one and only special people), these texts are focusing not on Israel as unique but on Israel as united. However,

5. However, Arie van der Kooij argues, on the basis of 11QT 57.13, that the term refers to people sitting together—that is, an assembly ("The *Yaḥad*—What's in a Name?," *DSD* 18 [2011]: 109–28).

6. Mark Adam Elliott refers also to Ps. 133:1; Hosea 1:11; Ezra 4:3, which are possible but less likely sources (*The Survivors of Israel: A Reconsideration of the Theology of Pre-Christian Judaism* [Grand Rapids: Eerdmans, 2000], 347n112). For the Qumran community's interpretation of Micah as prophecy being fulfilled in their own time, see 1QpMic; CD-A 4.20–21.

7. Raymond E. Brown goes so far as to suggest, "It is not impossible that the Johannine *hen*, 'one,' literally translates the concept of *yaḥad*" in 1QS (*The Gospel according to John [XIII–XXI]: Introduction, Translation, and Notes*, AB 29A [New York: Doubleday, 1966], 777). But Mark L. Appold thinks that the case for a close connection between the Qumran term and the Johannine oneness notion "has since lost its plausibility" (*The Oneness Motif in the Fourth Gospel: Motif Analysis and Exegetical Probe into the Theology of John*, WUNT 2/1 [Tübingen: Mohr Siebeck, 1976], 191).

8. Richard Bauckham, *The Testimony of the Beloved Disciple: Narrative, History, and Theology in the Gospel of John* (Grand Rapids: Baker Academic, 2007), chap. 6.

an interesting transition occurs when the prophets connect that unity of the people with the thought that they will have one king—in a restoration of the monarchy of David and Solomon. Ezekiel says that they will have one king or one shepherd (a metaphor for king), Hosea that they will have one head. Here the thought is of uniqueness: one king, not many. There is a readily intelligible connection between a *unified* people and their *unique* ruler. The people are unified by the leadership of a single king. The two dimensions of the meaning of oneness come together here, one characterizing the people, the other their leader. (It is not difficult to think of many examples of a singular something uniting a group of people. For example, fans of the musician Elton John are united by their adulation of one man. They are a united group, he is a unique individual.)

A prayer based on these passages in the Hebrew Bible is included in the so-called Amidah or Eighteen Benedictions, a Jewish liturgical prayer that goes back in some form to the first century,[9] though probably there was no one fixed wording of the blessings in that period. So we can suppose that very likely the Amidah in first-century usage included, as do the versions we know from later periods (see table 2.2), a prayer for the regathering of the exiles of Israel, but we cannot be sure what words would have been used. The texts of this benediction are identical in the two versions we know, except that the Babylonian version contains an additional phrase that is not in the Palestinian version: "gather us together from the four corners of the earth." That line echoes Mic. 2:12, including the word *yaḥad*, "together" or "as one." Whether or not with such a specific reference to the uniting of the exiles, first-century Jews probably would have been familiar with the regular use of a liturgy that blessed God as "the one who gathers the dispersed of his people Israel" (a phrase borrowed from Isa. 56:8)[10] and thereby with the prophetic passages as echoed in the liturgy more closely than with the passages in the prophets themselves.

Even more interesting and relevant for our present purposes are passages from first-century Jewish literature that exemplify the correlation of "one God" and "one people." The most relevant of these appear in table 2.2.[11]

9. David Instone-Brewer, *Prayer and Agriculture*, vol. 1 of *Traditions of the Rabbis from the Era of the New Testament* (Grand Rapids: Eerdmans, 2004), 107–8.

10. See also the hymn that occurs between 51:12 and 51:13 in the Hebrew text of Ben Sira (manuscript B), which includes the line "give thanks to him who gathers the dispersed of Israel."

11. Other such passages are 2 *Bar.* 78.4; 85.14; Josephus, *Ant.* 5.112; *Ag. Ap.* 2.193; Philo, *Spec.* 1.67; *Conf.* 170. In the Hebrew Bible a parallel between the unique God and his unique people is drawn only in 2 Sam. 7:22–23 = 1 Chron. 17:20–21. Passages of this kind in Philo and Josephus are discussed by Waaler, *Shema*, 172–78. Philo also speaks of "one humanity" and "one world," reflecting concepts of the unity of humanity current in the Roman world,

They connect Jewish faith in the one and only God with the uniqueness of his people, his temple, and his law. A pagan might well ask why the Jews did not have many temples. The answer given by Josephus is that the one God should be worshiped in one temple where his one people worship him. This may not immediately seem to make logical sense. Why should not the one God be worshiped in many temples? But the correlation of one God, one temple, one law, and one people makes much more sense when we realize that at work in these passages is the idea that God's people are unified by their allegiance to one God. (It's like the fans of Elton John.) God's people compose one people because they are united in their devotion to the one God, whose one law they obey and in whose one temple they gather to worship him.

Philo makes this quite clear and develops a very interesting variation on this thought, which is peculiarly relevant to the Gospel of John. Devotion to the one God unites the one people of God, he says, in a bond of love for each other. Not only does God's law command them all to love one another, but also, Philo seems to be claiming, their belief in the one God inspires in them the love that unites them with each other.

(Ephesians 4:4–6 is evidently a Christian version of this Jewish tradition of aligning the uniqueness of God with his one people and with the various unique things that that people have in common and that bind them together.)[12]

The Reuniting of God's People

With this background in place, we may turn to the Gospel of John and focus first on references to the oneness of the people of God. John uses the word "one" of the people of God six times (10:16; 11:52; and four times in Jesus's prayer in chap. 17). In these passages we find clear echoes of the passages from the prophets that we have reviewed. As in the prophets, the thought is not of the uniqueness of the people of God but of their unity. In every case it is a matter of *becoming* one. The people of God need to be gathered and united together, and Jesus prays—very prominently among the topics of his great prayer in chapter 17—that they may become one, climaxing in the goal that they should become completely one (17:23).

The connection with the hope of the prophets we find first in chapter 10, the great parabolic discourse of Jesus about the shepherd and the sheepfold.

---

but it does not seem to me that this theme as such is to be found in John's Gospel, despite its frequent reference to "all people" and "the world." In relation to humanity, the Gospel seems to stress totality or comprehensiveness rather than "oneness."

12. This passage is discussed by Waaler, *Shema*, 251–55.

Ezekiel is undoubtedly in the background to this whole discourse. The climax comes when Jesus declares himself to be the good shepherd who lays down his life for the sheep. Then he continues: "I have other sheep that do not belong to this fold. I must bring them also, and they will listen to my voice. So there will be one flock, one shepherd" (10:16). As in Ezekiel, there appear to be two, divided parts of the people of God, who will be brought together to form a single people (the one flock) united by their one shepherd, the Messiah. The unitedness of the people is related to the uniqueness of their leader. This general thought is more important for our present purposes than the rather more puzzling issue of the actual identity in John of "this fold" and the "other sheep." In Ezekiel it is a question of the two divisions of divided Israel, the northern and the southern tribes, Ephraim and Judah. John certainly has transmuted that thought in some way, most likely by thinking of, on the one hand, Jewish believers in Jesus ("this fold"), and, on the other, Gentile believers ("other sheep").[13] He may well have done so on the basis of another prophetic passage about the gathering of the dispersed, Isaiah 56:8: "I will gather others to them besides those already gathered." If the "other sheep" are Gentiles, John is not rejecting Ezekiel's hope that all twelve tribes of Israel will be regathered; he is extending the hope to include the Gentiles also. Moreover, whereas the prophets also entertain expectations of the conversion of the Gentiles to the worship of the one God, John's claim that "there will be one flock, one shepherd" goes further in anticipating the uniting of Jews and Gentiles into a single people of God. This is the Johannine version of Paul's concern that Jewish and Gentile believers should not be two separated communities but rather form one people of God (while remaining Jews and Gentiles).

In the context of John 10 it seems that the people of God are to be unified not just by their allegiance to one shepherd (although there is a strong emphasis on the shepherd's sheep knowing his voice and following him) but also by the fact that the shepherd lays down his life for the flock. That thought connects the passage with the other key echo of the prophets among these Johannine texts, which is to be found in 11:52. In this context the Jewish authorities have gathered to decide what to do about the threat posed by Jesus. The high priest Caiaphas, in persuading them that Jesus must die, uses this argument: "It is better for you to have one man die for the people than to have the whole

---

13. This is probably the majority view among the commentators. Another possibility is that "this fold" refers to believers among Jews in the land of Israel, while the others are Jews and Gentiles outside the land. John A. Dennis thinks that the "other sheep" are Diaspora Israelites (*Jesus' Death and the Gathering of True Israel: The Johannine Appropriation of Restoration Theology in the Light of John 11.47–52*, WUNT 2/217 [Tübingen: Mohr Siebeck, 2006], 300–301).

nation destroyed" (11:50). In Caiaphas's intention this is a straightforward political calculation, but it is also a prime instance of the Johannine irony by which characters say more than they think they say. Caiaphas, John explains, "prophesied that Jesus was about to die for the nation, and not for the nation only, but to gather into one the dispersed children of God" (11:51–52). The biblical background here is obvious,[14] but the echo perhaps is, even more tellingly, of the tenth benediction of the Amidah.[15] It is worth noticing that John could have said simply "to gather the dispersed children of God," using, as he does, the verb *synagein*, which means "to gather *together* [*syn*]." This is actually how the Septuagint Greek version of the Old Testament translates the passages in the prophets that lie in the background to John's words here. But John has chosen a somewhat redundant translation "to gather *into one* [*eis hen*]," which echoes the Hebrew of the prophets more literally, evidently because he wanted to stress here the word "one" that links this passage with his other texts that refer to the unity of the people of God.

The language in 11:52 is a direct echo of the words of the prophets, and the same question arises as in the case of 10:16: how does John mean his readers to understand the identity of the people of God, made up of two components? Are we to think of Israel in the land ("the nation") and Israel in exile ("the dispersed children of God")? This is the obvious meaning, but John must be once again transmuting the meaning, especially as in John's Gospel it is clear that a child of God is what one must become by spiritual birth from above, not what belongs to Jews merely by ethnic descent from Abraham (1:12; 3:3–7; 8:37–47). So the most likely meaning is this: not for the people of Israel only but also for the Gentiles. The significance then is very much like what Jesus says in the next chapter: "I, when I am lifted up from the earth, will draw all people to myself" (12:32). The death of Jesus will be the means by which he gathers together all those, Jews and Gentiles, whom God calls to belong to his people in the last days.[16]

14. *Diaskorpizō* ("to scatter, disperse") is used in LXX for the scattering of Israel among the nations, often in connection with regathering (Deut. 30:1, 3; Neh. 1:8–9; Tob. 13:5 [S text]; Jer. 23:1–2; Ezek. 20:34, 41; 28:25). The image of gathering the scattered is also connected with the shepherd image, as used in John 10 (cf. Zech. 11:16; 13:7). For "children of God" as perhaps connected with the theme of gathering, see Dennis, *Jesus' Death*, 281–84.

15. Walter Grundmann, "The Decision of the Supreme Court to Put Jesus to Death (John 11:47–57) in Its Context: Tradition and Redaction in the Gospel of John," in *Jesus and the Politics of His Day*, ed. Ernst Bammel and Charles F. D. Moule (Cambridge: Cambridge University Press, 1984), 295–318, here 308–10.

16. Note the insightful comments of Stephen C. Barton: "[John 10:16 and 11:52] imply an inclusive solidarity where the boundaries of the people of God are able to be redrawn because of Jesus's sacrifice in death. But boundaries remain: they are redrawn but not discarded. To put it another way, because the centre—understood now in terms of the death of the Good

These passages therefore connect the singularity, the uniqueness of Jesus, the one shepherd, the one man who dies for the people, with the uniting of the people of God. If we read on into chapter 17, we find a much more remarkable thought: Jesus prays that his disciples may be one "as we [Jesus and his Father] are one" (17:11, 22). In order to understand this, we must move from the unity of the people of God to the unity of God (after which we will return to the people of God).

The Unity of God

We can begin from the presumption that in the context of first-century Judaism (which is the primary context of John's Gospel) any use of the word "one" in relation to God would inevitably call to mind the Shema. The most straightforward case is in 8:41, where the Jewish leaders, in dispute with Jesus, claim to be children of God: "We have one father, God."[17] Here the word "one" has its usual sense, in relation to God, of uniqueness. They mean that they are children of the one and only divine Father, perhaps in order to rival Jesus's claim to be the Son of that divine Father.

However, when we move to the other texts in which "oneness" is related to God, we find something remarkable that has no precedent in previous Jewish usage. In 10:30 Jesus claims: "I and the Father are one [*hen*]." Commentators tend not to notice the allusion to the Shema here, but the word "one" (even though here it is necessarily neuter) could not fail to recall the Shema for any Jewish hearer or reader. The uniqueness of the one God, as asserted by the Shema, must therefore be evoked.[18] But at the same time the other dimension of oneness language—unity, being at one with one another—must here also be intended. The Father and the Son are one in their communion with each other. Jesus is claiming that the unique deity of the God of Israel *consists in* the communion between Father and Son.[19] To assert this kind of oneness,

---

Shepherd—has shifted, the periphery has shifted (but not dissolved) also, allowing the inclusion of some previously excluded and the union of some previously separated" ("The Unity of Humankind as a Theme in Biblical Theology," in *Out of Egypt: Biblical Theology and Biblical Interpretation*, ed. Craig Bartholomew et al., SHS 5 [Milton Keynes: Paternoster; Grand Rapids: Zondervan, 2004], 233–58, here 252).

17. The words are virtually a quotation from Mal. 2:10, which itself is probably an echo of the Shema (see Waaler, *Shema*, 110–14).

18. I am less sure that John 20:28 (where "one" does not occur) is an echo of the Shema, as Andreas Köstenberger and Scott Swain claim (see Andreas J. Köstenberger and Scott R. Swain, *Father, Son, and Spirit: The Trinity and John's Gospel*, NSBT 24 [Nottingham: Apollos; Downers Grove, IL: InterVarsity, 2008], 174).

19. See Bauckham, *Testimony*, 250–51.

the oneness of personal community, of God is unprecedented in early Judaism. Not that early Jewish writers say anything that necessarily excludes it; it simply did not occur to them to think of the oneness of God otherwise than as uniqueness.

This remarkable adaptation of the Shema is not without parallel in the rest of the New Testament, for Paul does something similar, though not identical, in 1 Cor. 8:6. There Paul takes the words of the Shema and divides them between the two persons of God the Father and the Lord, Jesus Christ, thus: "For us there is one God, the Father, from whom are all things and for whom we exist, and one Lord, Jesus Christ, through whom are all things and through whom we exist." This can only be understood as an interpretation of the Shema, rather than a repudiation of the Shema, amounting to a radical rejection of Jewish monotheism, if the one God and the one Lord, the Father and Jesus Christ, *compose* the one God of the Shema.[20] Where this formulation differs from that of John 10:30, however, is that Paul does not here explicitly call Jesus "the Son" and so does not explicate the unity of God as the community of the Father and the Son. Paul's reformulation of the Shema looks outwards, at the one God's relationship to creation and his people, whereas John's, in 10:30, grounds the outward unity of the divine activity in the community of persons internal to God.

In John's narrative the reaction of the Jewish leaders to this claim of Jesus is to take up stones to stone him, because, as they themselves explain, they consider him guilty of blasphemy in that "you, though only a human being, are making yourself God" (10:33). Jesus's self-defense then climaxes in another claim, equally audacious, that the Jewish leaders again perceive as blasphemous. He says, "The Father is in me and I am in the Father" (10:38). We surely should take this second claim as effectively equivalent to or a further explication of the first. The "in-one-another" language refers to the uniquely intimate communion that unites the Father and the Son. This strongly supports the view that the unity between the Father and the Son is not just their unity of will in Jesus's mission from the Father, the unity of words and works by which Jesus conveys what he has heard from the Father and does the works of the Father.[21] Together with the allusion to the Shema in 10:30,

20. Richard Bauckham, *Jesus and the God of Israel: God Crucified and Other Studies on the New Testament's Christology of Divine Identity* (Grand Rapids: Eerdmans, 2008), 210–18; Waaler, *Shema*, passim.

21. Contra Johan Ferreira, *Johannine Ecclesiology*, JSNTSup 160 (Sheffield: Sheffield Academic Press, 1998), 128, 134. He seems to think that the only alternative to his understanding of the oneness between Father and Son as a unity in action would be "a unity in essence." He misses the notion of personal communion in love.

the "in-one-another" language of 10:33 points to a relational intimacy of Jesus and the Father within the identity of the one God. We might also be reminded of the statement at the end of the prologue to the Gospel: the Son is in the bosom of the Father (1:18). This intimacy of relationship is not the same thing as, but the ground and source of, the unity of action played out in the sending of the Son by the Father into the world.

The progression of thought within the prologue itself in this respect is very significant. It begins with a self-differentiation of God in terms of the Word: "the Word was with God and the Word was God" (1:1). This is a differentiation within God that is apparent in his creation of the world through the Word (1:3). Implicitly, the differentiation is between God as speaker and God as the Word spoken. However, the Word appears for the last time in the whole Gospel when the prologue announces that "the Word became flesh" (1:14). In the incarnation the Word is revealed as Son (1:14). Therefore the prologue ends with a more profound form of divine self-differentiation: the intimacy of the Father and the Son (1:18), a relationship internal to God. This personal communion within God, announced at the end of the prologue, is then further explicated through the course of the Gospel, climaxing in Jesus's prayer to the Father in chapter 17.

Armed with this understanding of the unity of Jesus with his Father, we can now return to Jesus's petition, in chapter 17, that believers may be one as he and the Father are one. This petition is important enough to occur four times, first with reference to Jesus's disciples (17:11), subsequently with reference to those who will come to faith in Jesus through the disciples' witness (17:21, 22, 23). On the last occasion we find the climactic expression "that they may be perfectly one" (17:23). A more literal translation would be "that they may be perfected into one" (*teteleiōmenoi eis hen*), recalling the expression "gathered into one" in 11:52. The unity of believers is evidently, then, not a static fact but a dynamic process of becoming one, to be complete only eschatologically. The location of these passages in the final part of Jesus's prayer to the Father, a crucial turning point in the Gospel's narrative structure, suggests the key importance of this thought—that believers are to be one as Jesus and the Father are one—for the Gospel's theology. The early references to the motif of oneness are here integrated into a passage that both extends and completes them.

But how exactly are the unity of Jesus with his Father and the unity of believers connected? Believers are to be one "as" (*kathōs*) Jesus and his Father are one. *Kathōs* is a favorite Johannine word, but that does not mean that it is always used in the same way. For example, it features in the phrase "as it is written" that is used to introduce scriptural citations in John, but that usage scarcely helps to illuminate the usage that presently concerns us. Passages that are relevant, however, are the rather numerous ones in which something about the believers is connected, by *kathōs*, with something about Jesus and/or the Father, such that the former is understood to reflect the latter. For example,

Just as [*kathōs*] I have loved you, you also should love one another. (13:34)

Just as [*kathōs*] the living Father sent me, and I live because [*dia*] of the Father, so whoever eats me will live because of [*dia*] me. (6:57)

As the Father has sent me, so I send you. (20:21)

I know my own and my own know me, just as [*kathōs*] the Father knows me and I know the Father. (10:14–15)

There is a unique concentration of such sayings in chapter 17, which contains five of them (17:14, 16, 18, 21b, 23) in addition to the three that refer to the oneness of believers (17:11, 21, 22). The range of such sayings shows that *kathōs* in 17:11, 21, 22 has its usual comparative force, not, as some have suggested, a causative sense (that they may be one because we are one).[22] It is in any case rather dubious that *kathōs* can bear such a sense, while John has other ways of expressing causation (cf. 17:9, 19, 24, 26). This means not that the oneness of the believers does not, in some way, depend on the unity of Jesus and the Father but only that the *kathōs* sayings themselves do not say so. They state an *analogy* between the unity of Father and Son and that of the Christian community. Such an analogy does not require that the two correspond completely, that the oneness of believers is exactly like the unity of Jesus and the Father. We do not have to conclude that the unity of the Father and the Son is no more than the kind of unity that can exist between human persons, but only that there is a resemblance.[23]

If we now ask how it comes about that the oneness of believers resembles that of the Father and the Son, we find ourselves back with "in-one-another" language. Such language is closely connected with the prayer for oneness, and it is this language that establishes more than a resemblance between divine and human community. In fact, Jesus never says that just as he is in the Father and the Father in him, so believers will be in one another. What he says is that just as the Father is in him and he is in the Father, so may they be "in us"

22. Ferreira, *Johannine Ecclesiology*, 118–19.
23. See Miroslav Volf, *After Our Likeness: The Church as the Image of the Trinity* (Grand Rapids: Eerdmans, 1998), 211.

(17:21). Again, he prays "that they may be one, as we are one, I in them and you in me" (17:22–23). These thoughts are then perhaps further explicated when he prays "that the love with which you have loved me may be in them, and I in them" (17:26). The general sense (not precisely stated, as is typical of Johannine discourse) is that from the loving communion between the Father and the Son flows the love with which Jesus loved his disciples, a love that enables them to enjoy an intimate, "in-one-another" relationship with Jesus and his Father, and it is from this overflowing of divine love into the world that the oneness of believers among themselves stems.

The Social Trinity

The Gospel of John has exercised a strong and appropriate influence on trinitarian theology down the centuries,[24] and the passages that I have been discussing are among the most important in this regard. In at least one important respect the theological tradition has gone beyond the Gospel. Although this Gospel has much to say about the Holy Spirit or the Paraclete and leaves us in no doubt that the Spirit in its own way belongs to the identity of the one God, the passages that we have examined, those that use "oneness" and "in-one-another" language, are binitarian rather than trinitarian. The Gospel does not use that language to characterize the relation of the Holy Spirit to the Father and the Son but only to characterize the relation between the Father and the Son. Although it has been suggested that the Spirit is present anonymously in chapter 17,[25] there is certainly no explicit reference to the Spirit in that passage. My point is not that the Gospel's comprehensive understanding of God is not trinitarian, but simply that the "oneness" and "in-one-another" language is used only in a binitarian way, to refer to the relationship of the Father and the Son. (An examination of the ways that the Gospel characterizes the relationship of the Spirit with the Father and the Son must be left for another occasion.) From the perspective of the theological tradition, doubtless it legitimately and appropriately extended the Johannine language of oneness and in-one-anotherness to the relations between all three persons of the Trinity. But as exegetes, we must be clear that this was an extension.

24. For the Fathers, see T. E. Pollard, *Johannine Christology and the Early Church*, SNTSMS 13 (Cambridge: Cambridge University Press, 1970); Maurice Wiles, *The Spiritual Gospel: The Interpretation of the Fourth Gospel in the Early Church* (Cambridge: Cambridge University Press, 1960). For the Reformers and later, see Tord Larsson, *God in the Fourth Gospel: A Hermeneutical Study of the History of Interpretations*, ConBNT 35 (Stockholm: Almqvist & Wiksell, 2001).
25. Köstenberger and Swain, *Father*, 176–78.

The second half of the twentieth century saw a remarkable renaissance in trinitarian theology in the work of theologians such as Wolfhart Pannenberg, Jürgen Moltmann, Miroslav Volf, John Zizioulas, and Catherine LaCugna.[26] These theologians share (with a variety of different emphases and nuances) what is commonly called a doctrine of the social Trinity.[27] It has at least these four common elements:

1. Unlike much of the tradition, these theologians do not give priority to the one divine substance over the three Persons in God. The three Persons are irreducible.[28]

2. They understand the three Persons to be acting and relating subjects, not the three modes of being of a single personal subject. As Stanley Grenz puts it, in most contemporary trinitarian theology "the psychological model [of the Trinity] has given way to variations on the theme of divine sociality."[29]

3. They use the concept of perichoresis (or coinherence or mutual indwelling) to point to a kind of relationship among the three Persons that actually constitutes their unity. (This point is of critical importance in protecting the notion of the social Trinity from any kind of projection of the autonomous human self of Western modernity.)

4. They see a correspondence between the relations within the Trinity and the kind of human relationships, whether in ecclesial or political society, that reflect the trinitarian sociality of God.

Broadly, it seems to me that these trinitarian concepts reflect quite well the binitarian thought of the Gospel of John. The idea of perichoresis, or coinherence, corresponds well, as these theologians are aware, to the "in-one-another"

26. Stanley J. Grenz offers a useful, brief summary of the concept of the Trinity in each of these theologians apart from Volf (*The Social God and the Relational Self: A Trinitarian Theology of the* Imago Dei [Louisville: Westminster John Knox, 2001], 41–57).

27. For criticism of this development, see Karen Kilby, "Perichoresis and Projection: Problems with Social Doctrines of the Trinity," *NBf* 81 (2000): 432–45; Stephen R. Holmes, *The Quest for the Trinity: The Doctrine of God in Scripture, History, and Modernity* (Downers Grove, IL: IVP Academic, 2012).

28. In the third-century controversy over "modalism" it was debated whether texts such as John 10:30 mean that the "duality" of Father and Son is ultimately reducible to "oneness," as was argued by the modalists, who thought that "Father" and "Son" (as well as "Holy Spirit") were temporally limited modes of appearance that God adopted, one after another, in his dealings with the world. This view cannot plausibly be attributed to the Gospel once it is understood that 10:30 ("I and the Father are one") alludes to the Shema and that it is further explicated by 10:39 ("the Father is in me and I am in the Father").

29. Grenz, *Social God,* 57.

language of the Gospel. Moltmann defines it as "this special unmixed and undivided community of the one and the other" (where "unmixed and undivided" derives from the Council of Chalcedon's statement about the relation between the human and divine natures in Christ), which entails "community without uniformity" and "personhood without individualism."[30] Moltmann also takes advantage of the spatial image that the "in-one-another" language of John evokes to speak of the mutual indwelling of the Persons, and, extending the notion to God's relation to the world, he speaks of "the indwelling and inhabitable God."[31] Volf also keeps the spatial image when he says that the three Persons are "mutually internal"[32] and speaks of their "reciprocal interiority."[33]

These theologians most obviously break with the Western theological tradition when they see the divine unity not as something prior or additional to the relations between the trinitarian Persons, but as actually constituted by those relations.[34] Those relationships both differentiate them and unite them. This is not tritheism, nor is it a purely "moral" union of will, because the three Persons do not exist prior to their relationships but are constituted as persons in those relationships.[35] As far as it goes, the Johannine "oneness" concept points in this direction. The unity of the Father and the Son comprises and consists in their "in-one-anotherness."

As for the correspondence between divine community and human community, it can be deployed in a misleading fashion when the thought is simply that the Trinity provides a model to which human community should correspond. Such a purely external relationship between the Trinity and human community is woefully inadequate, even though a superficial reading of the Johannine Jesus's prayer ("that they may be one, as we are one") might suggest it. In

---

30. Jürgen Moltmann, "God in the World—the World in God: Perichoresis in Trinity and Eschatology," in *The Gospel of John and Christian Theology*, ed. Richard Bauckham and Carl Mosser (Grand Rapids: Eerdmans, 2008), 369–81, here 372. For a fuller presentation of Moltmann's trinitarian theology, see Jürgen Moltmann, *The Trinity and the Kingdom of God: The Doctrine of God*, trans. Margaret Kohl (London: SCM, 1981).

31. Moltmann, "God," 369. He makes the illuminating comment that his theology has moved "from Eschatology to Ecology . . . from the concept of Time in the progress of human history to the concept of Space in the life-giving organism of the earth." It could be illuminating to reflect further on the spatiality of Johannine theology, with its depiction of Jesus as the new temple or place of God's presence and its language of above and below, ascending and descending.

32. Volf, *After Our Likeness*, 208.

33. Volf, *After Our Likeness*, 209.

34. They differ in their attitudes toward the Greek patristic and Eastern theological notion of the "monarchy" of the Father.

35. See Volf, *After Our Likeness*, 210n88, defending Moltmann against criticism on this point.

fact, however, these theologians think of human community as formed by participation in the divine community. Commenting precisely on John 17:21, Moltmann characteristically asserts that the divine unity is not a "closed" unity, but a "wide open, inviting and integrating unity."[36] The mutual love of the divine Persons overflows so as to include creatures within it,[37] something that occurs when the Son of God takes human beings "into his own intimate relationship with his God and Father."[38] But Moltmann is also careful to distinguish the perichoretic unity between persons of the same nature, the trinitarian Persons, and the perichoretic community between divine and human persons.[39]

Finally, in discussing the correspondence between divine community and human community, Volf carefully insists that there are limits to the analogy, since, he claims, the "indwelling of other persons is an exclusive prerogative of God."[40] No human being, he explains, can be internal to another self as a subject of action, not even in mutual love. "Human persons are always external to one another *as subjects*."[41] This requires him also to say that the indwelling of human persons by God the Holy Spirit is not strictly reciprocal, for the Spirit of God can be internal to human persons, but human persons cannot be internal to the person of the Spirit. They can only, he says, "indwell *the life-giving ambience of the Spirit*, not the person of the Spirit."[42] In the case of relationships between humans, Volf claims that humans cannot be interior to one another as persons; "only the *interiority of personal characteristics* can correspond [on the human level] to the interiority of the divine persons."[43]

These distinctions may help us to understand why the Gospel of John uses "in-one-another" language of the relations between the Father and the Son and of their relations with humans, but not of interhuman relationships. However, I am concerned that Volf turns "in-one-anotherness" into something strictly without analogy and therefore unintelligible. I prefer to think that the degree to which human persons can become internal to one another, especially in intimately loving relationships, gives us some real purchase on the image, even though the divine community exceeds this.

36. Moltmann, "God," 375.
37. According to Moltmann, all creation will be included, eschatologically, in this integrating community of God with creatures.
38. Moltmann, "God," 376.
39. Moltmann, "God," 376.
40. Volf, *After Our Likeness*, 211.
41. Volf, *After Our Likeness*, 211.
42. Volf, *After Our Likeness*, 211.
43. Volf, *After Our Likeness*, 211.

From Divine Community to the World

We must return to John 17, for we have not yet pursued the implications of the "oneness" concept to their limit. Mark Appold, in the only monograph devoted to the "oneness" concept in John, points out how the Gospel's whole theology can be seen to stem from the unity of the Father and the Son.[44] From this theological or christological reality derives the Gospel's soteriology and from that the Gospel's ecclesiology and finally the church's mission to the world. We shall see how each of these aspects appears in the prayer of Jesus in John 17.

The love between the Father and the Son is the source of the Son's mission, whose goal, as the very last words of the prayer express it, is that "the love with which you [the Father] have loved me may be in them, and I in them" (17:26). This inclusion of believers in the love of the Father and the Son, through the "in-one-another" relationship of God and believers, is surely the heart of Johannine soteriology. Its result is the oneness of believers, reflecting the oneness of Jesus and the Father—surely the key to Johannine ecclesiology. But there is a further stage in the way the love of the Father and the Son takes effect in the world. Twice Jesus prays that believers may be one "so that the world may believe/know" (17:21, 23). This is the climax of the "oneness" language:

> so that they may be one, as we are one, I in them and you in me, that they may become completely one, so that the world may know that you have sent me and have loved them even as you have loved me. (17:22–23)

The loving community of believers witnesses to the love of God in Christ for all the world to see.

This final thought has occurred already in embryo at 13:34–35, where Jesus introduces his new commandment:

> I give you a new commandment, that you love one another. Just as I have loved you, you also should love one another. By this everyone will know that you are my disciples, if you have love one for another.

What is new about the commandment is not that it requires love for one another, but that the disciples are to love as Jesus has loved them. Love for one another (in the Greek *agapēn en allēlois*, literally: "love between one another") is the nearest that humans come, in the Gospel's terminology, to being "in" one another. It is the human community's correspondence to divine community. So

44. Appold, *Oneness Motif*, 285–88.

the missional aspect is not just the obvious thought that people will see that they are Jesus's disciples because they are obeying his command, but the more profound dimension that emerges more clearly in chapter 17: the world will recognize God's love as it is at work and reflected in the Christian community.

It is sometimes rather held against this Gospel that in it the disciples are commanded to love one another but not other people, and this is easily connected with the contention that the community the Gospel allegedly reflects was a sectarian group, turning in on itself in the face of the hostile world. But what is unequivocal in John is that *God* loves the world. In the famous words of 3:16, "God so loved the world that he gave his only Son." By the end of chapter 17 we know that this love of God for the world comprises the whole movement of God's love that begins in the mutual loving communion of the Father and the Son, entails the Son's mission to include humans in that divine love, creates the loving community of disciples of Jesus, and thereby reaches the world.[45] Disciples are not explicitly told to love the world, but they are caught up in that movement of God's love that has nothing less than the world as its goal.

45. It could be asked why, in that case, Jesus says that he is praying not for the world but only for those the Father has given him, his disciples (17:9). The reason probably relates to the multivalent character of "the world" (*kosmos*) in Johannine usage. It can have a strongly negative sense: the world in its opposition to God and rejection of the truth. It is the world in this sense that has hated both Jesus and his disciples because they do not belong to the world (17:14–16). It is for the world *qua* world-against-God that Jesus does not pray. But when he goes on to expect "that the world may believe that you have sent me" (17:21 [cf. 17:23]), he speaks of the world as God's creation and as redeemable through believing in Jesus (cf. 3:17). The witness of the disciples to the world will provoke both hostility and belief, confronting the world with the possibilities of responding to God's love for it (3:16) or remaining resolutely in darkness (3:19–21). See also Barton, "Unity," 252–54.

3

Glory

Glory is a key theme in the Gospel of John, as most readers and commentators readily recognize, but it is rarely given extended exposition. This chapter is a preliminary attempt at an analytic overview of the theme. We shall see that, among its functions, glory helps to explicate the relationship between the Sinai covenant, on the one hand, and the incarnation and cross of Jesus, on the other. "Glory" is also a term John uses to penetrate the meaning of Jesus's ministry and miracles. Above all, glory is a theme that John uses, very distinctively among the New Testament writers to highlight, by paradox, the extraordinary nature of the love of God for the world in going to the lengths of Jesus's abject dying in the pain and shame of crucifixion.

We must begin with the words. This is truly a case of "Greek words with Hebrew meanings,"[1] a case where John's usage is determined less by ordinary Greek usage than by biblical Greek usage. In other words, he adopts a kind of Jewish Greek that reflects the Hebrew of the Hebrew Bible.

1. See David Hill, *Greek Words and Hebrew Meanings: Studies in the Semantics of Soteriological Terms*, SNTSMS 5 (Cambridge: Cambridge University Press, 1967). Since Hill wrote, the concept of Jewish use of Greek words with Hebrew meanings has been subject to criticism, but in the case of *doxa* it seems clearly valid.

1. Words

In Hebrew and Greek the words often translated within the Bible by the English word "glory" (*kābôd*, *doxa*) both have a range of meaning, but the range is significantly different in each case (see table 3.1). The Hebrew noun *kābôd*, as used in the Hebrew Bible, has three categories of meaning. It comes from the verbal root *kābad* ("to be heavy"), and it is possible to see how the three meanings of *kābôd* develop from this root meaning. First, it can mean "wealth, power, importance." (The English word "weighty," in the sense of "important," provides an analogy for this meaning.) Because prestige was attached to those things and honor was given to people with those things, the second category of meaning is "honor, prestige, good reputation." In the ancient world, honor and prestige often had visible manifestation in clothes, jewelry, and general magnificence, and so the third—very important—category of meaning is "visible splendor." This is what God has when people see his glory. Glory in this sense is always something visible.

The Greek word *doxa*, in nonbiblical Greek usage, comes from the verb *dokeō* ("to think, to suppose, to believe"), and the most common use of it is in the sense "opinion." It can also mean "reputation, honor" (the high opinion that people have of someone). So there is an overlap of meaning with the Hebrew word *kābôd*, but the overlap is quite small. It was the translators of the Hebrew Bible into Greek who changed this situation. They used *doxa* to translate the word *kābôd* in very many instances and shifted its meaning to accommodate the meaning of the Hebrew. So in the Greek Bible *doxa* never has its common Greek meaning, "opinion," and acquires a meaning that it never had in Greek before this: "visible splendor." The New Testament follows the usage of the Greek Bible. *Doxa* in the New Testament has the two different categories of meaning: "honor, reputation" and "visible splendor."

Most New Testament writers use *doxa* in both these senses, and usually they mean either one or the other, not both at once. But, of course, when a word has more than one meaning, this coincidence can be deliberately exploited, by bringing the two meanings together in a single use of the word or by slipping back and forth from one meaning to the other. John, as we shall see, does just this.

The corresponding Greek verb *doxazō*, which in ordinary Greek means "to have an opinion," usually in the Greek Bible and the New Testament means "to honor, to praise" (as in "to give glory to God," "to glorify God"), but it can sometimes mean "to endow with visible splendor."

Table 3.1 provides some statistics for New Testament occurrences of these words. The Gospel of John equals 2 Corinthians in using *doxa* more than

Table 3.1 Glory Words

Meanings

Hebrew, *kābôd,* כבוד root: כבד, to be heavy	importance wealth power	honor prestige reputation	visible splendor
Greek, *doxa,* δόξα verb: δοκέω, to think, believe, suppose	opinion	reputation (usually good = honor)	
Greek Old Testament (LXX), *doxa,* δόξα		honor prestige reputation	visible splendor
New Testament, *doxa,* δόξα		honor prestige reputation	visible splendor

New Testament Frequency

doxa, δόξα	John 19× 2 Cor. 19×; Rev. 17×; Rom. 16×; Luke 13×; 1 Cor. 12×; etc.
doxazō, δοξάζω	John 23× Luke 9×; Acts 5×; Rom. 5×; Matt. 4×; 1 Pet. 4×; 2 Cor. 3×; etc.

Occurrences of *doxa* (δόξα) and *doxazō* (δοξάζω) in John

Reference	*doxa,* δόξα	*doxazō,* δοξάζω	Reference	*doxa,* δόξα	*doxazō,* δοξάζω
1:14	x		12:28		x
1:14	x		12:41	x	
2:11	x		12:43	x	
5:41	x		12:43	x	
5:44	x		13:31		x
5:44	x		13:31		x
7:18	x		13:32		x
7:18	x		13:32		x
7:39		x	13:32		x
8:50	x		14:13		x
8:54		x	15:8		x
8:54	x		16:14		x
8:54		x	17:1		x
9:24	x		17:1		x
11:4	x		17:4		x
11:4		x	17:5		x
11:40	x		17:5	x	
12:16		x	17:10		x
12:23		x	17:22	x	
12:28		x	17:24	x	
12:28		x	21:19		x

other New Testament writings, but others are not far behind, and, when one takes comparative length into account, John's high usage is not very remarkable. But in the case of *doxazō*, John's usage is way ahead of most other New Testament books. (If we took comparative length into account, only 1 Peter would be ahead of John, and 2 Thessalonians not far behind.) This is due to its connection with *doxa* and does suggest that there might be something special about the theme of glory in John's Gospel.

Table 3.1 also provides a chart of the distribution of these two words throughout the Gospel. It shows that more than half of the occurrences (24 of 42) are in chapters 12–17, with eight occurrences in chapter 12 and eight in chapter 17. Nearly all of these occurrences are in words of Jesus (the exceptions, in 12:28, are in words of God to Jesus). These statistics show that Jesus uses the language of glory especially as he approaches and contemplates his own glorification and God's glorification in the event of his death-and-exaltation.

2. Glory Seen in Jesus Christ (John 1:14)

The word *doxa* first appears in the Gospel of John in 1:14, a key verse of the prologue that announces the incarnation of the Word in flesh. In fact, the word *doxa* appears twice in that verse, in swift succession, emphasizing its programmatic significance for the Gospel as a whole. But we need to approach this verse via its Old Testament background. (See table 3.2 for a presentation of the texts referred to here.)

2A. Glory: The Visible Manifestation of God in Israel's History

From the first appearance of the glory of the Lord in the wilderness after the exodus until Ezekiel sees it depart from the temple before its destruction by the Babylonians, the glory of the Lord is conceived as a fiery radiance that can be seen but only in a veiled form, hidden within a cloud. Only when the glory returns to the new temple, in Ezekiel's vision, and lights up the new Jerusalem with glory visible to all people will the glory appear without the cloud. Thus in Israel's history God is revealed only in hiddenness. What is revealed is both the holy otherness of the God who is a consuming fire and the gracious presence of God in the midst of his people, dwelling among them.

2B. Only a Glimpse of Glory (Exod. 33:17–23; 34:5–7)

The story of Moses's glimpse of the glory of God on Mount Sinai is one of the key revelatory events of the biblical narrative because it contains the

Table 3.2 Seeing the Glory of God
(Old Testament)

Glory: The Visible Manifestation of God in Israel's History

1. First appearance (Exod. 16:7, 10)
2. Mount Sinai (Exod. 24:15–17; 33–34)
3. Tabernacle (Exod. 40:34–35)
4. Temple (2 Chron. 5:11–14; 7:1–3)
5. Departure (Ezek. 10)
6. Return (Isa. 35:2; 40:5; 60; Ezek. 43:1–6)

In cases (1–5) the glory (fiery radiance) is hidden in the cloud; only when the glory returns to the new temple (6) is there no cloud. What is revealed is both the holy otherness of God (a consuming fire) and the gracious presence of God in the midst of his people (dwelling among them).

Moses: Only a Glimpse of Glory (Exod. 33:17–23; 34:5–7)

Exod. 33:18–23 LXX:
> And he [Moses] says, "Show me your own glory!" [19]And he [the Lord] said, "I will pass by before you in my glory, and I will call by my name 'Lord' before you. And I will have mercy on whomever I have mercy, and I will have compassion on whomever I have compassion. [20]And he said, "You shall not be able to see my face. For a person shall never see my face and live." [21]And the Lord said, "Look, a place is near me. You shall stand on the rock. [22]Now, whenever my glory passes by, then I will put you in a hole of the rock, and I will cover you with my hand until I pass by. [23]And I will take my hand away, and then you shall see my hind parts, but my face will not appear to you." (*NETS*)

Exod. 34:5–7 LXX:
> And the Lord descended in a cloud, and he stood beside him [Moses] there, and he called in the name of the Lord. [6]And the Lord passed by before his face, and he called,
>
> > "The Lord, the Lord God is compassionate and merciful,
> > patient and very merciful and truthful
> > [7]and preserving righteousness and doing mercy for thousands,
> > taking away acts of lawlessness and of injustice and sins,
> > and he will not acquit the guilty person,
> > bringing lawless acts of fathers upon children and upon children of
> > children, upon the third and fourth generation." (*NETS*)

Exod. 33:18–23 MT:

> Moses said, "Show me your glory, I pray. [19]And he [the LORD] said, "I will make all my goodness pass before you, and will proclaim before you the name, 'The LORD'; and I will be gracious to whom I will be gracious, and will show mercy on whom I will show mercy. [20]But," he said, "you cannot see my face; for no one shall see me and live." [21]And the LORD continued, "See, there is a place by me where you shall stand on the rock; [22]and while my glory passes by I will put you in a cleft of the rock, and I will cover you with my hand until I have passed by; [23]then I will take away my hand, and you shall see my back; but my face shall not be seen."

Exod. 34:5–7 MT:

> The LORD descended in a cloud and stood with him there, and proclaimed the name, "The LORD." [6]The LORD passed before him, and proclaimed,

> "The LORD, the LORD,
> a God merciful and gracious, slow to anger,
> and abounding in steadfast love and faithfulness,
> [7]keeping steadfast love for the thousandth generation,
> forgiving iniquity and transgression and sin,
> yet by no means clearing the guilty,
> but visiting the iniquity of the parents upon the children
> and the children's children,
> to the third and fourth generation."

Isaiah Saw His Glory

Isa. 6:1 LXX:

> I saw the Lord sitting on a throne, lofty [*hypsēlou*] and raised up, and the house was full of his glory. (*NETS*)

Isa. 52:13–14; 53:2b–3 LXX:

> See, my servant shall understand,
> and he shall be exalted [*hypsōthēsetai*] and glorified [*doxasthēsetai*]
>   exceedingly.
> [14]Just as many shall be astonished at you—
> so shall your appearance be without glory from humans [*adoxēsei*
>   *apo anthrōpōn*]
> and your glory [be absent] from humans [*hē doxa sou apo tōn*
>   *anthrōpōn*]
>
> [53:2]. . . he has no form or glory [*doxa*],
> and we saw him, and he had no form or beauty.

> ³But his form was without honor [*atimon*], failing beyond all people,
> a man struck down [*en plēgē*] and knowing how to bear weakness;
> because his face is turned away,
> he was dishonored and not esteemed. (*NETS* altered)

Isa. 6:1 MT:
> I saw the Lord sitting on a throne, high and lofty [*rām wĕniśśā'*]; and the
> hem of his robe filled the temple.

Isa. 52:13–15a; 53:2b–3 MT:
> See, my servant shall prosper;
> he shall be exalted and lifted up [*yārûm wĕniśśā'*], and shall be very
>   high.
> ¹⁴Just as there were many who were astonished at him—
> so marred was his appearance, beyond human semblance,
> and his form beyond that of mortals—
> ¹⁵so shall he startle many nations. . . .
>
> ⁵³:² . . . he had no form or majesty that we should look at him,
> nothing in his appearance that we should desire him.
> ³He was despised and rejected by others;
> a man of suffering and acquainted with infirmity;
> and as one from whom others hide their faces
> he was despised, and we held him of no account.

definitive character description of God that is echoed throughout the rest of the biblical literature, including John's Gospel. It is a strange and evocative story that conveys a subtle theological message in highly anthropomorphic form. For our purposes it is best read in the Greek version that John's readers knew, although I am sure that John himself habitually consulted the Hebrew text as well as the Greek. (Table 3.2 provides both the Greek [LXX] and Hebrew [MT] texts for comparison.)

The context is the renewal of the Sinai covenant after Israel's shocking apostasy in the incident of the golden calf, for which God in his surprising grace forgives them. Moses asks to see God's glory, and God replies,

> I will pass by before you in my glory, and I will call by my name "Lord" before you. . . . [But] you shall not be able to see my face. For a person shall never see my face and live. . . . Now, whenever my glory passes by, then I will put you in a hole of the rock, and I will cover you with my hand until I pass by. And I will take my hand away, and then you shall see my hind parts, but my face will not appear to you. (Exod. 33:19a, 20, 22–23 LXX *NETS*)

When the moment for the revelation comes, the Lord passes by Moses, calling out,

> The Lord, the Lord God is compassionate and merciful, patient and very merciful and truthful and preserving righteousness and doing mercy for thousands. (Exod. 34:6 LXX *NETS*)

Thus Moses is granted only a passing glimpse of God's visible glory, because no one can see the face of God, but he receives a revelation nonetheless. He may not see who God is, but he hears who God is. He hears from God himself God's identity: his name ("YHWH," represented in the Greek version by "the Lord") and his character. As Israel so much needs to know, Moses hears that God is merciful, compassionate, forgiving, and faithful to his covenant promises. The story seems to suggest that God's glory is the radiance of his character, of his goodness, of who he truly is. (In fact, the Hebrew uses the phrase "all my goodness" [Exod. 33:19] as equivalent to "my glory.") This is what the face of God would reveal, if Moses could see it. A person's identity is made visible in the person's face. Moses cannot see, but he does hear.

2C. God's Glory Revealed in the Flesh of the Only Son (John 1:14–18)

One of the functions of the prologue to John's Gospel is to indicate to readers how, starting with the Old Testament, they should read the story of Jesus. That they should start with the Old Testament should be obvious, because the opening words repeat literally the opening words of Genesis. For the meaning of the first five verses of the prologue the opening verses of Genesis are crucial, but for the last five verses of the prologue the key text is Exodus, more specifically Moses at Sinai. John presents the incarnation of the Word, Jesus Christ, as the eschatological fulfillment of the Sinai covenant, a revelation of glory that fulfills the Sinai covenant by qualitatively surpassing it:

> And the Word became flesh and dwelt among us, and we have seen his glory, the glory as of the Only One from the Father, full of grace and truth. . . . From his fullness we have all received, grace in addition to grace. The law was given through Moses; grace and truth came through Jesus Christ. No one has ever seen God. It is God the Only One, who is close to the Father's heart, who has made him known. (NRSV altered)

The Word became flesh. In other words the audible word became visible flesh. This is why Jesus is never called "the Word" in John's Gospel after this sentence. From now on he is not only audible but also visible. Surpassing the divine words of the Sinai covenant, the incarnation manifests God visibly. But since no one can see the face of God and live, as Moses and others in the Old Testament narratives learned, why was the incarnation not fatal to those who saw Jesus? The answer is that God is manifested in something not divine, in flesh, in a human life. The glory that was hidden in the cloud in the Old Testament narratives remains hidden, now veiled in flesh, but the veil is of a kind that permits a visible form of revelation. Isaiah expected the time when "the glory of the Lord will appear, and all flesh shall see the salvation of God" (Isa. 40:5 LXX). All flesh will see the glory when it is revealed in flesh.

The Word became flesh and dwelt [eskēnōsen] among us. This phrase echoes the dwelling of God's glory in the tabernacle and the temple, God's gracious presence at the heart of his people's life. Now the glory in the flesh of Jesus Christ is God's tent-dwelling among his people.

The Word became flesh and dwelt among us, and we have seen his glory. Who are "we"? Contrary to many of the commentators, the "we" are not Christians in general, but the eyewitnesses who saw the flesh of Jesus with their physical eyes.[2] When John means to speak of all Christians, in verse 16, he says "we all" to make clear the transition. This point is theologically important, because what is seen is the glory in the flesh of Jesus Christ. Precisely the visibility of the flesh is the point. If we take "we have seen" to refer to something purely spiritual, we negate the incarnation. Of course, no one could see the glory in the flesh merely with physical eyes. Spiritual perception was also necessary, but physical sight was required. In John's vocabulary, one can believe without seeing, as is shown by the beatitude that Jesus pronounces on those who, unlike Thomas, do not see but yet have come to believe (20:29b). But those who must believe without seeing need the testimony of those who did see, which John's Gospel was written to provide.[3]

We have seen his glory, glory as of the Only One from the Father. This does not mean the only Son *of* the Father, but the only Son who came into the world *from* the Father, the Son who became incarnate. The glory is his, but it fully reflects the glory of his Father. But how can the glory be seen in the flesh?

2. See Richard Bauckham, *Jesus and the Eyewitnesses: The Gospels as Eyewitness Testimony* (Grand Rapids: Eerdmans, 2006), 380–81, where I suggest that "we" may in fact refer only to one eyewitness, the Beloved Disciple, who wrote the Gospel, using the idiom of the "we" of authoritative testimony (a strengthened form of "I").

3. See Bauckham, *Jesus and the Eyewitnesses*, 403–6.

Glory as of the Only One from the Father, full of grace and truth. John alludes to the famous character description of God that Moses had heard. In the Hebrew it reads, "The LORD, the LORD, a God merciful and gracious, slow to anger, and abounding in steadfast love and faithfulness" (Exod. 34:6). John's "full of grace and truth" (*plērēs charitos kai alētheias*) is a precise Greek equivalent of the phrase "abounding in steadfast love and faithfulness" (*rab-ḥesed we'ĕmet*).[4] For such a key biblical text, John certainly would not depend only on the Septuagint, whose rendering here is not very literal. He provides a more literal equivalent. The glory is the radiance of the character of God, the grace and truth about which Moses heard, but which the disciples of Jesus have seen in his human person and life.

The law was given through Moses, grace and truth came through Jesus the Messiah. Here, in verse 17, John refers to Moses explicitly. Again we have the contrast between hearing and seeing. The law was grace and truth in words. The same grace and truth of God "became" through Jesus—happened and were seen in his life and death. Jesus spoke the words of God's grace and truth, certainly, but he also enacted God's grace and truth. Probably the best illustration of the relationship is the new commandment that Jesus gave his disciples: "Love one another as I have loved you" (13:34). The command to love one another is, of course, an old commandment, already found in Leviticus (19:18), already regarded as a summary of the whole Mosaic law. What is new is the "as I have loved you." It is new because Jesus himself has lived it—and died it, we might say. He has loved to the utmost. He has incarnated the kind of divine love that the disciples are called to imitate. They not only hear his commandment, as they could in the synagogue; they see it on the cross.

No one has ever seen God. It is the Only One, himself God, who is in the bosom of the Father, who has made him known. This concludes the prologue. John is not denying the visions of God that Scripture narrates; but no one has seen God in the full sense that was denied to Moses, no one has seen his face, no one has seen who God is in the holy splendor of his face. But the Only One, because he is uniquely close to the Father, because he gazes into the face that expresses the infinite goodness of God, he alone has described him (*exēgēsato*). Ben Sira, the Jewish sage, summoned his readers to glorify the Lord with all their powers, because they could never match his inexpressible greatness (Sir. 43:30). He asks, "Who has seen him and can describe him?"

4. This is demonstrated in detail by Alexander Tsutserov, *Glory, Grace, and Truth: Ratification of the Sinaitic Covenant according to the Gospel of John* (Eugene, OR: Pickwick, 2009).

(Sir. 43:31). It is a rhetorical question, but John, in effect, answers it. Only the utterly Unique One has seen him and so can describe him. That description is the life and death of Jesus. More than once the Gospel says that whoever has seen Jesus has seen the Father (12:45; 14:9). The extraordinary message of the Gospel is that only human flesh in its visibility could make that true.

Before leaving the prologue, we need to return to the phrase in which John uses the word "glory" for the first time: "we have seen his glory." The last time John uses the word "glory" is in Jesus's prayer in chapter 17, and again the reference is to Jesus's disciples seeing his glory (17:24). In fact, these are the only two explicit references to the disciples seeing Jesus's glory in the Gospel, forming a surely deliberate *inclusio*. Toward the end of his prayer, looking forward to his return to the Father, Jesus prays,

> I desire that those also, whom you have given me, may be with me where I am, to see my glory, which you have given me because you loved me before the foundation of the world. (17:24)

Jesus's disciples, those who have seen his glory in his earthly life, where it is veiled under the conditions of this world, will see him in his manifest glory in heaven. And this time, because by this point in his prayer Jesus has extended his purview from his personal disciples to include also those who will come to believe in him in the future (17:20), all believers are included.

3. Jesus and God Glorified

3A. Isaiah Saw His Glory

In John 12:41 the evangelist tells us, "Isaiah said this because he saw his [Jesus's] glory and spoke about him." The words "Isaiah said this" refer back not only to 12:40 (a quotation from Isa. 6:10) but also to 12:38 (a quotation from Isa. 53:1). He has in mind both Isaiah's vision of the Lord on his exalted throne in chapter 6 and Isaiah's prophecy of the Servant who suffers and is exalted in chapters 52–53. There are key verbal connections between the two passages, which encouraged early Christians to read them together (following the Jewish exegetical practice that brought together in a connected interpretation passages of Scripture in which the same words or phrases occurred). One of these connections is more apparent in the Hebrew text than in the Greek translation, though it is partly preserved in the latter: the Lord's throne is "high and lifted up" (*rām wĕniśśā'* [6:1]), while the Servant also is exalted and lifted up (*yārûm wĕniśśā'* [52:13]). But what the Greek version loses in this respect it gains in another, creating a connection between the Lord's "glory" (*doxa* [6:1]) and the prophecy that the Servant will be "glorified" (*doxasthēsetai* [52:13]) (see the presentation of the texts in table 3.2). In my view, John knew both versions, but it is the Greek version, with its four occurrences of *doxa* words in 52:13–14; 53:2, that he has in mind at John 12:41 and in other references to Jesus's glory and glorification.

John appears to have taken the opening of the Suffering Servant passage (52:13: "he shall be exalted and glorified exceedingly") as a kind of heading for the whole of the subsequent passage, which describes the Servant's humiliation, suffering, death, and exaltation beyond death. According to this way of reading the prophecy, it is not only at the end of this sequence that the Servant is exalted and glorified. *The whole sequence is his exaltation and glorification.* This is the exegetical source of John's remarkable and distinctive way of speaking of the exaltation ("lifting up") and glorification of Jesus as taking place through his humiliating death as well as his subsequent resurrection. The point of Jesus's deepest humiliation is, paradoxically, also his glorification. Whereas the more common early Christian way of thinking envisaged humiliation followed by exaltation, suffering followed by glory, John sees exaltation and glory in the humiliation and death.[5]

Following the introductory rubric (52:13), the Suffering Servant passage continues in the Greek version thus:

> Just as many shall be astonished at you—so shall your appearance be without glory from humans [*adoxēsei apo anthrōpōn*] and your glory [be absent] from humans [*hē doxa sou apo tōn anthrōpōn*]. . . .
>
>   . . . he has no form or glory [*doxa*], and we saw him, and he had no form or beauty. But his form was without honor [*atimon*], failing beyond all people, a man struck down [*en plēgē*] and knowing how to bear weakness; because his face is turned away, he was dishonored and not esteemed. (52:14; 53:2b–3 *NETS* altered)

In considering how John and his readers would have understood this, we should recall that the word *doxa* can mean not only "visible splendor" but also "honor" or "praise." Both meanings come into play in Isaiah's prophecy. The Servant's visible appearance has no beauty or glory, but he is also without honor. He is humiliated and dishonored. John will have found this significant because crucifixion notoriously involved both dimensions: it was physically

---

5. For more detail, see Richard Bauckham, *Jesus and the God of Israel: God Crucified and Other Studies on the New Testament's Christology of Divine Identity* (Grand Rapids: Eerdmans, 2008), 35–37, 46–50.

disfiguring to a horrifying degree, and it was also the ultimate humiliation. The former was designed to achieve the latter. But we should notice especially that the Servant is said to be without glory "from humans," since this is an expression that we shall find John adopting. Finally, when the heading verse (52:13) uses the verb *doxazō*, we find that this verb can readily be understood in accordance with both meanings of *doxa*. The Servant is given the visible splendor that Isaiah saw in chapter 6, but he is also exalted to the highest position of honor. Here we have excellent prophetic precedent for John to move from one to the other meaning of both *doxa* and *doxazō*, or even to combine the two meanings.

3B. God's Glory Revealed in the Signs (John 2:11; 11:4, 40)

The most obvious way in which the glory of God is revealed in Jesus's ministry is the miracles, for which John uses the term "signs" (*sēmeia*). John makes explicit in the case of the first of the signs that Jesus "revealed his glory," with the result that "his disciples believed in him" (2:11). This function of the signs is made explicit again in the case of the sixth sign, the raising of Lazarus, which is said to reveal "the glory of God" (11:40). It is also said to be "for God's glory, so that the Son of God may be glorified through it" (11:4).[6] We should undoubtedly conclude that all of the signs reveal the glory of God, which is also Jesus's own glory, the divine glory revealed in him.

The signs are important because, as we have noticed, Jesus was not self-evidently the revelation of the glory of God. He revealed the glory *in the flesh*, and so, of course, people who encountered him had all sorts of opinions about him, as John records quite extensively. The signs function to alert people to wonder whether they are encountering something more than just flesh. The signs point beyond mere flesh in two ways. They do so, first, in their stupendous miraculousness, which John does not at all play down (see table 3.3). Indeed, he has selected some of the most stupendously miraculous of Jesus's miracles from among the many that he could have recounted. They are unheard-of marvels. But more than that, secondly, they mean something specific. Each of them says something about Jesus and the eternal life that he has come to give. In one way or another all of them are signs of the eternal life that Jesus will actually give only later. In both senses they exceed the flesh. Like Jesus

6. The immediate reference here is to Lazarus's illness, but the thought is that this will lead to his raising by Jesus, which will be for God's glory. At the same time, since it is the raising of Lazarus that provokes the decision of the Jewish authorities to put Jesus to death, there may be a further reference to the glorification of God and of Jesus in the death-and-exaltation of Jesus (see the next section).

himself, they are visible. That they are visible is essential. They are means of
seeing the glory of God (as Martha did at the raising of Lazarus [11:40]). As
visible events that exceed the flesh, they signal the presence of God's glory.

A minor observation that highlights the care with which John deploys the
word *doxa* is that, in its only occurrence on the lips of opponents of Jesus,

Seven signs	Called a "sign"	Details emphasizing the miraculous	Explicit indications of significance
1. Water into wine (2:1–11) "the beginning of his signs" (2:11)	2:11	6 water jars holding 20 or 30 gallons each (2:6)	
2. Healing the official's son (4:46–54) "the second sign" (4:54)	4:54	at the point of death (4:47); recovered at the hour Jesus spoke (4:52–53)	
3. Healing the lame man on the Sabbath (5:2–9)	6:2	ill for 38 years (5:5)	Jesus does God's work on the Sabbath (5:17)
4. Feeding the 5,000 (6:1–15)	6:14, 26	12 baskets left (6:13)	"I am the bread of life" (6:35)
5. Healing the blind man on the Sabbath (9:1–12)	9:16	blind from birth (9:1; cf. 9:32)	"I am the light of the world" (8:12; 9:5); "that those who do not see may see" (9:39)
6. Raising Lazarus from death (11:1–45)	12:18 (cf. 11:47)	already buried for four days (11:17, 39)	"I am the resurrection and the life" (11:25)
7. Resurrection of Jesus	2:18–19 (cf. 6:30; 20:30–31)	cf. 20:6–7, 12, 20, 27	
Miraculous events not called "signs" (not signs in the sense indicated by 20:31)			
Walking on the water (6:1–15)			
Stupendous catch of fish (21:4–11)		153 large fish, net not broken (21:11)	

Table 3.3 The Seven Signs

it forms a rarely noticed instance of Johannine irony. This is in the story of the fifth sign, the healing of the blind man. The Pharisees, obliged to admit that the man was blind and has acquired sight, nevertheless refuse to credit Jesus with the healing. To the man they say, "Give glory to God! We know that this man is a sinner" (9:24). Thus they refuse to see that God has been glorified not despite Jesus, but in his Son, whose glory is revealed in the sign. It is they who prove to be blind (9:40–41).

3C. God's Glory Revealed in Jesus's Self-Dedication to the Father

There are four passages in the Gospel where Jesus or the evangelist speaks of accepting glory, seeking glory, and loving glory (5:41–44; 7:18; 8:50–54; 12:43). If we put the expressions used in these passages together, we have a set of activities that are judged negatively (they are what Jesus does not do but what the Jewish authorities whom he criticizes do) and a corresponding set judged positively. Thus, negatively, what Jesus does not do is

accept glory from humans (5:41)

accept glory from one another (5:44)

seek his own glory (7:18; 8:50)

glorify himself (8:54)

love the glory of humans (12:43)

The obvious meaning of "glory" here is "honor" or "praise."[7] It is very human to want the approval of other people and to seek to advance one's reputation. The honor-shame culture of antiquity gave, as it were, cultural form and endorsement to this general feature of human motivation. We should note that one increases one's own honor by accepting honor from people. That is in the nature of honor.

In the corresponding set of expressions, evaluated positively, Jesus does

seek the glory that comes from the One who alone is God (5:44)

seek the glory of the One who sent him (7:18)

love the glory of God (12:43)

At first sight, one might think the contrast between the Jewish authorities and Jesus is simply this: the Jewish leaders seek honor from other people, Jesus seeks honor from God. But the difference is more profound. Whereas

---

7. Note in John 8:49 the use of the verb *timaō* as a synonym for *doxazō*.

the Jewish leaders are concerned only with their own reputation, Jesus seeks to promote not himself but God. The Jewish leaders are self-centered; Jesus is God-centered. He lives for the honor and praise of God. But, paradoxically, this can be called seeking the honor that comes from God—that is, Jesus's own honor given by God. By seeking only the glory of God, he wins God's approval. What goes largely unsaid in these particular passages (but cf. 8:49) but certainly is implied is that Jesus, by seeking God's glory and not his own, actually incurs dishonor and disgrace in the eyes of humans but approval from God. Seeking God's glory is the path of self-humiliation that Jesus follows to the cross.

Elsewhere in the Gospel Jesus says, "I seek not to do my own will but the will of him who sent me" (5:30), a statement reminiscent of Jesus's prayer in Gethsemane in the Synoptic Gospels. He also says that his "food is to do the will of him who sent me and to complete his work" (4:34), and there are many other statements in the Gospel that cohere closely with these. Jesus's life is dedicated to bringing honor to God by doing what the Father has given him to do even though he can only complete this task by suffering the utmost humiliation and shame when he is crucified.

But does "glory" in the passages that we have just considered bear only its obvious meaning, "honor," or is there at least a hint of the other meaning too? Arguably, there is a hint that by seeking only the glory of God, Jesus is revealing God's glory in the flesh.[8] The radiance of God's character is displayed in Jesus's humility before God and his obedience to God. By centering his life not in himself but in God, Jesus reveals God.

We may appreciate this better if we turn to a number of passages where the verb *doxazō* ("to glorify") is used with reference to the climax of the Gospel's story: the death and resurrection of Jesus.

3D. Jesus's Cross and Resurrection as Glorification

The whole Gospel story moves toward what it calls "Jesus's hour." By this, John seems to mean the complex of events that occur in chapters 12–20 (i.e., the passion, death, resurrection, and ascension of Jesus). This is the hour of Jesus's exaltation, when he is exalted on the cross in order to be exalted to heaven. The cross is the climax of the work that God has given Jesus to do, and so it is the climax of his life of seeking God's glory, not his own. It is therefore also the climax of the revelation of God's glory in the flesh.

8. Note the proximity of 12:43 to the statement that "Isaiah saw his glory" (12:41).

In order to make this point, John especially uses the verb *doxazō* ("to glorify"). This is the verb that is paired with *hypsoō* ("to lift up, to exalt") in Isa. 52:13 LXX. John uses *hypsoō* in a series of cryptic sayings that refer both to the physical elevation of Jesus on the cross and to the exaltation to heavenly glory that this entailed (3:14; 8:28; 12:32–34). Since *doxazō* accompanies *hypsoō* in Isa. 52:13, John uses this verb similarly to refer to the death-and-exaltation of Jesus, but he also multiplies its meaning by using it both of Jesus's glorification of his Father and the Father's glorification of Jesus, two movements of glorification that occur simultaneously. (For the texts discussed in this section, see table 3.4.)

In this context the most obvious meaning of the verb is "to honor." Jesus honors the Father supremely by completing the work that God has given him to do when he dies on the cross (17:4; cf. 19:30). God will honor Jesus when he vindicates him beyond death by exalting him to heaven. But it is not so simple. When Jesus prays, "Father, glorify me in your own presence with the glory that I had in your presence before the world existed" (17:5), I doubt that this refers mainly to honor, though honor is entailed. This glory in God's presence is a glory that can be seen (17:24). It is the manifest splendor, the

---

Table 3.4 Jesus's Cross and Resurrection/Exaltation as the Mutual Glorification of the Father and the Son

The hour has come for the Son of Man to be glorified. (12:23)

Father, glorify your name. . . .
I have glorified it, and I will glorify it again. (12:28)

Now the Son of Man has been glorified, and God has been glorified in him. If God has been glorified in him, God will also glorify him in himself and will glorify him at once. (13:31–32)

Father, the hour has come; glorify your Son so that the Son may glorify you. (17:1)

I glorified you on earth by finishing the work that you gave me to do. So now, Father, glorify me in your own presence with the glory that I had in your presence before the world existed. (17:4–5)

See also "Jesus was not yet glorified" (7:39) and "when Jesus was glorified" (12:16).

glory of God that no one can see on earth and live, the unveiled radiance of "who God is." Just as the prologue told us that this heavenly glory that the Son shares with the Father in eternity was seen in the flesh, in veiled form in the earthly life and death of Jesus, so the passion narrative tells us that it was seen in veiled form in the cross prior to Jesus's return to the presence of the Father to share once again the unveiled glory of the Father.

In John's use of the verb "glorify" the two meanings of glory—honor and splendor—coincide. What is for God's glory (honor) displays his glory (splendor). The double meaning characterizes both cross and exaltation. There is honor in the humiliation of the cross and splendor in the degradation of the cross. There is honor in the vindication of the resurrection and splendor in the Son's return to heavenly glory.

We are brought back once again to the importance in Johannine theology of the flesh of Jesus and its visibility. The last sentence of John's account of the crucifixion and death of Jesus is a quotation from Zechariah: "They will look on the one whom they have pierced" (19:37). It is sometimes suggested that, by referring to Jesus's death as his exaltation and glorification, John empties the cross of suffering and shame. It becomes like one of those very beautiful crucifixes made of gold and jewels that Christian Europe later produced. But John's account of the crucifixion actually does nothing to mitigate the bleak horror that crucifixion as such would suggest to ancient readers. Unlike the Synoptic evangelists, John recounts no supernatural accompaniments: no darkness at noon, no earthquake, no tearing of the temple veil. What happens is just what always happened at crucifixions, in all their pain and humiliation. What especially marks it out as different is the subsequent event of the resurrection, which, in my view, is the seventh of the Gospel's seven signs.[9] Like the other signs, it signals revelation of God's glory. As the seventh and climactic sign, it signals that revelation to which all the other signs have only pointed.

To this manifestation of God's glory, the ultimate such revelation in the flesh on earth, the resurrection is essential, but so is the cross. John's narration of the seventh sign is not complete until Thomas sees the risen Christ and the wounds of crucifixion in his hands and his side. This is not just a question of a need for evidence to believe that Jesus himself was risen; it is also a way of indicating that the degradation and the death of Jesus are not superseded by the resurrection. It is the degradation and the death, in the

9. I count seven events that the Gospel actually calls signs as the seven signs (see table 3.3). It is usually overlooked that the resurrection of Jesus is called a sign in John 2:18–19. The seventh of a series can have a distinctive significance that exceeds that of the other six, as in the days of the week.

light of the resurrection, that constitute the ultimate manifestation of God's glory to the world.

They are that, of course, because they are the ultimate point to which the love of God—his *ḥesed*, his *charis*, his *agapē*—can go for our sake. This is the character of God that Moses heard on Sinai now described in visible flesh on Golgotha. The paradox of the cross—honor in humiliation, visible splendor in disfigurement and death—exists to make us reckon with a love that is sufficient to resolve the paradox.

3E. Glory and the Disciples

Finally, we must take account, albeit briefly, of a number of passages in the Gospel that speak of glory in relation to Jesus's disciples. They are a rather miscellaneous group of statements. I have already discussed Jesus's prayer that the disciples see his glory in the presence of the Father (17:24). There is also one reference to the Paraclete, the Spirit of truth, glorifying Jesus when he reveals the significance of Jesus more fully to the disciples in the future (16:14). This is one of the ways in which this Gospel compares the relation between Jesus and the Paraclete with the relation between God the Father and Jesus. Just as Jesus in his earthly life and death glorified the Father, so the Spirit of truth will glorify Jesus. In a trinitarian theology this would be a basis for understanding the relationships between the trinitarian persons in terms of self-dedication to the Other and self-giving to the Other. Indeed, the Son's own glorification of the Father does not cease after the resurrection. When he does what the disciples ask in his name, says Jesus (14:13), the Father will be glorified in the Son.

Among the various references to glory and glorification in Jesus's great prayer to the Father are two that are especially difficult to interpret. Jesus speaks of his disciples as those whom the Father has given him, and says, "I have been glorified in them" (17:10). This is particularly puzzling in the context of the passion narrative, in which all the disciples, except the Beloved Disciple and the women, will desert Jesus, just as he has only recently predicted (16:32). The other statement is in the context of Jesus's prayer that the disciples may be one, as he and the Father are one. "The glory that you have given me," he says, "I have given them, so that they may be one, as we are one" (17:22). Here understanding the glory as the radiance of God's character makes good sense. Just as God's love, by which Jesus and the Father are one, has been reflected in the life and death of Jesus, so it is to be reflected in the disciples when they love one another. This reading is supported by a strong connection with chapter 15, where following the allegory of the vine, Jesus says that "the

Father is glorified by this, that you bear much fruit and become my disciples" (15:8). The passage goes on to expound this in terms of the commandment to love one another, as Jesus has loved them.

This general theme—that the glory of God seen in the flesh of Jesus is reflected also in the disciples when they follow his example—reaches an appropriately climactic expression in chapter 21, when Jesus predicts Peter's martyrdom. "He said this," comments the evangelist, "to indicate the kind of death by which [Peter] would glorify God" (21:19).

4

Cross, Resurrection, and Exaltation

This is a very large topic, since the whole of John's theology is strongly focused on the death-and-resurrection/exaltation of Jesus, just as the narrative moves relentlessly toward Jesus's "hour" (2:4; 7:6, 8, 30; 8:20; 12:23, 27; 13:1; 17:1). That Jesus's destiny is to die is first announced by John the Baptist, the primary witness to Jesus (1:7), whose witness is "Here is the Lamb of God who takes away the sin of the world!" (1:29). The first of many cryptic indications of Jesus's coming death-and-resurrection/exaltation comes in the first of the twenty-five sayings of Jesus that are highlighted by the introduction "Amen, amen, I say to you . . ." (1:51).[1] More such riddling sayings come thick and fast through the rest of John's narrative up to the events themselves (2:17, 19–21; 3:14–16; 6:51, 62, 70–71; 7:33–36; 8:21–22, 28; 12:7–8, 24–25, 33–34; 13:21, 28, 33, 36; 14:2–4, 19, 28–31; 16:5–7, 16–22, 28). At the same time the determination of the authorities to put Jesus to death gathers force (5:18; 7:1, 19–20, 25; 8:37, 40, 58–59; 10:30–39; 11:45–53, 56–57; cf. 11:16; 13:2), though they are not able to do so before his "hour" arrives (7:30; 8:20; 10:39; 11:54). The one point at which Jesus says with clarity that he is going to die and rise again is designed to counter any impression that his death will be other than voluntary (10:11–18; cf. 15:13). All this material for understanding John's interpretation of the death-and-resurrection/exaltation of Jesus occurs even

---

1. See chap. 7, "Dimensions of Meaning in the Gospel's First Week."

before the narratives of the arrest, the trials, the crucifixion, the burial, and the resurrection appearances.

In this chapter I shall attempt a fresh approach to this topic by taking up in turn the four big theological words of the Gospel: "love," "life," "glory," and "truth."[2] I call these "big" words because their meaning is abundant and cannot be constrained within any particular exposition. As windows on the meaning of Jesus's death and resurrection, they open vistas to contemplate. They do not afford a totally comprehensive account of the subject,[3] but they do provide an approach that encompasses a great deal of the relevant material in the Gospel.

I have used the phrase "the death-and-resurrection/exaltation of Jesus" because John does not usually work with a threefold sequence (death-resurrection-exaltation), but rather, like other early Christian writers, with two pairs: death-and-resurrection and death-and-exaltation. The second terms in each case are not at all the same thing. Resurrection is Jesus's "return" to life and to his disciples; exaltation is his return to the Father. In our first two sections we are concerned with death-and-resurrection, in the third with death-and-exaltation.

Love

It is a distinctive theme of John's Gospel that Jesus gave his life in love for his disciples, whom the Gospel calls "his own" (10:3–4, 14; 13:2; cf. 15:19) and Jesus calls his "friends" (15:13–15; cf. 11:11). His death is the most costly possible act of love for those he loves. By representing Jesus as giving his life for the circle of his disciples, those specific people whom he knew and loved as friends, John gives concrete narrative form to the love of God for the world that Jesus lives out in his actual path to death.

"No one has greater love than this, to lay down one's life for one's friends" (15:13).[4] This has the ring of a well-known adage, but there is no evidence that it was. It does, however, summarize a common sentiment of Greco-Roman

2. All occur in the prologue with the exception of "love." But "grace" (*charis*), used in the prologue (1:14, 16, 17) but nowhere else in the Gospel, is the equivalent word that John uses in the prologue because he wishes to echo Exod. 34:6 ("abounding in steadfast love and faithfulness" = "full of grace and truth"). Thereafter he speaks of "love" (*agapē*).

3. Significant themes not treated in this chapter are Jesus's death as a sacrifice for sin and Jesus's death as his victory over the devil. I do not intend to minimize the significance of these themes, but they require separate treatment.

4. When speaking of the love of friends (*philoi*), John can use *agapaō* interchangeably with *phileō* (note especially the disciple whom Jesus "loved" [*agapaō* in 13:23; 19:26; 21:7; *phileō* in 20:2] and Jesus's questions to Peter in 21:15–17), but he does not use *phileō* otherwise except in

philosophies: true friendship entails willingness to give one's life for one's friend. The philosophers recommend this as a hypothetical ideal, but they mention examples only from the mythological and far distant past. Jesus takes up the maxim when he is on the point of actually practicing it.[5]

In its context in John it forms the basis for Jesus's "new commandment" to "love one another as I have loved you" (15:12; cf. 13:34). To love one another is not, as such, a new commandment. It went back to Moses (Lev. 19:18), as all Jews were well aware. What was new was to love as Jesus loved his friends—that is, so as to lay down his life for them. By comparison with the commandment to love the neighbor "as oneself" (Lev. 19:18), this might seem to demand loving them more than oneself or at least to require that "as oneself" has a profounder meaning than the self-protective limitation that one might otherwise put on it. Thus, John's version of the command that sums up all of one's duties to others is (unlike the Synoptic versions) explicitly and decisively colored by Jesus's death.

That it is this unlimited love for his friends that takes Jesus to the cross is first indicated in chapter 10, where the parable of the good shepherd provides an essential interpretative background for reading, first, the narrative of the raising of Lazarus in chapter 11, and, secondly, the passion narrative itself. "The good shepherd lays down his life for the sheep" (10:11). Although love is not explicitly mentioned, a remarkable degree of care for the sheep is indicated. A shepherd might risk his life for the sheep, as did David, the shepherd king, when he was literally a shepherd (1 Sam. 17:34–35), but to lay down his life for the sheep, knowing that he was excluding any possibility of saving it, deliberately giving his life in exchange for that of the sheep, is more than anyone could reasonably demand of a shepherd. It is not even part of the shepherd parable on which Jesus's parable is based (Ezek. 34:1–24) but rather a fresh development of it. As happens in many parables, of course, this feature breaks the bounds of the analogy, suggesting something extraordinary.

Jesus spells out the obvious meaning: he himself is the shepherd; the sheep are "his own," those he knows and who know him; it is he who will lay down his life for them (10:14–15). Although this meaning is explicitly open to the wider people of God whom he intends to gather in through his death (10:16), the immediate reference is to those he knows personally and who know him personally, his friends (this is clear from 13:1; cf. 15:14; 17:12). For the significance of what follows, it is also essential that Jesus here characterizes his

---

5:20 (the Father loves the Son); 15:19 (the world's love for its own); 16:27 ("the Father himself loves you because you have loved me"). Otherwise, for God's love John always uses *agapē* and *agapaō*.

5. Sjef van Tilborg, *Imaginative Love in John*, BIS 2 (Leiden: Brill, 1993), 149–54.

death as in the fullest sense voluntary: "I lay down my life in order to take it up again. No one takes it from me, but I lay it down of my own accord. I have power to lay it down, and I have power to receive it again" (10:17–18). This makes it an act of pure love.

Now that Jesus's intention of laying down his life for his own has become quite clear to the readers, he actually begins to do so in the story of the raising of Lazarus, which is the greatest of Jesus's "signs," short of the climactic one to which all the others point, his own resurrection. It is a story that John tells at length with all his considerable storytelling skill, and in John's narrative it is the event that leads most immediately to Jesus's death, since it is because of the reputation it gives Jesus that the high priest and his council form the determination to put Jesus to death at the earliest opportunity (11:45–53). That Jesus is in fact already in serious danger in Jerusalem is clear in 10:39, at which point Jesus escapes to the safety of a distant region (10:40). When he opts to return to the Jerusalem area, out of his love for his friend Lazarus and the sisters Martha and Mary, it is obvious to the disciples that he is walking into mortal danger. "Let us also go, that we may die with him," says Thomas, with well-meant bravado. It is essential that the narrative of the raising of Lazarus be understood with reference to the rather tight narrative connections that John has given it, both with what precedes in chapter 10 and especially with what follows in the passion narrative. (More so than the Synoptic Gospels, John's narrative has a clearly developing plot.)

When Jesus, facing the prospect of approaching Lazarus's tomb, weeps, "the Jews" say, "See how he loved him!" (11:36). It is a case (one of several in John) where people say more than they mean. They think that Jesus weeps because Lazarus is dead. In reality, Jesus already knows that he will bring Lazarus back to life, but he also knows that this act of love for his friend will lead to his own death. The strong emotion that John attributes to Jesus in this story, with remarkable emphasis ("he was greatly disturbed in spirit and deeply moved" [11:33], "again greatly disturbed" [11:38]),[6] is the combined effect of his love for the Bethany sisters, whose distress he feels, and the knowledge that, in acting on his love for them, he is, in effect, laying down his own life. John uses this language only once more, when Jesus, in a kind of Johannine moment of Gethsemane, shrinks from the death that he knows is his destiny: "Now is my soul troubled" (12:27).

6. Interpretations of Jesus's emotion here are unconvincing if they do not take account of the similar language in 12:27, the only other occurrence of such language in John. Thus the suggestion that Jesus is angry at death, which has taken his friend Lazarus from him, is implausible because this cannot be the meaning in 12:27.

In the Lazarus story John foreshadows for us the human reality of the passion. Jesus provokes the plot that will lead to his death *in order to save his friend from death*. He lays down his life for his friend. But this is also a "sign." Jesus brings Lazarus back to mortal life as a sign of the eternal life that his own death will acquire for his friends. The paradox of the cross—of life through death—(to which we shall return in the next section) is signaled in this story by the fact that Jesus declares himself to be "the resurrection and the life" (11:25) in the course of ensuring that he himself will die.

The Lazarus story is the beginning of the turn that the Gospel narrative takes from Jesus's ministry to the people (which ends with the summary of his message in 12:44–50) toward his attention to "his own." The turn is definitively announced at the outset of the last day of his earthly life:

> Jesus knew that his hour had come to depart from the world and go to the Father. Having loved his own who were in the world, he loved them to the end [*eis telos*]. (13:1)

The *eis telos* could mean "to the utmost" or "to the end." It surely means both, for the utmost of love is to die for one's friends. It anticipates Jesus's dying words in 19:30, "It is finished!" (*tetelestai*, from *teleō*, "to complete" [cf. 19:28]).

It is a well-known puzzle that John's account of the Last Supper, unlike all of the Synoptics, has no "institution of the Eucharist" narrative. Part, at least, of the reason for this becomes clear when we notice the real function of the "institution of the Eucharist" narratives in the Synoptics. Although, of course, readers know that Jesus is performing an act that his followers will continue, this is not why the Synoptic Gospels tell the story (though it is why Paul does so in 1 Cor. 11:23–26). In Matthew and Mark there is actually no indication that the disciples are to repeat these symbolic acts of Jesus at the supper. The Synoptic writers include them because they supply the meaning of the death of Jesus that they then go on to narrate. The "eucharistic" acts are there to interpret the ongoing narrative, giving it sacrificial significance. (Luke's "given for you" and "poured out for you" [22:19–20; contrast "for many" in Matthew and Mark] are the nearest the Synoptics get to John's very concrete picture of Jesus dying for those who are having supper with him.) Unlike the Synoptics, John has announced the sacrificial meaning of Jesus's death already in John the Baptist's witness (1:29) and then works a sacrificial interpretation into the way he tells of the death of Jesus itself (19:34–36). He does not need the bread and wine for this purpose.

Instead, he tells of a different symbolic act of Jesus at the supper, one that anticipates the meaning of the cross in a different way.[7] Jesus washes his disciples' feet. It is the act that no one but a slave could ever be expected to perform for another. If someone other than a slave did it, exceptionally, it was as an expression of the deepest love, the love that makes one willing to be a slave to the beloved, to perform the most humiliating of acts of service. So it prepares for the fact that Jesus is to die the most humiliating of deaths, the death of a slave or an outcast, for his friends. He washes *their* feet. This is an example for the disciples to follow (13:12–16), something that they can readily understand (if not easily accept), but it also has a further meaning that they cannot yet understand. Jesus says, "You do not know now what I am doing, but later you will understand" (13:7). This is how John regularly speaks of what they could only understand after Jesus's death and resurrection (2:22; 12:16; 20:9). In Jesus's utter giving of himself for them there is both something unique, that only he can do for them, and something imitable, which he will by his self-giving actually enable them to imitate.[8]

I am inclined to think that Jesus's words from the cross to his mother and the Beloved Disciple (19:26–27) take their meaning from this Johannine understanding of the death of Jesus as death for his friends. These are the two people most dear to him in a fully human sense: his mother and his best friend. Though in excruciating pain that might be expected to turn him in on himself, Jesus gives loving attention to his mother and his friend. He provides for their life without him—without him in a genuine sense, though not in another. He asks them, in fact, to love each other in his place, to be the loving son and the loving friend that he has been. His destiny does not override his human love for them, as we might have supposed from his earlier words to his mother (2:4). He loves them not least when he is fulfilling that destiny by dying. To die for those dearest to him is actually part of that destiny.

It is the human tenderness of Jesus's love for his friends that John's exquisitely told narratives are able to evoke as nothing else could.[9] We see it incomparably in the story of his meeting with Mary Magdalene in the garden (20:11–18). It is a reunion of friends, the reunion that Jesus had

7. For this paragraph, see in more detail Richard Bauckham, *The Testimony of the Beloved Disciple: Narrative, History, and Theology in the Gospel of John* (Grand Rapids: Baker Academic, 2007), chap. 9.

8. Contrast Peter's declared willingness, before the cross, to lay down his life for Jesus (13:37), which he proved unable to do, and Jesus's prediction, after the resurrection, that Peter, in his restored and renewed love for Jesus, will in fact do so (21:15–19).

9. It has had little attention from scholars, perhaps because of an assumption that it is not really "theological"—unlike God's love for the world. But van Tilborg's *Imaginative Love* is a perceptive and illuminating study.

promised his friends after the supper (16:16–22). For Jesus, it is a reunion with one of the only four friends who stood by him in the extremity of his giving his life for them (19:25–26). Moreover, very significantly, the encounter echoes the parable of the good shepherd. Like the sheep in the parable (10:3, 14),[10] Mary recognizes Jesus's voice when he says her name. She is one of his own who knows him personally, as he knows her. It is for her that he has laid down his life and received it again. His love for her has not been extinguished by death but has proved stronger than death. There is a sense in which love proves stronger than death whenever someone lays down his or her life out of love. That person's love has not been deterred by death; on the contrary, it has made death into the supreme expression of love. But in the Gospel narrative Jesus's love does more than this. By loving "to the end," he is able to go on loving his friends beyond the end. The end becomes a new beginning.

This story of Jesus's love for his friends John tells as the central story within the great narrative that runs from the eternity before creation (1:1) to the future coming of Jesus to bring all creation to its fulfillment (21:23). It is the story of the Father's love for the Son from "before the foundation of the world" (17:24) and of God's love for the world, which was so great that he gave his Son for the life of the world (3:16) and the Son gave himself for the life of the world (6:51). This love is not, of course, limited to the small group of Jesus's friends within his historical story. But had Jesus not loved like that the people he actually knew and humanly loved, his death could not have been the expression of God's love for the world. If we took this element out of John's story, we would have a Jesus who, obedient to his Father, carried out the destiny decreed for him, the divine plan for the world, but we could not believe that he did so in love for the world. It is only because God's love for the world took the concrete, human, incarnate form of Jesus's love for the flesh-and-blood particular people who were close to him that the love of God in him could also reach people who did not know him in the flesh (17:20–24; 20:29). In Jesus's love for his friends God's love took human, historical form in order to embrace the world.

This aspect of the Gospel story is probably the most theologically important way in which the Gospel depicts Jesus as God incarnate in humanity. It is strangely missed by those who find the Jesus of this Gospel more divine than human. It is in this thoroughly human love of Jesus for his friends that the divine love for the world takes human form. In this way "the Word became flesh . . . full of grace" (1:14).

10. John 10:3 is the only reference in the Bible to animals having names.

Life

The motif of Jesus's love for his own does not in itself tell us why he needed to lay down his life for them or what he thereby gained for them. He did not strike a bargain with the Jewish authorities that they would leave his friends alone if he gave himself up. The Gospel will not allow us to suppose that Jesus died only because he remained faithful to his mission despite the mortal danger into which it led him. It represents his death rather as something he had to do, actually the most important thing he had to do, to which his earlier ministry was merely preparatory. As we have already seen implied in the story of the raising of Lazarus, the Gospel claims that Jesus died to give others eternal life: "God so loved the world that he gave his only Son [to die], so that everyone who believes in him should not perish but may have eternal life" (3:16 [cf. 20:31]). It recognizes the strange paradox of saying that his death is life-giving. Just as the Israelites in the wilderness, dying of snakebite, gained life through looking at a snake raised up like an ensign, so by looking to the dead Jesus raised up on the cross people will gain life (3:14–15; cf. 12:32).

Of course, this is conceivable only because Jesus did not remain dead. The resurrection appearance stories show, among other things, that he did not simply pass through death as though it was in the nature of death to be a universal gateway into postmortem immortality. Rather, he nullified death. What led the Beloved Disciple to believe that Jesus had risen from death was the sight of Jesus's grave clothes lying abandoned in the empty tomb (20:5–8). Jesus had left death behind—tomb and grave clothes abandoned, but no corpse. The story of Thomas, who saw the wounds in Jesus's wrists and side (20:24–29), is of key importance in the Gospel's narrative because it shows that Jesus had nullified death *in* his own human and corporal identity. As he was incarnate in flesh (1:14) and gave his flesh in death for the life of the world (6:51), so his fleshly humanity was raised. Only this makes his death and resurrection life-giving for fleshly and mortal humans. For those not privileged to see this, as only Thomas and the other disciples who met the risen Christ could, it is entirely essential that those disciples *did see*. Jesus's beatitude in 20:29 ("Blessed are those who have not seen and yet have come to believe") is grossly misunderstood when it is taken to mean that it would have been better if Thomas and others had not needed to see. John tells the stories because later believers need to hear the testimony of those who did see. Otherwise they could not believe. Even the Beloved Disciple's precocious resurrection faith (21:6–7) was enabled by seeing what no later believers can see.

John tells us, somewhat subtly, that he uses the term "eternal life" (or, often, just "life") as equivalent to the term "kingdom of God" in other Gospels or

Gospel traditions.[11] The only two occurrences of "kingdom of God" in this Gospel are early in the narrative, associated with "birth from above," and are followed by a transition to talk of "eternal life" (3:3–16), which then becomes a frequent usage. This may seem to shift the emphasis from God's eschatological renewal of human life in society in all its dimensions to something more narrowly spiritual. On the face of it, it might seem that, whereas in the Synoptic Gospels Jesus's "acts of power" are part of the way he goes about doing good (cf. Acts 10:38), healing the concrete ills of life in this world, Jesus's "signs" in John's Gospel merely signify something other than themselves: the eternal life that Jesus will give through his death and resurrection. Thus, to the crowds he has miraculously fed, John's Jesus says, "Do not work for the food that perishes, but for the food that endures to eternal life, which the Son of Man will give you" (6:27). But this is really saying much the same as the Synoptic saying "Strive first for the kingdom of God and his righteousness, and all these things will be given to you as well" (Matt. 6:33 [//Luke 12:31]). Even in the Synoptic Gospels the feeding miracles signify more than feeding the temporarily hungry. They anticipate the eschatological banquet in the presence of God when God's people will celebrate even the abolition of death, as well as of every sort of suffering and want (Isa. 25:6–8).

Eternal life in John is much more than the goods of earthly, mortal life, but it is certainly not less than them. It surpasses them by including them, not leaving them behind. This is, again, why it is essential that the risen Jesus is still Jesus in his fully bodily reality. He takes his fleshly reality up into a new form of life beyond the reach of death. So, for example, when, in the third of the signs (5:1–9), Jesus gives the paralyzed man bodily health and strength, along with the enhancement of his life that these bring, this is not just a sign of something purely spiritual and entirely different. It is a good that participates in the character of the surpassing good to which it can therefore point. The sequence of signs is designed to suggest what eternal life may mean. It is the renewal of the whole of life through participation in the divine life.

One of John's distinctive ways of thinking is in pairs of opposites: light and darkness, God and the world, life and death.[12] So, negatively, eternal life is life beyond the reach of death (11:25–26). But death manifests itself not only in the final loss of life, but also in all that damages and impairs life before death. So eternal life is the healing and transfiguration of life in all the ways that mortal life falls short of life in its fullness. But it is more than the putting right of what is wrong, important though that is. Eternal life is also the fulfillment of all

---

11. In fact, there is precedent for this in Mark 9:43, 45, 47.
12. See chap. 6, "Dualisms."

that is good. It is significant that the first of Jesus's signs (2:1–11) does more than meet a need. Running out of wine at a wedding feast would certainly be a serious source of social humiliation for the family, but Jesus does much more than solve a problem for them. The quantity and the quality of the wine that he provides are far in excess of need. What wine, enjoyed in a social context of this kind, does is to enhance life a little, especially the enjoyment of fellowship. The miracle points to the greater enhancement of life to which Jesus refers when he says that he came "that they may have life, and have it abundantly" (10:10 [in the context of being the gate of the sheepfold]).

This is an opportunity to illustrate John's frequently rich pattern of allusion to Scripture. The wedding feast at Cana anticipates the eschatological banquet, which the Lord "will make for all peoples . . . a feast of well-aged wines" (Isa. 25:6). But the Isaianic context links this banquet with the universal abolition of death (25:7–8; one of the very few texts in the Hebrew Bible that expect this).[13] So there is a scriptural connection between the first sign and not only the sixth sign (the raising of Lazarus), but also, even more importantly, the seventh, climactic sign, which is Jesus's own resurrection.[14] The eternal life that Jesus gives is not only, negatively, the abolition of death and all its lesser minions, but also, positively, the enhancement of human life to the utmost in joyful fellowship with God.

Finally, the motifs of love and life in relation to Jesus's death and resurrection are closely linked because life in John's Gospel is understood relationally: "This is eternal life, that they may know you, the only true God, and Jesus Christ whom you have sent" (17:3). The eternal life of the Father and the Son is sustained by their eternal fellowship in love, and so the eternal life Jesus gives entails participation in that fellowship (17:21–24).

Glory

Glory is the visible manifestation of God.[15] In John's usage it is the visible revelation of God's character, what one would see if one could see the very

13. Isaiah 25:6–8 was an important text for other early Christian writers too: 1 Cor. 15:54; Rev. 7:17; 21:4; and compare Jesus's saying in Mark 14:25. Perhaps Jesus's encounter with Mary Magdalene in the garden is intended to recall Isa. 25:8.

14. Seven events are actually called "signs" in the Gospel (see table 3.3). The resurrection is identified as a sign in 2:18–19. This may seem an obscure way to indicate that the resurrection is the last of the series of signs, but John's Gospel frequently makes its points in a less than obvious way. The fact that 20:30–31 follows the resurrection appearance to Thomas also confirms that the Gospel treats the resurrection of Jesus as one of the signs.

15. For more detail, see chap. 3, "Glory."

face of God. Moses was denied this, but instead he heard God's character revealed (Exod. 33:17–23; 34:5–7). This provides the implied contrast between Jesus and Moses in 1:14–18. The eternal Son, who as Son uniquely shares his Father's glory, manifests the glory of God in human flesh. As incarnate human, just as in the divine eternity, he is "full of grace and truth" (1:14), a paraphrase and summary of the divine character description given to Moses (Exod. 34:6: "abounding in steadfast love and faithfulness"). So Jesus reveals God's glory in his signs and especially in his death-and-exaltation.

Other early Christian writers thought of the death and exaltation of Jesus as a sequence: suffering followed by glory, humiliation followed by exaltation. They saw this pattern in the prophecy of the Suffering Servant (Isa. 52:13–54:12, echoed especially in Phil. 2:6–11). John did something theologically remarkable when he collapsed this sequence into what he can speak of as a single event of Jesus's exaltation ("lifting up") or glorification. In both cases he is both basing himself on exegesis of Isaiah and exploiting the double meaning of the words. John reads Isa. 52:13 ("my servant . . . shall be exalted and lifted up and very high"; LXX: "exalted and glorified exceedingly"), not as referring to the Servant's exaltation following his suffering and humiliating death, but rather as a kind of rubric covering the whole story. So the Servant is exalted in his death and through it; he is glorified in his suffering and death. Building on this exegetical foundation, John uses the verb "to lift up" (*hypsoō* [as in Isaiah]) in riddling references to Jesus's death (3:14; 8:28; 12:32), implying that his physical elevation above the earth on the cross (12:32–33) is at the same time his exaltation to heaven, where he returns to the Father to share his glory. Of course, John is not denying the temporal sequence of death-resurrection-ascension that he sets out clearly in chapters 19–20. He is viewing the cross as exaltation rather than humiliation—or rather, as exaltation in humiliation, since nothing could rid crucifixion of its meaning (for all citizens and subjects of Rome) as the most abject humiliation.

Similarly, the word "glorify" (*doxazō*) John takes from Isa. 52:13 and uses with reference not just to the glory that follows Jesus's suffering and death, contrasted with them, but to the whole event of Jesus's "hour"—both his passion and his exaltation to heaven, where he shares once more the heavenly glory of his Father (e.g., 12:23, 28; 13:31; 17:1, 4–5). Had the cross been Jesus's end, it would not have revealed God. But, seen in the light of his manifest glory in heaven, it is the supreme revelation on earth of God's glory. It is what 1:14 ("we have seen his glory, full of grace and truth") especially refers to. This investment of the horror and shame of the cross with glory makes sense because glory is the manifestation of God's character. The cross as the supreme enactment of God's love is also the supreme revelation of his glory—of who he is. What Moses *heard* is actually *seen* in Jesus's path to abject suffering and death.

Everyone knew the shame and acute suffering of crucifixion. John has no need to spell those out when he tells the story of Jesus's death. The ordinary facts of crucifixion sufficiently evoke them. John is not, as has been alleged, suppressing the horror and shame in order to turn the death of Jesus into a glorious act of divine heroism. This would negate the whole purpose of John's use of the language of glorification, which is that the horror and shame of the event constitute the extraordinary lengths to which God's love for the world went.

Truth

Of the four big words, "truth" is the hardest to define in John's usage. "True" in the Gospel of John can mean "true as opposed to false," but it can also mean something more like "real" as opposed to "provisional." Jesus is "the true light," "the true bread from heaven," "the true vine." That John the Baptist was not "the light" (1:8) does not mean that he did not in fact give light (see 5:35), but that his "light" consisted in testifying to Jesus. Its reality consisted in or depended on its reference to the ultimate reality of Jesus. Similarly, that the manna in the wilderness was not "the true bread from heaven" (6:32, 58) does not mean that it was not genuinely a gift of God for the sustenance of his people, but that its fullest meaning consisted in foreshadowing Jesus, who is God's gift from heaven for the eternal sustenance of all people.

One way in which "truth" illuminates John's understanding of Jesus's death-and-resurrection/exaltation is therefore the manifold ways in which in death and resurrection Jesus "fulfills" Scripture. He is, for example, the true Passover Lamb, slain to effect the new exodus from the empire of sin (1:29; 19:33, 36). He is the true temple of the messianic age from which the water of life flows (7:38; 19:34; 21:11; cf. Ezek. 47:1–12).[16] He is the true righteous king of the psalms of David, protected by God even in his abandonment to deathly affliction (13:18; 19:24, 28, 36). He is the truth of Jacob's ladder, raised up on the cross to reach heaven (1:51). By fulfilling Scripture, in these and many other ways, Jesus enacts God's faithfulness. In him God proves true to his word. When the prologue speaks of the incarnate one as "full of grace and truth" (1:14), it echoes the character description of God as "abounding in steadfast love and faithfulness ['*emet*]" (Exod. 34:6). The Hebrew '*emet* (in

16. Bauckham, *Testimony*, 278–80.

the LXX often translated *alētheia*, "truth") means "faithfulness, reliability, trustworthiness, truth" and is frequently used of God. If the sense of "faithfulness" carries over into John's use of *alētheia*, at least in 1:14, then we can understand the importance he attaches to Jesus's fulfillment of Scripture. It is a matter of God's character, his faithfulness to his promises, manifested in Jesus.

The frequent use of "truth" and "true" in John's Gospel is not often explicitly related to Jesus's death. During his interrogation by Pilate, Jesus says, "For this was I born, and for this I came into the world, to testify to the truth" (18:37). This relates to the overarching theme of a cosmic trial that unites the language of witness and judgment throughout the Gospel,[17] but the Gospel does not seem to portray Jesus's death itself as a form of witness.

More relevant to our topic is Jesus's claim actually to be the truth: "I am the way, and the truth, and the life" (14:6). In context (14:1–5), "the way" is the way to his Father's house, the way that Jesus is about to go, so that he can later return and take his disciples to the place he will have prepared for them there. This is the way Jesus takes when he goes to his death—and exaltation. Thus it is Jesus crucified and exalted who is "the way," just as it is Jesus crucified and exalted who is the ladder reaching from earth to heaven, seen in Jacob's dream (1:51). Similarly, it is as the crucified and risen one that Jesus is "the life," and so it would seem that this must also be the sense in which he is "the truth." In his death-and-resurrection/exaltation he incarnates the true character of God and the true way for humans to come to God.

17. See especially Andrew T. Lincoln, *Truth on Trial: The Lawsuit Motif in the Fourth Gospel* (Peabody, MA: Hendrickson, 2000).

5

Sacraments?

Although many aspects of the interpretation of the Gospel of John are controversial, there can hardly be a topic on which modern scholarship has exhibited
such a wide range of views as that of sacraments. The various interpretations
of this Gospel's stance on the sacraments have been labeled anti-sacramental,
non-sacramental, sacramental, and ultra-sacramental or hyper-sacramental.[1]
But greater clarity about the issues can be had by distinguishing two different,
though related, areas of disagreement.

First, there is the question of how often, if at all, John's Gospel alludes
to sacraments. Rudolf Bultmann's view, often taken by scholars as a starting point for their own discussions, was that the present text of the Gospel
refers to sacraments on three occasions: to Christian baptism in 3:5 (the word
"water"), to the Eucharist in 6:51c–58, and to both together in 19:34. But he
held that these three allusions are late additions to the Gospel text, made by
the "ecclesiastical redactor" who edited the Gospel in order to bring it closer
to the theology of the mainstream church.[2] Few contemporary scholars accept

1. See, for example, Raymond E. Brown, "The Johannine Sacramentary," in *New Testament Essays* (New York: Paulist Press, 1965), 51–76, here 51–56; R. Wade Paschal, "Sacramental
Symbolism and Physical Imagery in the Gospel of John," *TynBul* 32 (1981): 151–76, here 155–56.

2. Rudolf Bultmann, *The Gospel of John*, trans. George R. Beasley-Murray (Oxford: Blackwell, 1971), 11, 138–39n3, 218–20, 677–78.

Bultmann's view that these passages are interpolations,[3] but in each of the three cases there are scholars who deny any sacramental allusion.[4] Some deny that any of these three passages refer to sacraments, and that there are any sacramental references in the Gospel at all.[5] Others maintain that the Gospel (in these and other passages) uses symbolism drawn from the sacraments, but to refer to other subjects, not to the sacraments themselves.[6]

At the other extreme, Oscar Cullmann found allusions to baptism or the Eucharist or both in most chapters of the Gospel.[7] As a Protestant, Cullmann thought only of baptism and the Eucharist as sacraments, but the Roman Catholic exegete Bruce Vawter, extending Cullmann's approach, also found allusions to Christian matrimony in 2:1–11 and to the sacrament of anointing in 12:1–11, while suggesting his agreement with the traditional Roman Catholic understanding of 20:22–23 as a reference to the sacrament of penance.[8] Such maximal views of sacramental reference in John have precedents in the literature and art of the early church from the second century onwards, as Cullmann and others were aware, while Paul Niewalda regarded such early interpretation of the Gospel as a reliable guide to the meaning intended in the Gospel.[9]

Since water, wine, and bread are, on any account, prominent in the Gospel of John and often undoubtedly carry symbolic meaning, it is not difficult to

3. Urban C. von Wahlde envisages three editions of the Gospel and assigns these three passages (characterized along with others by "the importance of the material and physical") to the third edition (*The Gospel and Letters of John*, ECC [Grand Rapids: Eerdmans, 2010], 1:331–35).

4. See, for example, on 3:5: Ben Witherington, *John's Wisdom: A Commentary on the Fourth Gospel* (Louisville: Westminster John Knox, 1995), 97; Klyne R. Snodgrass, "That Which Is Born from ΠΝΕΥΜΑ Is ΠΝΕΥΜΑ: Rebirth and Spirit in John 3:5–6," in *Perspectives on John: Method and Interpretation in the Fourth Gospel*, ed. Robert B. Sloan and Mikeal C. Parsons (Lewiston, NY: Edwin Mellen, 1993), 181–205, here 190–91; on 6:51–58: Witherington, *John's Wisdom*, 162–63; Herman N. Ridderbos, *The Gospel according to John: A Theological Commentary*, trans. John Vriend (Grand Rapids: Eerdmans, 1997), 235–42; on 19:34: Donald A. Carson, *The Gospel according to John* (Leicester: Inter-Varsity; Grand Rapids: Eerdmans, 1991), 624; Craig S. Keener, *The Gospel of John: A Commentary* (Peabody, MA: Hendrickson, 2003), 1151–54.

5. For example, J. Ramsey Michaels, *The Gospel of John*, NICNT (Grand Rapids: Eerdmans, 2010), 182–85 (where he allows that his interpretation of 3:5 "does not exclude a baptismal reference" but requires a wider view), 395–96 (where he concludes that the eucharistic interpretation of 6:54–58 "belongs to the 'reception history' of the text rather than to the Gospel writer's intention"), 969; cf. 729–32.

6. For example, Paschal, "Sacramental Symbolism."

7. Oscar Cullmann, *Early Christian Worship*, trans. A. Stewart Todd and James B. Torrance, SBT 10 (London: SCM, 1953), 37–119. Baptism: 1:19–34; 3:1–21; 3:22–36; 4:1–30; 5:1–19; 9:1–39; Eucharist: 2:1–11; 2:12–22; 6:1–13, 26–65; 13:31–17:26; baptism and Eucharist: 13:1–20; 19:34.

8. Bruce Vawter, "The Johannine Sacramentary," *TS* 17 (1956): 151–66.

9. Paul Niewalda, *Sakramentssymbolik im Johannesevangelium? Eine exegetisch-historische Studie* (Limburg: Lahn-Verlag, 1958).

find allusions to baptism and the Eucharist if the reader is looking for such allusions. Reacting against what he called "the ultra-sacramental view of John," exemplified by Cullmann and others, Raymond Brown attempted to deploy more rigorous criteria for identifying sacramental symbols in the Gospel.[10] He judged that nine passages meet his criteria, four referring to baptism (3:1–21; 4:1–30; 7:38; 9:1–39), three to the Eucharist (2:1–11; 6:1–3, 26–65; 15:1–8), and one to both (19:34).[11] He judged the probability of these cases variously: in the case of an allusion to baptism in the healing of the man born blind, he thought the evidence "reasonably probative," while an allusion to the Eucharist in the miracle at Cana has "good probability," and an allusion to baptism in the story of the footwashing is "solidly probable."[12] Brown's view of the extent of sacramental symbolism places him midway between, on the one hand, the "ultra-sacramental" views of Cullmann and Niewalda, and, on the other, not only Bultmann's position but also the views of a significant number of more recent scholars who judge there to be few if any sacramental allusions. For example, in the case of the healing of the man born blind, most recent commentaries either fail even to mention the possibility of a baptismal allusion[13] or dismiss it very cursorily.[14] In fact, I have not found a single scholar writing in the last twenty years who does see a baptismal allusion in the healing of the man born blind, though doubtless there are some. Probably several other passages among those Brown judges to meet his criteria for sacramental allusion are similarly lacking almost any support from recent Johannine scholarship. The tide of opinion seems to have been running strongly in the direction of minimal reference to sacraments in John. Probably only 3:5; 6:52–58; 19:34, the texts admitted to be sacramental by Bultmann (though he thought them interpolated), continue to enjoy much support.[15]

10. Brown, "Johannine Sacramentary."
11. Brown, "Johannine Sacramentary," 75–76.
12. Brown, "Johannine Sacramentary," 66, 70, 63.
13. Witherington, *John's Wisdom*; Francis J. Moloney, *The Gospel of John*, SP 4 (Collegeville, MN: Liturgical Press, 1998); D. Moody Smith, *John*, ANTC (Nashville: Abingdon, 1999); Keener, *John*; Ridderbos, *John*, 337; Colin G. Kruse, *The Gospel according to John*, TNTC (Leicester: Inter-Varsity, 2003); Andrew T. Lincoln, *The Gospel according to Saint John*, BNTC (Peabody, MA: Hendrickson; London: Continuum, 2005); Michaels, *John*.
14. Carson, *John*, 365n1; Andreas J. Köstenberger, *John*, BECNT (Grand Rapids: Baker Academic, 2004), 283n25. For arguments against a baptismal interpretation, see Paschal, "Sacramental Symbolism," 158; Craig R. Koester, *Symbolism in the Fourth Gospel: Meaning, Mystery, Community* (Minneapolis: Fortress, 1995), 180; Ridderbos, *John*, 337; Larry Paul Jones, *The Symbol of Water in the Gospel of John*, JSNTSup 145 (Sheffield: Sheffield Academic Press, 1997), 176.
15. Among English-speaking Catholic scholars of the generation after Brown, Francis Moloney is probably the foremost specialist on John. He followed up Brown's attempt to define criteria for identifying sacramental allusions in his own essay, "When Is John Talking about

In addition to the question of whether and, if so, how often John refers to sacraments, there is a second area of disagreement among scholars: how important does John consider the sacraments to be? Answers to this question do not necessarily correspond closely to answers to the first question. It is fairly obvious that those who take the "ultra-sacramental" view of John will also suppose that the sacraments were of great importance to him. But those who find minimal reference to the sacraments (two, three, or at most four references) may well see those references that John does make as indicating their considerable importance. For example, Udo Schnelle thinks that 3:5 treats "baptism as the 'condition of admittance' into the reign of God and thus an initiatory rite that is necessary for salvation."[16] Similarly, he sees in 6:53 an "emphasis on the Eucharist as the indispensable condition for salvation."[17] He sees this emphasis on the indispensability of the sacraments as an anti-docetic polemic against docetists who deprived the sacraments of significance. James Dunn, on the other hand, while agreeing that chapter 6 is anti-docetic, finds there also a secondary concern to counter "sacramentalism" and links this with the notable absence of an account of the institution of the Eucharist in chapter 13. Emphasizing 6:63, he holds that "John is concerned lest too much attention be given to the ritual act and lest eternal life be thought somehow dependent on or given through the physical elements"; John's message, as far as the Eucharist is concerned, is "one of caution and warning."[18] Likewise, of 3:5 Dunn remarks, "John seems to be challenging any sacramentalism which he assumes on the part of his readers."[19]

Although the absence of a eucharistic institution narrative in chapter 13 is important for some scholars in this regard, and the absence of explicit reference to Jesus's own baptism seems significant to some, for the most part the

Sacraments?," in "A Hard Saying": The Gospel and Culture (Collegeville, MN: Liturgical Press, 2001), 109–30. There he approves of Brown's criteria (and adds two more of his own) and seems to accept Brown's case for a baptismal allusion in John 9 (pp. 119–20), as well as stating that he is "in general agreement with those scholars who see regular references to the sacraments in John" (p. 115). Yet in his commentary (Moloney, John) he refers to sacramental allusions only at 3:5; chap. 6 (including 6:11); 13:1–11, 26; 19:34. He argues for a eucharistic understanding of 13:26 in "A Sacramental Reading of John 13:1–38," CBQ 53 (1991): 237–56.

16. Udo Schnelle, Antidocetic Christology in the Gospel of John: An Investigation of the Place of the Fourth Gospel in the Johannine School, trans. Linda M. Maloney (Minneapolis: Fortress, 1992), 185.

17. Schnelle, Antidocetic Christology, 204.

18. James D. G. Dunn, "John VI—A Eucharistic Discourse?," NTS 17 (1970–71): 328–38, here 337.

19. James D. G. Dunn, Baptism in the Holy Spirit: A Re-examination of the New Testament Teaching on the Gift of the Spirit in Relation to Pentecostalism Today, SBT 2/15 (London: SCM, 1970), 190. A rather similar approach is taken by C. Kingsley Barrett, Essays on John (London: SPCK, 1982), 80–97, who calls John's acceptance of sacraments "a critical acceptance" (p. 97).

real issue about the theological status of the sacraments in John's theology is not so much how many references there are as the character of those references. Do they indicate the importance of the material aspect of the rites of baptism and Eucharist, or do they, without altogether rejecting the material rites, play them down out of a theological concern to undercut reliance on them in favor of the really important factors: Spirit, Word, and faith?

Finally, even the view that John's Gospel does not refer at all to Christian baptism or the Eucharist need not entail that John attached no or little importance to these. Raymond Brown pertinently asks What sort of reference to sacraments can be expected "in *a gospel*?"[20] The Synoptic Gospels refer to the Eucharist only in their accounts of its "institution" at the Last Supper.[21] (In fact, it may be more accurate to say that only Luke does so [22:19], since the accounts in Matthew and Mark provide no indication that Jesus instituted a rite that was to be repeated by his followers.) Among the Synoptics, only Matthew refers to Christian baptism—in a postresurrection context (28:19).[22] The view that John's Gospel, unlike the Synoptics, merges or mixes the time of Jesus's earthly ministry with the time after his resurrection, such that subjects of concern to the church or to "the Johannine community" should be expected to be treated within the Gospel even if they were not part of the tradition of the words and acts of Jesus before his death, is mistaken (see, e.g., 2:22; 12:16; 13:7; 16:13, 25). Provided that John's failure to recount the "eucharistic" words and acts of Jesus at the Last Supper can be adequately explained without supposing that he did not think the Eucharist important (see below), a general silence of the Gospel on the subject of the sacraments can be understood as no more than an implication of the Gospel genre.

However, we must also question whether the category "sacraments" is appropriate at all. Barnabas Lindars observes that there can be no "sacramental theology" in the New Testament because its writers had no category "sacraments" with which to classify baptism and the Eucharist (let alone other rites) as two of the same kind of thing.[23] What Paul wrote in 1 Cor. 10:1–4 is at least evidence that baptism and the Eucharist were seen as the two principal rites of the Christian movement, in which all believers participated, as John 19:34 would be, if it were rightly taken to refer to both the rites. But we should be

---

20. Brown, "Johannine Sacramentary," 59.

21. Jesus's actions with the bread in the feeding miracles may well be evocative of the Eucharist (called "breaking of bread" in Acts), but only at a secondary level of meaning that is not required for understanding the accounts in their narrative contexts.

22. See also the longer ending of Mark (16:16).

23. Barnabas Lindars, "Word and Sacrament in the Fourth Gospel" (first published in 1976), in *Essays on John*, ed. Christopher M. Tuckett, SNTA 17 (Louvain: Leuven University Press; Peeters, 1992), 51–65, here 51–54.

wary of supposing that John had a theological concept of "the sacraments." In view of the controversial nature of our topic, it will be best to proceed by examining in detail the verse that has the most scholarly support as a reference to baptism (3:5) and the passage that has the most scholarly support as a reference to the Eucharist (6:52–58). Unless these references can be sustained, it is doubtful if any other references to sacraments in John will be plausible.

Born from Water and Spirit (3:5)

The most likely reference to Christian baptism in John occurs early in Jesus's dialogue with Nicodemus, the aristocratic Pharisee who professes to "know that you are a teacher who has come from God" (3:2). This degree of recognition is sufficient for Jesus to take up immediately this role of teacher by stating, as a matter of first importance, what Nicodemus needs to learn: "Very truly, I tell you, no one can see the kingdom of God without being born from above" (3:3). The word *anōthen*, here translated "from above," is understood by Nicodemus in the sense of "again." He takes Jesus to be talking about a second birth of the same sort as the first, and is therefore mystified: "How can anyone be born after having grown old? Can one enter a second time into the mother's womb and be born?" (3:4). Jesus repeats his statement, but with additions designed to make clear that he is speaking of a very different kind of birth: "Very truly, I tell you, no one can enter the kingdom of God without being born of water and Spirit [*ex hydatos kai pneumatos*]. What is born of the flesh is flesh, and what is born of Spirit is spirit" (3:5–6).

This reference to birth "from water and Spirit" is the most likely of alleged references to Christian baptism in John's Gospel. The words have been variously interpreted, both in support of a baptismal reference and against one. To guide us through this interpretative debate, I suggest a set of five criteria for a plausible reading of the phrase in its context:

1. A plausible interpretation must make sense in its narrative context, which is Jesus's conversation with Nicodemus, a Pharisaic member of the Jewish ruling council, in Jerusalem at an early stage of Jesus's earthly ministry. This criterion should not be confused with an assumption that the narrative is a historical report of a conversation that actually took place.[24] Even if the narrative is entirely fictional, the criterion applies because it is entailed by the

---

24. Unfortunately, Brown does not see this distinction when he writes "if we posit some kind of historical tradition behind the Nicodemus incident, then we must allow a primary, nonsacramental meaning to Jesus's words, a meaning which Nicodemus could have understood" ("Johannine Sacramentary," 59).

literary genre of the text as a narrative set in the past. Some scholars work with this criterion, while also allowing for a secondary level of meaning, available to readers of the Gospel but not to the characters within the narrative.[25] We certainly can leave that option open, while insisting that the primary meaning must be one that makes sense within the narrative context. This rules out interpretations such as Schnelle's, which maintains that in "John 3:5 the standpoint of the post-Easter community is articulated."[26]

2. In this particular narrative context a plausible interpretation should be one available to Nicodemus.[27] It is true that in verses 3, 5, 6, and 8 Jesus's words are, as often in the Gospel, cast in aphoristic form, such that they can be lifted out of their context and stand alone as meaningful independent sayings. But they are also appropriate to their context in the conversation. This is clear from the fact that the second person pronouns and verbs in these verses are singular. The reader must read them as words addressed to Nicodemus. This is true even in verse 7 ("Do not be astonished that I said to you [singular], 'You [plural] must be born from above'"), where the plural "you" refers back to Nicodemus's "we" in verse 2 (including himself among a group of colleagues for whom he acts as spokesperson).[28]

It is true that Jesus in John's Gospel frequently makes enigmatic or riddling statements that are not understood by the characters in the story, and that the evangelist sometimes indicates that these could not have been understood until after Jesus's resurrection (2:19; 13:7). All or almost all of these are references to Jesus's coming death-and-exaltation. However, it is clear that what Jesus says to Nicodemus in 3:3–10 is not of this kind, because Jesus concludes the dialogue with a clear indication that, as "the teacher of Israel," Nicodemus should have understood "these things" (3:10).

3. More precisely, Jesus's saying in 3:5 (as well as 3:6–8), which is a reformulation of the saying in 3:3, should function plausibly as a clarification in

25. Raymond E. Brown, *The Gospel according to John (I–XII): Introduction, Translation, and Notes*, AB 29 (New York: Doubleday, 1966), 141–44; Brown, "Johannine Sacramentary," 59–60; Xavier Léon-Dufour, "Towards a Symbolic Reading of the Fourth Gospel," *NTS* 27 (1981): 439–56, here 440–41, 445.

26. Schnelle, *Antidocetic Christology*, 185.

27. Contrast Francis J. Moloney's statement: "There is a rebirth 'of water and the Spirit' that understandably puzzles Nicodemus, but the reader has already learned of a close association between water and the Holy Spirit" (*Belief in the Word: Reading the Fourth Gospel, John 1–4* [Minneapolis: Fortress, 1993], 111).

28. As is often observed, Nicodemus drops out of the picture after 3:12. This is because in 3:13–21 Jesus goes on to matters that he does not expect Nicodemus to be able to understand (3:12). But the resemblances between 3:13–21 and what Jesus says later in the Gospel show that Jesus's speech does continue as far as 3:21. On the transition from dialogue to monologue, see Léon-Dufour, "Symbolic Reading," 445.

response to Nicodemus's misunderstanding in 3:4. Since the only difference between verses 3 and 5 that could function as clarification is that the words "from water and Spirit" replace "again/from above [*anōthen*]," those words in particular should function as clarification. It is worth noting that Jesus does not blame Nicodemus for his misunderstanding, but proceeds to explain his meaning more fully. Only in response to Nicodemus's subsequent expression of incredulity (3:9) does Jesus speak negatively of his failure to understand. So it would be incongruous if, following verse 4, Jesus did not attempt quite seriously to help Nicodemus reach an understanding of his message. (Readers, of course, may well see Nicodemus's misunderstanding as crass, but for them too it functions as the occasion for Jesus to provide a fuller account of his meaning.)

4. A plausible interpretation must do justice to the close association of the two terms "water" and "Spirit." This pair of anarthrous nouns (i.e., nouns without the article) connected by *kai* resembles other pairs in John's Gospel: "grace and truth" (1:14; cf. 1:17), "spirit and truth" (4:23, 24), "spirit and life" (6:63).[29] In 3:5, as in 4:23, 24, the two nouns are governed by a single preposition.[30] The relation between the two nouns cannot be quite the same in all these cases, and so we cannot identify a consistent use of hendiadys in John. As Craig Keener observes, "the grammatical argument by itself is not decisive" for the interpretation of 3:5,[31] but clearly in all four cases the two nouns are closely associated and some kind of conceptual unity is implied. It would seem very unlikely that "water" and "Spirit" are *contrasted* in 3:5.

5. While explaining the close association of the two terms "water" and "Spirit," a plausible interpretation must also explain the specific presence of the first term in 3:5, in contrast to the shorter phrase "born from the Spirit" in 3:8. The fuller phrase must say something that the shorter phrase does not, and the "added value" of "water and Spirit" must be a value specifically appropriate to the clarification required by Nicodemus's misunderstanding in 3:4.

We are now in a position to assess the various proposals for the significance of "water" in 3:5.

a. The phrase "born of water and Spirit" refers to Christian baptism—that is, water baptism in close association with the gift of the Spirit,[32] understood

29. But note that in 6:63 *estin* occurs after each noun.

30. Compare 1 John 5:6, discussed below. For a longer list of "pairs in tension" (more loosely defined), see Gary M. Burge, *The Anointed Community: The Holy Spirit in the Johannine Tradition* (Grand Rapids: Eerdmans, 1987), 166n68.

31. Keener, *John*, 550.

32. For example, Barnabas Lindars, *The Gospel of John*, NCB (London: Marshall, Morgan & Scott, 1972), 152; Moloney, *John*, 99; Smith, *John*, 95.

as effecting new birth. This view clearly fails my criterion 1, which allows an allusion to Christian baptism only at a secondary level of meaning.[33] A primary meaning must be established before such a secondary level of meaning can be considered.

b. A number of proposals connect "water" with various Jewish ritual uses of water about which Nicodemus could have known: John the Baptist's practice of baptism,[34] of which readers of John also know (1:31; 3:23), proselyte baptism,[35] or other forms of ritual purification.[36] Some proposals of this kind bring John's baptism together with the practice of baptism by Jesus and his disciples, according to 3:22, which would seem to have much the same sort of significance as John's baptism.[37] Often such proposals serve to support a secondary reference to Christian baptism. Their common weakness is that in all these cases the use of water symbolizes cleansing (from impurity or sin), not new birth. In none of these Jewish practices is there any connection with a notion of new birth.[38] Cleansing, on the other hand, is completely absent from the discussion of Jesus with Nicodemus. Some interpreters wish to see in 3:5 a reference to cleansing as required in addition to renewal by the Spirit, but it must be admitted that the word "water" is the only element in 3:3–10 that could convey such a reference to cleansing. This seems too much weight to place on this one word, especially

33. Ignace de la Potterie maintains a primary reference to Christian baptism that does not have to be intelligible to Nicodemus because the author of the Gospel added the words "water and" only at a late stage of composition ("To Be Born Again of Water and the Spirit," in *The Christian Lives by the Spirit*, by Ignace de la Potterie and Stanislaus Lyonnet, trans. John Morriss [New York: Alba House, 1971], 1–36, here 23–24).

34. Edwyn Clement Hoskyns, *The Fourth Gospel*, ed. Francis Noel Davy (London: Faber & Faber, 1947), 214; Burge, *Anointed Community*, 163–64.

35. Keener, *John*, 549–52. It is disputed whether Jewish proselyte baptism is pre-Christian, but it was most likely practiced by the time John's Gospel was written (see Keener, *John*, 444–47; Everett Ferguson, *Baptism in the Early Church: History, Theology, and Liturgy in the First Five Centuries* [Grand Rapids: Eerdmans, 2009], 76–82).

36. Koester, *Symbolism*, 163–64. Commentators often refer to the ritual use of water in connection with repentance and purification from sin in 1QS 3.6–9 (e.g., George R. Beasley-Murray, *John*, WBC 36 [Waco: Word, 1987], 49), though not usually with the implication that Nicodemus would think specifically of the practice of the Qumran sect. I do not agree with Keener's broader view (see Keener, *John*, 441–42), that John (in a number of places) is engaged in an argument with the synagogue about the nature of true purification. This reads far too much into 2:5 and 3:25.

37. For example, Brooke Foss Westcott, *The Gospel according to St. John* (London: John Murray, 1889), 50; Hoskyns, *Fourth Gospel*, 214; Beasley-Murray, *John*, 49.

38. It is misleading to suppose that a saying of Rabbi Yose (second century CE), "A proselyte at the moment of conversion is like a new-born baby" (*b. Yebam.* 48b), has any relevance to John 3 (e.g., Keener, *John*, 549; Köstenberger, *John*, 124n30), since the saying refers only to the fact that such proselytes have not yet learned the details of Torah (see C. Kingsley Barrett, *The Gospel according to St. John: An Introduction with Commentary and Notes on the Greek Text*, 2nd ed. [Philadelphia: Westminster, 1978], 206).

when the alternative significance of water as life-giving was just as available in the cultural and scriptural context and, in fact, predominates in John's Gospel (4:7–15; 7:37–39). Water as life-giving has a much more obvious connection with the context. It may also be doubted whether, for Nicodemus, a reference to a Jewish rite of purification in water could connect closely enough with birth "from the Spirit" to satisfy my criterion 4.[39]

c. "Water" refers to semen, and so either the phrase "water and Spirit" refers to two "begettings," natural and spiritual,[40] or human semen is used metaphorically for divine "semen" (cf. 1 John 3:9) and the whole phrase thus refers to divine begetting.[41] These two views have been refuted far more often than they have been proposed. There are two main objections. First, the use of the Hebrew word *ṭîpâ*, meaning "drop of liquid," for semen in some rabbinic texts (e.g., *m. 'Abot* 3.1),[42] is a completely inadequate basis for supposing that "water" in John 3:5 could have been understood to mean "semen."[43] Second, whereas the verb *gennaō* most often refers to the male role in procreation ("to beget"), it can refer to the female role of giving birth to the child, especially in the passive (e.g., John 16:21), which is used throughout John 3:3–8. It is quite clear that in 3:4 Nicodemus understands Jesus's use of it to mean "to be born," and so more than the word "water" (which can more readily refer to the process of birth [see below]) would be needed to correct this. It is easier to assume that throughout 3:3–8 the passive verb means "to be born."[44]

39. Jesus would, in this case, mean "born by means of a rite of purification in water and by means of the Spirit." This is a complicated notion for someone to apprehend who had never connected a rite of purification in water with new birth.

40. I have not found precisely this proposal in the literature, but if "water" can be understood as semen, it is a possible one.

41. Hugo Odeberg, *The Fourth Gospel Interpreted in Its Relation to Contemporaneous Religious Currents in Palestine and the Hellenistic-Oriental World* (Amsterdam: Grüner, 1968), 48–64; Leon Morris, *The Gospel according to John*, NICNT (Grand Rapids: Eerdmans, 1971), 216–18; Sjef van Tilborg, *Imaginative Love in John*, BIS 2 (Leiden: Brill, 1993), 49–52.

42. Odeberg, *Fourth Gospel*, 49–51.

43. Van Tilborg, *Imaginative Love*, 49–50. In addition, it is often said that, in this Gospel, we would expect the same usage as in 1:13 (*ex haimatōn*), but the meaning of the latter is unclear and may refer to both paternal and maternal contributions to the formation of the embryo (see the full discussion in van Tilborg, *Imaginative Love*, 33–47). The ordinary word for "semen" is *sperma*. Ben Witherington sees a reference to semen as water in Prov. 5:16 ("The Waters of Birth: John 3:5 and 1 John 5:6–8," *NTS* 35 [1989]: 155–60, here 156), but if this is correct, it occurs in a highly metaphorical context, where water has a variety of meanings connected with procreation and sexual pleasure. It does not follow that a reference to water outside such a poetic context could be understood as referring to semen.

44. See, for example, Dorothy A. Lee, *The Symbolic Narratives of the Fourth Gospel: The Interplay of Form and Meaning*, JSNTSup 95 (Sheffield: Sheffield Academic Press, 1994), 43–44; Judith M. Lieu, "Scripture and the Feminine in John," in *A Feminist Companion to the Hebrew Bible in the New Testament*, ed. Athalya Brenner, FCB 10 (Sheffield: Sheffield Academic Press,

d. "Water" refers to the amniotic fluid of the womb, and so "water and Spirit" refers to two births, one natural and the other spiritual.[45] References to the amniotic fluid as "water" are not easily adduced for the relevant period,[46] but the release of watery fluid from the womb in childbirth is an obvious feature of the process of birth and so recognizing a reference to it here does not really need textual support.[47] In its favor is that the reference to water in 3:5 follows immediately Nicodemus's reference to birth from "his mother's womb" in 3:4. In favor of the proposal generally, it can be said that the phrase "water and Spirit" then parallels the two kinds of birth described in the next verse (3:6).[48] According to Sandra Schneiders, then, what Nicodemus is asked to understand is that "it is necessary not only to be born into the Covenant of Israel but also to be born anew in the Spirit because what is born of flesh is fleshly while what is born of the spirit [sic] is spiritual."[49] However, there are two main objections to the proposal. First, it fails my criterion 4 because,

---

1996), 225–40, here 237–38; Lieu, "The Mother of the Son in the Fourth Gospel," *JBL* 117 (1998): 61–77, here 76. Lieu points out the maternal image of God in Deut. 32:18: "God who gave you birth" (see also Isa. 46:3).

45. Russell Fowler, "Born of Water and the Spirit (John 3⁵)," *ExpTim* 82 (1971): 159; D. G. Spriggs, "Meaning of 'Water' in John 3⁵," *ExpTim* 85 (1974): 149–50; Margaret Pamment, "John 3:5: 'Unless One Is Born of Water and the Spirit, He Cannot Enter the Kingdom of God,'" *NovT* 25 (1983): 189–90; Sandra M. Schneiders, "Born Anew," *ThTo* 44 (1987): 189–96; Witherington, "Waters"; Witherington, *John's Wisdom*, 97.

46. *4 Ezra* 8.8 speaks of the preservation of the embryo in the womb in "fire and water" (the reference to "fire" is unparalleled and obscure). In 1QH 11.7–12 (Sukenik's numbering: 3.7–12) there is a highly poetic description of the pain and danger of childbirth, which employs wordplay between *mišbār* ("wave of the sea") and *mišbēr* ("mouth of the cervix"), portraying the process of childbirth as like a perilous storm at sea (see also 11.14–17), but it is not at all clear that this includes reference to the waters released from the womb in childbirth. Whether Prov. 5:18 or Song 4:15 refers to the water of childbirth (Witherington, "Waters," 156) seems dubious; sexual pleasure is a more appropriate meaning in Song 4:15 and Prov. 5:15 (cf. vv. 13–14), while Prov. 5:18 may well refer to offspring but hardly specifically to water from the womb. The clearest references to amniotic fluid, among those adduced, are the ancient Mesopotamian ones (note by the editors added to Pamment, "John 3:5," 190; Witherington, "Waters," 157–58), but they are quite remote in time from John's Gospel.

47. Clement of Alexandria (*Strom.* 4.160.2) says that Christians have been "born from the womb of water" (γεγέννηκεν ἐκ μήτρας ὕδατος), evidently in dependence on John 3:5. He is comparing the water of baptism with the womb from which a child is born, a thought that may have been prompted by the presence of "water" in a pregnant woman's womb. Later patristic writers also think of the water of baptism as the womb from which the baptizands are born again—for example, John Chrysostom (see Annewies van den Hoek and Claude Mondésert, *Clément d'Alexandrie: Les Stromates; Stromate IV*, SC 463 [Paris: Cerf, 2001], 323n7) and Theodore of Mopsuestia (quoted in Joel C. Elowsky, ed., *John 1–10*, ACCS 4a [Downers Grove, IL: InterVarsity, 2007], 111–12).

48. But I doubt that this can be called "an example of Semitic parallelism" (Witherington, "Waters," 155).

49. Schneiders, "Born Anew," 192.

especially in view of 3:6, "water" and "Spirit" would be in contrast to each other rather than in any kind of association.[50] Second, it is difficult to see why natural birth needs mentioning in 3:5. Nicodemus does not need to be told that it is necessary. If the meaning were "To enter the kingdom, not only (as you know already) must one be born naturally, but also one must be born again spiritually," we should expect a more explicit signaling of the "not only . . . but also." The phrase "born from water and Spirit" seems naturally to refer to one birth only, in parallel with "born from above" and "born from the Spirit."

e. Both "water" and "spirit" (also translatable as "breath") refer, at a literal level, to natural birth ("the infant must pass through the *waters* of childbirth and breathe into its *nostrils* the breath of life"), which is here used as a metaphor for spiritual birth.[51] The difficulty in this proposal is that if the whole phrase "water and Spirit" can be understood adequately as a reference to natural birth, how does 3:5 serve to correct Nicodemus's misunderstanding? How is he supposed to see that the literal meaning is intended as a metaphor for spiritual birth? Jesus's play on the meaning of *pneuma* as either "wind" or "Spirit" in 3:8 is different, since the use of the word in the sense of "Spirit" has already been clearly established in 3:7, if not 3:6.

f. Whereas all the proposals discussed so far take "water" and "Spirit" to refer to distinct, even if closely related, entities, this next proposal, which seems to be increasingly popular among commentators, takes "water and Spirit" as a true hendiadys in which both terms refer to the same entity, and the *kai* ("and") is epexegetical.[52] The meaning, then, is "water, that is to say, Spirit." Water is a symbol of the Spirit,[53] as it is explicitly in 7:37–39 and implicitly in 4:7–15.

To explain how Nicodemus could understand this, most proponents appeal to biblical prophecies of a future divine gift of the Spirit imaged (as often in the Hebrew Bible)[54] as water. Reference is made especially to Ezek. 36:25–27,

---

50. On 1 John 5:6–8, cited as a parallel by Witherington, "Waters," see below. Even if, as Witherington ("Waters," 160) interprets this passage, "water" refers to the birth of Jesus and "blood" to his death, these are not contrasting realities in the way natural birth and spiritual birth are in the context of John 3:5.

51. Dorothy A. Lee, *Flesh and Glory: Symbol, Gender, and Theology in the Gospel of John* (New York: Crossroad, 2002), 69; see also p. 70 (she comes close to opting definitely for this view).

52. Carson, *John*, 194; Snodgrass, "That Which Is Born," 190–91; Kruse, *John*, 107–8; Lincoln, *Saint John*, 150–51; Köstenberger, *John*, 123–24; Michaels, *John*, 184; Jones, *Symbol of Water*, 74; Keener, *John*, 550–51 (he combines this with proposal *b* by suggesting that Jesus means "a *spiritual* proselyte baptism"). This was also Calvin's view (John Calvin, *The Gospel according to St. John 1–10*, trans. Thomas H. L. Parker [Grand Rapids: Eerdmans, 1961], 65).

53. "The two terms are functional equivalents, with water serving as a symbol of the Spirit" (Lincoln, *Saint John*, 150).

54. The image of the Spirit as water is implicit whenever it is said to be "poured out" by God (e.g., Joel 2:28–29).

which predicts that God will "sprinkle clean water" on Israel to purify them
(v. 25), put a new heart within them, replacing the heart of stone with one of
flesh (v. 26), and "put my spirit within you" (v. 27). The text does not explicitly use water as a symbol for the Spirit, but, since it seems implausible that
God would use literal water, it was natural to interpret the cleansing water
of verse 25 as referring to the Spirit of God. This is how the text is read in
1QS 4.20–22, which says that God "will sprinkle over him [man] the spirit
of truth like lustral waters" (4.21). Rabbinic literature also reads Ezek. 36:25
in this way.[55] However, there is a difficulty in seeing this text as the scriptural
background of John 3:5 in that the water has a purifying, not a life-giving
function, and proponents of this view therefore find cleansing as well as renewal
in the birth of which John 3:5 speaks.[56] In commenting on proposal *b* I have
already pointed out that cleansing is foreign to this context and imports an
unnecessary complication into a text where the obvious symbolism of water
in connection with birth is water as life-giving (as in John 4:7–15; 7:37–39).
A remedy for this problem would be to refer rather to texts where the prediction is that God will pour his Spirit like water on dry ground so that new life
will spring up from it (Isa. 32:15; 44:3–4).[57] (Another difficulty with seeing
a primary reference to Ezek. 36:25–27 is that the contrast between "stone"
and "flesh" there differs strikingly from John's contrast between "flesh" and
"spirit.")

Another possible problem with this proposal relates to my criterion 5. Why
would "born from Spirit" not have been an entirely adequate clarification of
"born again/from above [*anōthen*]"? What does "water" add? The answer
could be that it directs Nicodemus to the scriptural prophecies more clearly
than "Spirit" alone would have done. This might be an adequate explanation, but the issue prompts me to offer a new proposal, one that combines, I
believe, the strengths of proposals *d* and *f*:

g. "Water" refers to the amniotic fluid of the womb, and the phrase is a
hendiadys in which the two terms refer to the same entity. The phrase should
thus be understood as "the womb-water that is Spirit." Jesus is clarifying his
earlier saying in direct response to Nicodemus's misunderstanding of it in 3:4,
which refers to birth from a human mother's womb. Nicodemus's mistake

55. Keener, *John*, 551–52.
56. For example, Carson, *John*, 194; Keener, *John*, 550–51. Linda Belleville appeals to these
biblical prophecies to argue that "water and Spirit" represent two distinct aspects of new birth:
cleansing and participation in divine nature ("'Born of Water and Spirit': John 3:5," *TJ* 1 [1980]:
125–41, here 139–41).
57. Many commentators refer to the second of these texts, but few to the first. Belleville
("Born," 139) is one who does.

is to think that Jesus is speaking of another birth of the same kind as the first. So Jesus clarifies: "To enter the kingdom of God, one must be born not from the womb-water of a human mother, but from the womb-water that is Spirit." This takes up the common symbolism of water as life-giving, used to symbolize God's Spirit as his life-giving activity, and gives it a new twist that incorporates it into the metaphor of birth. To understand "water," Nicodemus has only to see that it picks up his own reference to the womb, while "Spirit" shows him that he has been mistaken in thinking of another birth of the ordinary kind. The phrase "water and Spirit" leads him from natural birth, which is all that has occurred to him so far, to the notion of another sort of birth, stemming directly from the life-giving activity of God.[58] The following verse (3:6) further clarifies the difference.

This proposal gives "water" a precise function in connecting 3:4 and 3:5 and so explains why it occurs only at this point in Jesus's exposition of new birth. It also does full justice to the close association of "water" and "Spirit" suggested by the grammatical structure.

Following Jesus's further attempt to help Nicodemus grasp the idea of a birth "from above" or "from the Spirit," this time starting with the phenomenon of wind (3:8), Nicodemus expresses incredulity (3:9), and Jesus says, "Are you a teacher of Israel, and yet you do not understand these things?" (3:10). The most likely reason why a Jewish teacher should have understood what Jesus has been saying about the necessity for birth "from above" or "from the Spirit" for entrance to the kingdom of God is that Nicodemus can be expected to know the Scriptures (cf. 5:39; 7:52). Here the prophecies of a future outpouring of the Spirit are clearly relevant. We might note that Isa. 32:15 speaks of "a spirit from on high" (LXX: *pneuma aph' hypsēlou*).[59] *Jubilees* 1.23–28, in a prophecy of the eschatological restoration of Israel, links Ezek. 36:27 with the promise that at that time Israel will be called "children of the living God" (Hosea 1:10). This shows that such texts could be associated in Jewish tradition, linking the gift of the Spirit from heaven with a new birth of the people as God's children. This scriptural background explains Jesus's expectation that Nicodemus could have understood the idea of birth from the Spirit, but there is no need to insist that "water" in particular must have a scriptural background of this kind.

---

58. The attempt by Jesus, here and in 3:8, to lead Nicodemus to understanding by starting with a feature of the ordinary world (physical birth, the wind) is probably what Jesus means by saying that he has spoken "about earthly things" (3:12). See Tom Thatcher, *The Riddles of Jesus in John: A Study in Tradition and Folklore*, SBLMS 53 (Atlanta: Society of Biblical Literature, 2000), 269–70. But for a different interpretation, see Jan G. van der Watt, "Knowledge of Earthly Things? The Use of ἐπίγειος in John 3:12," *Neot* 43 (2009): 289–310.

59. Note also Wis. 9:17: "you sent your holy Spirit from the heights [*apo hypsistōn*]."

A Secondary Reference to Baptism in 3:5?

If a text can be shown to have a primary meaning that is adequate to explain it, as I think proposals *f* and *g* do in the case of "water and Spirit" in 3:5, then it is difficult to establish criteria for detecting a secondary meaning. One might be that the meaning is sufficiently clear for readers to be reasonably expected to see it, but this is, of course, difficult to gauge. A second criterion might be that the secondary meaning must be coherent with the first. For example, to argue that 3:5 makes baptism necessary for salvation, as has been done in much of the history of interpretation, can hardly be justified in the light of the finding that, in the primary meaning of the text, "water" refers to the same entity as "Spirit," not to some other factor additional to "Spirit."

I have argued that the motif of cleansing or purifying is absent from the discussion of new birth in 3:3–10, and so "water" should not be understood as a symbol of purification, especially since water was just as commonly used to symbolize what is life-giving, and this has a much more obvious connection with the theme of new birth. It follows that a secondary reference to baptism cannot be established on the basis of early Christian views of baptism in which the water is understood to symbolize purification. The image of washing away impurity or sin was deeply rooted in Jewish practices of ritual use of water and was presumably also in play in John the Baptist's practice of baptism (cf. John 3:25). We find this understanding of the symbolism of water also in several early Christian references to the water of baptism (Acts 22:16; 1 Cor. 6:11; Eph. 5:26; Heb. 10:22–23; cf. *Barn.* 11.11).

In order to see a reference to baptism in John 3:5, we need evidence of an understanding of the symbolism of the water in baptism that would make it possible to say that the baptized person is "born from water." Baptism is associated with new life in the Pauline literature (Rom. 6:3–4; Col. 2:11–13), but in these passages the image is of being buried with Christ and raised with him. However, there is one New Testament passage that appears to come close to a baptismal understanding of John 3:5. According to Titus 3:5–6, God

> saved us . . . through the bath (washing) of a new beginning and renewal of the Holy Spirit [*dia loutrou palingenesias kai anakainōseōs pneumatos hagiou*] which he poured upon us richly through Jesus Christ our Savior.

The syntax of the phrase I have given in Greek is debatable. Most probably we should understand it this way: "through the bath of a new beginning and through renewal effected by the Holy Spirit."[60] Though *palingenesias* is commonly translated "regeneration," and it is hard to find a satisfactory alternative, I have avoided that translation because it suggests the image of rebirth and thus brings the passage closer to John 3:5 than is strictly justified.[61] The word is connected not with *gennaō* but with *ginomai* and means something more like "new genesis" or "re-creation."[62] Its meaning is very close to *anakainōseōs*. Most scholars take *loutrou*, whether they understand it as a reference to baptism or purely figuratively,[63] to refer to washing or cleansing (as in Eph. 5:26), and suppose that the cleansing effects renewal. But it may be that, as a reference to baptism, it refers simply to a ritual act of immersion in water, with the connotation of cleansing not active on this occasion. In that case, the image may be of water as life-giving and the whole phrase quite close in significance to John 3:5.

In support of the likelihood that readers would find an allusion to baptism in John 3:5, we could appeal to a passage in Justin Martyr's *First Apology* (ca. 151–155 CE), referring to baptism:

> From there they are brought by us where there is water, and are born again [*anagennōntai*] in the same manner of rebirth [*anagennēseōs*] by which we ourselves were born again [*anagennēthēmen*], for they then receive washing [*loutron*] in water in the name of God the Father and Maker of all, and of our Savior, Jesus Christ, and of the Holy Spirit. For Christ also said, "Except you are born again [*anagennēthēte*], you will not enter into the Kingdom of heaven." Now it is clear to all that it is impossible for those who have once come into being to enter into their mothers' wombs. (*1 Apol.* 61.3–5)[64]

Because of the differences between the saying of Jesus as cited by Justin and John 3:3, 5, some scholars have argued that Justin is quoting not from the

60. See I. Howard Marshall and Philip H. Towner, *A Critical and Exegetical Commentary on the Pastoral Epistles*, ICC (Edinburgh: T&T Clark, 1999), 316–18; George W. Knight, *The Pastoral Epistles: A Commentary on the Greek Text*, NIGTC (Grand Rapids: Eerdmans, 1992), 341–44; Jerome D. Quinn, *The Letter to Titus*, AB 35 (New York: Doubleday, 1990), 218–20.

61. Quinn (*Titus*, 223) suggests that it is used deliberately to avoid the difficulty posed by language of sexual generation, as used in John 3:3–10.

62. I have taken the translation "a new beginning" from Knight, *Pastoral Epistles*, 342.

63. A purely figurative meaning (without allusion to baptism) is proposed by Dunn, *Baptism*, 168–69; Knight, *Pastoral Epistles*, 343–44; Ben Witherington, *A Socio-Rhetorical Commentary on Titus, 1–2 Timothy and 1–3 John*, vol. 1 of *Letters and Homilies for Hellenized Christians* (Downers Grove, IL: InterVarsity, 2006), 159–60. Compare Marshall and Towner: "It is more likely that the term refers primarily to that spiritual cleansing which is outwardly symbolized in baptism with water" (*Pastoral Epistles*, 318). But Everett Ferguson says that a figurative use of the word *loutron* "would be unprecedented" (*Baptism*, 163).

64. Translation from Leslie William Barnard, *St. Justin Martyr: The First and Second Apologies*, ACW 56 (New York: Paulist Press, 1997), 66.

Gospel of John but rather from an independent tradition of the same saying. But Justin's obvious dependence on John 3:4 in his comment following the saying of Jesus makes it clear that Justin does have this passage of John in mind. He has doubtless quoted from memory (hence "of heaven" rather than "of God") and substituted for John's *gennēthē* the verb that he himself has just used,[65] at the same time changing to the second person plural, which is more appropriate to the general context in which he cites the saying.[66] His quotation approximates to John 3:3 rather than John 3:5 because it lacks reference to "water and Spirit," but we must presume that his association of the Johannine passage with baptism is related to the use of "water" in John 3:5 as well as with an understanding of baptism as regeneration.

Thus, Justin provides evidence of a second-century reading of John 3:3–5 that understood it to refer to baptism. Since he goes on to refer to washing as cleansing from sin, with reference to Isa. 1:16–20, he probably understood the Johannine passage as referring both to baptismal regeneration and to the water as symbolic of cleansing from sin. As we have seen, this is not a plausible understanding of the primary sense of the text, but it is not difficult to understand how, given an understanding of Christian baptism as rebirth and cleansing from sin, the text could be read in this way. It has been read in the same way frequently in the history of the text's reception,[67] though not unanimously so.

We should probably admit that we do not know whether the earliest readers of John are likely to have perceived a secondary reference to baptism in this text. What the history of reception demonstrates is that the text is open to such an interpretation, given a view of baptism informed by other passages of the New Testament, such as Titus 3:5–6. This could be understood as a canonical dimension of the meaning of the text or as a *sensus plenior*, properly discerned in the church's tradition of interpretation and sacramental practice. At the same time, however, responsible interpretation should not allow such a secondary reference to replace the primary meaning of the text. The latter should be allowed to determine the way in which the text is related to baptism. The water used in baptism may be understood to symbolize the activity of the Spirit, but it is the Spirit, not the water, who effects rebirth.[68]

---

65. It is the verb used in 1 Pet. 1:3, 23, which refers to rebirth by the word of God, with no explicit allusion to baptism.

66. Perhaps this form of the saying was in use, addressed to the baptizands, in the practice of baptism known to Justin.

67. For examples from the Fathers, see Elowsky, *John 1–10*, 111–12. Many more examples can be found in Ferguson, *Baptism*.

68. Compare Calvin: "He connects water with the Spirit because under that visible sign He testifies and seals the newness of life which by His Spirit God alone effects in us" (*St. John 1–10*, 64).

Eating and Drinking Jesus (John 6:31–59)

In an exegetical tradition going back to some of the church Fathers,[69] there have been many modern scholars who have held that this whole discourse, from start to finish (6:31–59), is eucharistic, identifying the "bread from heaven" throughout not only with Jesus but also with Jesus present in the bread and wine of the Eucharist.[70] However, this view, which usually depends on reading the whole discourse in the light of verses 53–58, is rarely found in recent scholarship, where the focus of debate has been on those verses alone. Some scholars hold that at verse 52 there is a transition from non-eucharistic to eucharistic reference,[71] a view that has often been accompanied by the explanation that verses 52–58 are a secondary addition to the discourse, which in itself is non-sacramental. The addition can be understood as an interpolation that diverges from the theology of the discourse (as Bultmann held)[72] or as harmonious with the rest of the discourse, added perhaps even by the author himself, developing the thought in an explicitly sacramental way.[73] Alternatively, especially in view of strong arguments for the unity and coherence of the whole discourse, including verses 53–58, an increasing number of scholars maintain that the whole discourse, including these verses, can be understood without reference to the Eucharist.[74] Some think that there

69. Craig R. Koester, "John Six and the Lord's Supper," *LQ* 40 (1990): 418–37, here 420–22.

70. Michel Roberge lists scholars who take this view up to 1978 ("Le discours sur le pain de vie (Jean 6,22–59): Problèmes d'interprétation," *LTP* 38 [1982]: 265–99, here 273n33). They include Hoskyns (*Fourth Gospel*, 281–307), though he does not take the reference to be exclusively eucharistic. Roberge calls the two forms of interpretation of John 6 "sapientielle" and "eucharistique," but this is misleading. Not everyone who interprets the passage without reference to the Eucharist thinks that it identifies Jesus with Wisdom.

71. Roberge ("Le discours," 276–77) lists and discusses scholars who take this view while holding to the literary unity of the whole discourse (including Schnackenburg, Dodd, Barrett). Add now Charles H. Talbert, *Reading John: A Literary and Theological Commentary on the Fourth Gospel and the Johannine Epistles* (London: SPCK, 1992), 138–40.

72. Roberge ("Le discours," 278–84) lists and discusses scholars who take this view (including Bultmann).

73. Roberge ("Le discours," 285–89) lists and discusses scholars who take this view (including Brown, Forestell). Brown repeats his view in *An Introduction to the Gospel of John*, ed. Francis J. Moloney (New York: Doubleday, 2003), 231–32. Those who think that the addition was made by the evangelist himself are listed and discussed by Roberge, "Le discours," 293–98 (including Boismard). Add now Schnelle, *Antidocetic Christology*, 201–8.

74. In 1982 Roberge ("Le discours," 267–68) was able to instance only four scholars who understand the whole discourse to make no eucharistic allusion, but to them can now be added Witherington, *John's Wisdom*, 162–63; Ridderbos, *John*, 235–42; Michaels, *John*, 395–96; Koester, *Symbolism*, 94–100, 259–62; Kruse, *John*, 174–76. Others think it possible that readers might be expected to think of the Eucharist, but they attach little importance to this: Carson, *John*, 296–97; Marianne Meye Thompson, *The Humanity of Jesus in the Fourth Gospel* (Philadelphia: Fortress, 1988), 44–48; Köstenberger, *John*, 217; Godfrey W. Ashby, "Body and Blood in John

is reference to the Eucharist, but only at a secondary level.[75] There are also those who think that eucharistic language is used but not with reference to the Eucharist (or perhaps even to warn against unacceptable sacramentalism).[76] A few scholars hold that the whole discourse can be read on two levels, with a non-eucharistic meaning that would have made sense to Jesus's hearers in the narrative context and a eucharistic significance intended for readers of the Gospel.[77]

We must first establish that the entire discourse (6:31–59) is a coherent whole in which verses 52–58 are an integral part. Most recent exegetes[78] have accepted Peder Borgen's argument that verses 31–58 have a homiletic structure in which the text cited in verse 31 (a conflation of Exod. 16:4 and 16:15; cf. also Ps. 78:24) is expounded step by step.[79] Jesus first expounds "He gave" (v. 32), then "bread from heaven" (vv. 33–48), then "to eat" (vv. 48–58). The conclusion (v. 58) forms an *inclusio* with verse 31, tying the whole discourse into the initial statement of the crowd and the scriptural text that they cited, as well as echoing the more recent statement in verse 50. Formally, therefore, verses 52–58 are integral to the structure of the discourse.

6:41–65," *Neot* 36 (2002): 57–61; Keener, *John*, 689–91. It may not be irrelevant that most of these scholars are evangelical Protestants.

75. To those listed by Roberge, "Le discours," 270–72 (including Lindars, Borgen and Moloney), add now Beasley-Murray, *John*, 95–96; Lee, *Symbolic Narratives*, 152–53; Lincoln, *Saint John*, 232–35.

76. To those listed by Roberge, "Le discours," 268–69 (including Dunn), add now Paul N. Anderson, *The Christology of the Fourth Gospel: Its Unity and Diversity in the Light of John 6*, WUNT 2/78 (Tübingen: Mohr Siebeck, 1996; repr., Valley Forge, PA: Trinity, 1997), 208, 212–13, 220 (he thinks that the reference is to solidarity with Jesus in his death); Paschal, "Sacramental Symbolism," 161–66; Maarten J. J. Menken, "John 6,51c–58: Eucharist or Christology?," *Bib* 74 (1993): 1–26. Note James D. G. Dunn's comment: "The 'eucharistic overtones' of the passage are secondary and negative in import" ("John VI—A Eucharistic Discourse?," *NTS* 17 [1970–1971]: 328–38, here 337).

77. Xavier Léon-Dufour, "Le mystère du pain de vie (*Jean VI*)," *RSR* 46 (1958): 481–523; Léon-Dufour, *Sharing the Eucharistic Bread: The Witness of the New Testament*, trans. Matthew J. O'Connell (New York: Paulist Press, 1987), 252–72. (Léon-Dufour is probably more successful in showing that the whole discourse can be read without eucharistic reference than in showing that, even on a secondary level, eucharistic reference is present from the start.) For others who take a similar view, see Roberge, "Le discours," 299n167; Frédéric Manns, "Jean 6," in *L'Évangile de Jean à la lumière du Judaïsme*, ASBF 33 (Jerusalem: Franciscan Printing Press, 1991), 141–61.

78. However, Anderson (*Christology*, 197) thinks that the main text is not the Old Testament quotation but "the narration of Jesus's ministry" in 6:1–24.

79. Peder Borgen, *Bread from Heaven: An Exegetical Study of the Concept of Manna in the Gospel of John and the Writings of Philo*, NovTSup 10 (Leiden: Brill, 1965). I am much less convinced by Borgen's argument that the discourse compares Jesus to Torah and Wisdom, an argument that depends heavily on Philo and rabbinic literature, but it has been very influential.

As well as the principal text from the Torah that Jesus expounds (v. 31), there are allusions to a secondary text from the prophets: Isa. 54:9–55:5.[80] As well as the explicit quotation (v. 45 = Isa. 54:13), there are a series of allusions to Isa. 55:1–3[81] ("thirst . . . come . . . eat . . . bread . . . come to me . . . so that you may live") in verses 35, 37, 40, 44, 45, 47, 51, 54, 57, 58.[82] The implied reading of this text from Isaiah is that, in contrast to the food and drink that cannot satisfy, God gives to those who come to him food and drink that truly sustain life. Especially important for the thematic coherence of the discourse is 6:35, which is both the first and fullest allusion to Isa. 55:1–3[83] and also the first of the Gospel's series of seven "I am" sayings with predicate: "I am the bread of life. Whoever comes to me will never be hungry, and whoever believes in me will never be thirsty." Jesus here identifies himself not only with the bread of the Exodus text, but also as the divine speaker[84] in Isa. 55, who offers both food and drink to those who come to him.[85] Jesus cites the "come to me" of that text and then interprets it as "believes in me," while implicitly equating it also with eating and drinking. The theme of eating *and drinking* is then taken up in verses 53–56. When Jesus says that "my flesh is true food and my blood is true drink," there is probably an allusion to Isa. 55:2, where "that which is not bread" and "that which does not satisfy" are contrasted with the food and drink that God gives. For the coherence of the whole discourse it is highly significant that, while verses 49–51 and 57–59 take up the motif of "eating bread" from Exodus, verses 53–56 take up the motif of "eating and drinking" from the key saying in verse 35 and its source text in Isa. 55:1–5.

80. See Aileen Guilding, *The Fourth Gospel and Jewish Worship: A Study of the Relations of St. John's Gospel to the Ancient Jewish Lectionary System* (Oxford: Clarendon, 1960), 63–64. On the relevance of Guilding's work, see Lindars, *John*, 251–52.

81. This text is connected with Exod. 16 by means of the Jewish exegetical technique of *gezerah shavah*: the words "bread" (Exod. 16:3, 4, 8, 12, 15) and "satisfy" (Exod. 16:3, 8, 12) occur in both texts. (The Hebrew texts, not the LXX, lie behind John 6.) John's phrase "bread of life" makes a transition from one text to the other.

82. Lincoln, *Saint John*, 224.

83. There may well be an earlier allusion in 6:27. See Lindars, *John*, 254–55; Anderson, *Christology*, 200.

84. Some commentators on John, following some Old Testament scholars, refer to the speaker in Isa. 55:1–3 as Wisdom, but we should not assume that first-century readers of Isaiah would have thought this.

85. Most scholars prefer to see allusions to Prov. 9:5 and Sir. 24:21 (e.g., Lindars, *John*, 259–60; Keener, *John*, 683) and make this the basis for the idea that Jesus here presents himself as the divine Wisdom. I do not think there is an adequate basis for what is often called the "sapiential" interpretation of John 6 (see Carson, *John*, 299). Isaiah 55:1–3 accounts for much more of what is said in John 6 than do the Wisdom passages and coheres with the quotation from Isa. 54:13 in John 6:45. Moreover, Isa. 55:1–3, read in context, can easily be understood as referring to the eschatological provision of God for his people. Remarkably, Borgen (*Bread*) makes no reference to Isa. 55:1–3.

The theme of "eating bread" is introduced in verses 49–51 in a way that makes it quite clear that it is equivalent to "coming to" Jesus and "believing in Jesus." The theme returns in verses 57–58 in very similar terms. Between these passages is the passage that speaks of eating Jesus's flesh and drinking his blood, the passage that is frequently said to be unmistakably eucharistic. The transitions between this language and that of "eating bread" used before and after it are carefully made. In verse 51 the bread is said to be Jesus's flesh. In verse 57 the language of eating his flesh and drinking his blood gives way to the simple "eats me," which enables a transition back to eating the bread that we have known since verse 35 is Jesus himself. So why is the language of eating Jesus's flesh and drinking his blood introduced in the four verses 53–56? Since the image of both eating and drinking was already announced in verse 35, why is it not taken up until verse 53, and why is it developed as eating *flesh* and drinking *blood*? It could be said that if one were to expand the image of eating Jesus into one of eating and drinking him, then to speak of eating his flesh and drinking his blood would be the obvious way to do so. But John need not have taken up the image of eating and drinking from Isa. 55:1 at all. He evidently did so in verse 35 precisely in order to develop it into the image of eating Jesus's flesh and drinking his blood in verses 53–56.

As many scholars have recognized, a key to the use of this language lies in verse 51c ("the bread that I will give for [*hyper*] the life of the world is my flesh"). Here Jesus alludes, for the first time in chapter 6 and somewhat cryptically, to his coming sacrificial death. Before chapter 6 Jesus has made a few even more cryptic allusions to his death-and-exaltation (1:51; 2:19; 3:14, 16). They will become more common after chapter 6 (7:33–34; 8:14, 21, 28; 12:23, 24, 32; 13:3–11, 31–33, 36; 16:16–22, 28) and in a few cases much more explicit (10:11, 15, 17–18; 12:7; 15:13). In some cases, Jesus says that his death will be "for" (*hyper*) people (10:11, 15; 15:13; cf. 11:52), and 6:51 is the first of these cases, perhaps indebted, as we shall see, to eucharistic language. Within the discourse, verse 51c makes the transition from the incarnation (Jesus as the bread that came down from heaven) to the cross (Jesus as the bread that he gives for the life of the world). This theme is then developed in the following verses, where "flesh" is expanded to "flesh" and "blood." "Flesh" is a reminder of the real and vulnerable humanity of Jesus (1:14), humanity vulnerable to violence and death.[86] The addition of "drinking blood" to "eating flesh" makes clear that Jesus's violent death has come into view: blood must be shed before it may be drunk (cf. Num. 23:24; Ps. 50:13; Ezek. 39:18–19). In this connection, some commentators refer to the use of the Hebrew phrase

---

86. Perhaps, in view of 6:51, a hint of death should already be seen in the use of *sarx* in 1:14.

"flesh and blood" in the sense of human nature (Sir. 14:18; 17:31; *1 En.* 15.4; Matt. 16:17; 1 Cor. 15:50; Gal. 1:16; Eph. 6:12; Heb. 2:14),[87] perhaps with an emphasis on its physicality and mortality. But more relevant may be texts in which "flesh" and "blood" occur separately but in parallel with reference to violent death (Ps. 79:2–3; Ezek. 32:5–6; Zeph. 1:17; 1 Macc. 7:17; 4 Macc. 6:6).[88] In any case, it is clear from the context in John 6 (cf. v. 57: "eats me") that the flesh and blood are Jesus himself, considered as crucified as well as incarnate. The transition in verse 51c is not from faith to the Eucharist as the means of eternal life,[89] but from believing in Jesus to believing in Jesus as the one who died a violent death for the life of the world.

However, it is likely that the *language* is drawn from the eucharistic "words of institution." It is true that in Jewish temple sacrifices "flesh" and "blood," the two component parts of a sacrificial animal, were separated (e.g., Lev. 1:3–9), and in some cases the flesh was eaten, but drinking blood was specifically forbidden (Gen. 9:4; Lev. 17:11, 14; Deut. 12:23). Only in the gruesome sacrifice that God makes of the armies of Gog and Magog is the blood to be drunk—by birds and animals (Ezek. 39:17–19).[90] In the context of the Last Supper itself (according to the Synoptic Gospels and Paul), Jesus makes the wine that would be drunk in any case on such an occasion a symbol of the blood he is about to shed, an innovatory move that may well have been aided by the traditional association of blood with red wine (Gen. 49:11; Deut. 32:14; Isa. 63:3, 6; Sir. 39:26; 50:15; 1 Macc. 6:34).[91] But in John 6 there is no reference to wine that could ease the introduction of the otherwise very shocking image of drinking blood.[92] It seems likely, therefore, that John had the eucharistic words of Jesus in mind when he wrote verses 53–56. (The Johannine words come closest to Matt. 26:26–28, where Jesus explicitly tells the disciples to "eat," though this is implied in the other versions.) This is the more likely because already verse 51c seems to use language from the words of institution (cf. Luke 22:19: "my body which is given for you" [*hyper hymōn*]). It is true that in all four versions of the words of institution in the New Testament, Jesus speaks of his "body" (*sōma*) rather than, as in John 6,

87. For example, Köstenberger, *John*, 216; Jane S. Webster, *Ingesting Jesus: Eating and Drinking in the Gospel of John*, SBLAB 6 (Atlanta: Society of Biblical Literature, 2003), 84.

88. Note also Eph. 2:13–14; Col. 1:20–22 with reference to the death of Jesus.

89. J. Terence Forestell, *The Word of the Cross: Salvation as Revelation in the Fourth Gospel*, AnBib 57 (Rome: Biblical Institute Press, 1974), 144.

90. The echo of this passage in Rev. 19:17–18 refers only to eating flesh, not drinking blood.

91. Joachim Jeremias, *The Eucharistic Words of Jesus*, trans. Norman Perrin, NTL (London: SCM, 1966), 223–24.

92. Isaiah 55:1 refers to wine along with water and milk, but none of these images is taken up in John 6:35.

his flesh (*sarx*). But Ignatius of Antioch, writing not long after John's Gospel, uses "flesh" and "blood" in his eucharistic references (*Trall.* 8.1; *Smyrn.* 6.2; *Rom.* 7.3; *Phld.* 4; cf. Justin, *1 Apol.* 66.2).[93] So it may have been an alternative and established usage known to John.[94] In any case, he could well have preferred "flesh" both because it belongs to the biblical language of sacrifice and because of the incarnational association that he had already given it in 1:14. The Word became flesh in order to give his flesh for the life of the world.

The use of eucharistic language does not mean that verses 53–56 are actually about participation in the Eucharist.[95] Rather, because John now wishes to stress that the faith that leads to eternal life is faith in the Jesus who gave himself in death, he employs language used in the rite in which Jesus's sacrificial death was symbolically portrayed and its benefits symbolically appropriated. The fact that John uses two different verbs for "to eat"—*phagein* (6:49–53, 58) and *trōgein* (6:54, 56–57)—has sometimes been held to show that he moves from a metaphorical sense of eating (i.e., faith) to a literal one (i.e., Eucharist).[96] But that John in fact uses the two words interchangeably seems clear from the strict parallel between verse 53a and verse 54a. In the Greek of the New Testament, *phagein* is used only in the future and aorist, while *esthiein* is normally used in the other tenses, but John never uses *esthiein* and always uses *trōgein* instead for the present participle (in 6:54–58; and also 13:18, quoting Ps. 41:9 [40:10 LXX], where the LXX uses *esthiein*). In this he apparently follows a popular usage[97] and intends no difference of meaning between *phagein* and *trōgein*.[98] Moreover, even if *trōgein* did mean "to munch" in John, there is no reason why this should be any less metaphorical than "to eat."[99]

93. Ignatius may be dependent on John 6 (Dunn, "John VI," 334; Charles E. Hill, *The Johannine Corpus in the Early Church* [Oxford: Oxford University Press, 2004], 432–34), in which case he would be the earliest witness to a eucharistic reading of John 6.

94. It is suggested that *sōma* and *sarx* are alternative translations of Aramaic *besar*.

95. Ignatius (*Trall.* 8.1; *Rom.* 7.3), too, can use eucharistic language for purposes other than speaking about the Eucharist, actually as often as he uses it to speak directly of the Eucharist.

96. For example, Hoskyns, *Fourth Gospel*, 298–99.

97. In the New Testament this is found elsewhere only in Matt. 24:38.

98. Barrett, *John*, 299; Maarten J. J. Menken, "The Translation of Psalm 41:10 in John 13:18," *JSNT* 40 (1990): 61–79, here 65; Menken, "John 6,51c–58," 17.

99. Francis J. Moloney (*Signs and Shadows: Reading John 5–12* [Minneapolis: Fortress, 1996], 55) still maintains a distinction of meaning between the two verbs, with *trōgein* indicating "the action of crunching with the teeth," but he thinks that the latter "renders concrete the notion of eating the flesh of Jesus," not necessarily in a eucharistic sense. For the distinction of meaning, he relies on Ceslas Spicq, "ΤΡΩΓΕΙΝ: Est-il synonyme de ΦΑΓΕΙΝ et d'ΕΣΘΙΕΙΝ dans le Nouveau Testament?," *NTS* 26 (1979–80): 414–19. In fact, Spicq shows that the three verbs are interchangeable, and his evidence scarcely supports his view that some particular nuance (different in different cases) can attach to *trōgein* in particular contexts.

Scholars who defend a non-eucharistic reading of this passage, at least at the primary level of meaning, make the obviously valid point that Jesus's hearers within the narrative context could not possibly have understood Jesus if he were teaching them about the Eucharist (before instituting it!).[100] The principle on which I insisted in my discussion of John 3:5, that words of Jesus in the Gospel must be understood in the first place within the narrative context within which John sets them, is important also for interpretation of John 6. We are kept fully aware of Jesus's interlocutors throughout 6:25–65. Indeed, it is they who introduce the topic of manna and cite the text that Jesus then expounds (v. 31). As they become more unresponsive to Jesus's words, "the crowd" (v. 22) gives way to "the Jews" (vv. 41, 52), who do not actually address Jesus but share among themselves their complaints that his words are incredible. Nevertheless, in both cases Jesus takes note of what they are saying and responds to it. As often in the Gospel, the problems that Jesus's hearers have with what he tells them function to move the discourse on from one aspect of a topic to another. Finally the focus shifts to Jesus's disciples (evidently a wider group than the twelve and so presumably also among the "crowd" of v. 22), many of whom also find Jesus's teaching hard to accept. Jesus's words in verses 61–65 form a kind of postscript to the discourse, in which Jesus responds to these dubious disciples, ending by referring back to what he had said in the discourse (v. 65; cf. v. 44).

We should also note the parallels with Jesus's discussion with Nicodemus. In 6:53 Jesus enunciates a condition of attaining eternal life that, in its negative formulation, parallels the sayings about entering the kingdom in 3:3, 5. Moreover, the skeptical questions of "the Jews" in 6:42 ("How [*pōs*] does he now say . . . ?") and 6:52 ("How can [*pōs dynatai*] this man give us his flesh to eat?") are strikingly similar to those of Nicodemus in 3:4 ("How can [*pōs dynatai*] a person be born after having grown old?") and 3:9 ("How can [*pōs dynatai*] these things be?"). Just as after Nicodemus's first question Jesus attempted to explain further what he meant, so he does in 6:43–51. But just as after Nicodemus's second question Jesus gave up the attempt to accommodate his discourse to Nicodemus's "earthly" perspective, so he does after the second question of "the Jews" in chapter 6. Verses 53–56 hardly serve to make what "the Jews" have found impossible to believe any more acceptable, but rather intensify the offense. It is notable that in both cases (Nicodemus and "the Jews") the point at which Jesus apparently ceases to hope for comprehension from his auditors is the point at which he begins to speak of his

---

100. For example, Carson, *John*, 278; Ashby, "Body and Blood"; Michaels, *John*, 396.

death-and-exaltation.[101] When it comes to Jesus's cryptic references to his death, the disciples before the event seem no more able to comprehend than "the Jews" are (cf. 2:19–22), and this is evidently the case in chapter 6 for the disciples who find it hard to accept Jesus's teaching (vv. 60–61). Moreover, an openness to misunderstanding characterizes the way Jesus continues to refer to his death after chapter 6. As Jesus's words in this chapter suggest cannibalism, so his later sayings about going away suggest that he may be intending to travel abroad (7:33–36) or to commit suicide (8:21–22).

Therefore, precisely because in 6:51c, 53–56 Jesus is speaking of the need for faith in himself as the one who will have sacrificed himself in death for the life of the world, we must understand the language of eating his flesh and drinking his blood to be deliberately riddling.[102] On a literal level the words can only suggest cannibalism, while to have access to their real meaning one must at least entertain the extraordinary notion that by dying a violent death voluntarily Jesus will provide eternal life to those who are united with him through faith. That neither "the Jews" nor even "many of his disciples" (v. 60) can penetrate the meaning of the riddle is because they lack the Spirit-given insight that will actually be available only after Jesus's death-and-resurrection (vv. 62–63; cf. 7:39). Some of them, lacking even the faith in Jesus that is possible at this point in the narrative, are not even prepared for receiving that insight when it comes (vv. 36, 44–45, 62–65).[103] Thus, while Jewish sacrificial thinking, perhaps especially with reference to the Passover lamb (cf. 6:4), might, in the narrative context, effect some entry into the meaning of Jesus's words in verses 51c, 53–56,[104] we should also recognize that in the Gospel's perspective this meaning could not but remain obscure until after the resurrection.[105]

The rather popular idea that in verses 53–56 John stresses the physical reality either of the incarnation and death of Jesus as such or of those realities as represented in the Eucharist *in order to counter docetic teaching*[106] has no

101. The parallel is not exact, since in chap. 6 Jesus refers to his death already in verse 51 (although it is clear from v. 52 that "the Jews" have not understood this), whereas in chap. 3 Jesus speaks of his death only after Nicodemus's second question.

102. Thatcher (*Riddles*, 285–86) discusses verse 51 as a riddle but seems to think that in verses 53–58 Jesus is "expounding the answer to the riddle" rather than continuing and intensifying it.

103. In verses 36 and 40 "see" refers to seeing Jesus physically, as the people in the story do, while in verse 62 (as in 1:51) it refers to seeing him after his resurrection, as the disciples who believed in him before his death did.

104. See especially Ashby, "Body and Blood."

105. Léon-Dufour, "Symbolic Reading," 452.

106. For example, Borgen, *Bread*, 183–92; Schnelle, *Antidocetic Christology*, 101–8; Moloney, "When Is John," 121.

support from the context.[107] The problem that "the Jews" have in this chapter is not with the material reality of Jesus, but rather, quite the opposite, with his divine origin (v. 42). Even if "the Jews" are regarded as no more than a mouthpiece for groups in the context of the "Johannine community," we should need more than verse 52 to indicate that a group different from that in verse 42 is now to be imagined.

Another misconception that needs to be laid to rest is the view that verse 63 is some kind of comment on verses 53–56,[108] asserting that the mere "flesh" of Jesus is useless apart from the Spirit.[109] This understanding has sometimes been used to support the view that John is referring to the Eucharist but only in order to counter a form of sacramentalism that ascribed salvific efficacy to the mere consumption of the physical elements.[110] In fact, verse 63 is a comment, not on the christological or eucharistic content of the discourse, but rather on these disciples' difficulty in understanding it. As Andrew Lincoln observes, John "employs 'flesh' positively when it is linked with Jesus [as in 1:14; 6:51c, 53–56] and negatively when it is linked with human response to the divine revelation [e.g., 8:15]." In the latter sense, "flesh"

> refers to the sphere of merely human existence which, without the activity of the Spirit, is alienated from God. . . . The flesh is of no avail in evaluating Jesus; merely human categories can only take offence at the claim that the flesh of the divine Son of Man must be offered up in death for the life of the world.[111]

What is useless is not the flesh of Jesus, but rather the merely fleshly perspective of the disciples.

We have seen that 6:51c, 53–56 makes an advance on the teaching of the preceding parts of the discourse in that the language of eating Jesus's flesh and drinking his blood represent believing, not only in Jesus as the incarnate one, but also in Jesus as the crucified one. But there is another aspect to the advance. It now becomes clear that eternal life is not just a divine gift to those who believe in Jesus; it is actual participation in Jesus's own life, made available

107. For an extended argument against the anti-docetic interpretation, see Menken, "John 6,51c–58," 18–23.

108. Or, alternatively, that verses 53–58 must be an interpolation because their use of "flesh" is incompatible with that in verse 63.

109. For example, Hoskyns, *Fourth Gospel*, 301; Barrett, *Essays*, 43; Dunn, "John VI," 334–38; compare Thomas L. Brodie, *The Gospel according to John: A Literary and Theological Commentary* (New York: Oxford University Press, 1993), 288.

110. For example, Burge, *Anointed Community*, 158.

111. Lincoln, *Saint John*, 237; so also Lindars, *John*, 273; Moloney, *Signs*, 62; Menken, "John 6,51c–58," 25; Smith, *John*, 162.

through his death.[112] This is the significance of verses 56–57. In verse 57 Jesus explains that he himself lives out of the eternal divine life of his Father, and so believers, participating in Jesus's life, are alive with this same divine life. In verse 56 he explains that faith in the crucified Jesus unites the believer with him in a union so intimate and enduring that it can be depicted as mutual indwelling and abiding. This language of the reciprocal indwelling of Jesus and the believer is itself, because of its reciprocity, an advance on the language of eating and drinking. John introduces it here as a means of connecting this discourse with the Last Supper Discourse, where the image of mutual indwelling recurs (10:14–23; 15:4–7) in the context of fuller discussion of the life of discipleship.

A Eucharistic Overtone? (6:51c, 53–56)

John used eucharistic language to speak, not of the Eucharist, but of faith in the crucified Jesus and participation in his life. But the case for a secondary allusion to the Eucharist is certainly stronger than the case for a secondary allusion to baptism in 3:5. Since it is distinctively eucharistic language that appears in 6:53–56, it will almost inevitably call the Eucharist to the minds of Christian readers familiar with that language. We must reckon seriously with this "overtone," but at the same time we should not allow it to replace the primary meaning of the text. Responsible readers who recognize the eucharistic overtone will understand it in a way that is consistent with the primary meaning of the text. There is nothing in the context to support the view that John was actually warning against an unacceptable sacramentalism in which too much importance was attached to the material elements of the rite. But the passage surely does resist any eucharistic reading of it in which the material elements of the rite take the place of the faith in the crucified Jesus that it is primarily about. In other words, the Eucharist can be relevant to a reading of the text only insofar as the Eucharist is understood precisely as an expression of faith in the crucified Jesus and as a symbol of participation in his life. Then the text can function to teach participants in the Eucharist what the sacrament is actually about. At the same time, it is vital to recognize that while the Eucharist is the communal rite that focuses what this text is about in the life of the church, the meaning of the text exceeds the Eucharist. The primary meaning is both more basic and more extensive than the sacramental overtone.

112. A few interpreters think that these verses mean that believers in Jesus must expect suffering and martyrdom (Anderson, *Christology*, 207–9). Arguably, Ignatius (*Rom.* 7.3), if he knew John 6, understood the text in this way, applying it to his approaching martyrdom, although he also applied it to the Eucharist.

Were there space here to explore the reception history of this text, we might well find that it confirms this conclusion, for, while this text has often been read as directly eucharistic (among the Fathers, for example, by Cyril of Alexandria and John Chrysostom), there has also been a significant tradition of non-sacramental interpretation (including Clement of Alexandria, Origen, Eusebius, Luther, and Calvin). For Augustine, Thomas Aquinas, and some of those who debated the issue at the Council of Trent, a decisive consideration was that the text promises eternal life to those who eat and drink, whereas this could not be said of mere reception of the sacrament. So, according to Aquinas, the promises refer to those who eat and drink "not only in a sacramental way, but also in a spiritual way."[113] A sacramental interpretation misleads unless it is allowed only a secondary place.

The Last Supper

The absence of an account of "the institution of the Eucharist" from John's account of the Last Supper has been variously explained. I suggest two main considerations. (1) I have argued elsewhere[114] that John presupposes that his readers know Mark's Gospel and deliberately does not repeat what could be read in Mark unless he has a specific reason for doing so. (2) To call Mark 14:22–25 and Matt. 26:26–29 accounts of "the institution of the Eucharist" is misleading because, unlike Luke (22:19) and Paul (1 Cor. 11:25), they contain no indication that what Jesus does is to be repeated by his disciples. The function of these accounts in Mark and Matthew is to provide readers, in advance of the narrative of Jesus's death, with a sacrificial interpretation of that death. John has no need of such an account for this purpose, because his narrative of the death of Jesus itself suggests a sacrificial interpretation (19:34). So, at the Last Supper he narrates instead another symbolic act of Jesus, the foot-washing (13:1–11), which also interprets the death of Jesus, in this case as the culmination of his ministry of loving service in the role of a slave.

Blood and Water from Jesus's Side (19:34)

This passage can be discussed here only briefly, but it requires some attention because a significant tradition of interpretation, represented most recently

113. Koester, "John Six," 420–25.
114. Richard Bauckham, "John for Readers of Mark," in *The Gospels for All Christians: Rethinking the Gospel Audiences*, ed. Richard Bauckham (Grand Rapids: Eerdmans; Edinburgh: T&T Clark, 1997), 147–71.

probably by Francis Moloney,[115] sees an allusion here to the two sacraments of the Eucharist and baptism, portrayed as vehicles of the efficacy of Jesus's sacrificial death.

Most interpreters see that, in the first instance, the flow of blood and water signifies that Jesus died a truly human death (and some appeal to ancient physiology for the view that water as well as blood would have this significance).[116] Most also account for the Gospel's emphasis on this point (and its appeal to eyewitness testimony in 19:35) by supposing that docetic denial of the real humanity of Christ is in view. However, it is possible to suppose that it was theologically important to John that Jesus died a real human death, just as the reality of the incarnation was fundamental for him (1:14), without necessarily construing this as polemic against docetism. Finding anti-docetic motivation in the Gospel is popular with exegetes probably because there is no doubt that the Johannine Epistles have docetic denials of Jesus's real humanity in view. But there the concern is quite explicit. If the same author wrote both the Gospel and the Epistles, as I think probable, it would make sense that in 1 John he addressed a specific context of controversy, drawing on the Gospel to do so, but that in the Gospel he had no such limited objectives in view. In the Gospel he wrote for Christian communities that might or might not have to deal with docetic teaching, but his concern was with the positive meaning of the incarnation and death of Jesus, not with countering any particular misleading views of them. This approach can recognize that the motif of John 19:34 (blood and water) is deployed in 1 John 5:6 against docetism without requiring the same to be the case in John 19:34 itself. Since in 1 John 5:6 the phrase "through water and blood" (*di' hydatos kai haimatos*) consists of a single preposition governing two anarthrous nouns, the two terms are best understood as referring to closely associated realities (as in the case of "water and Spirit" in 3:5) and so as referring to the description in John 19:34.[117]

Whether or not the stress on the reality of Jesus's death is seen as anti-docetic, most interpreters are not content to see only a physical fact in the flow of blood

115. Moloney, *John*, 505–6; see also Hoskyns, *Fourth Gospel*, 533; Barrett, *John*, 557; Schnelle, *Antidocetic Christology*, 209; Smith, *John*, 363.

116. For example, Koester, *Symbolism*, 191.

117. For a detailed discussion that comes to this conclusion, see Raymond E. Brown, *The Epistles of John: Translated, with Introduction, Notes, and Commentary*, AB 30 (Garden City, NY: Doubleday, 1982), 573–79; see also Matthew D. Jensen, *Affirming the Resurrection of the Incarnate Christ: A Reading of 1 John*, SNTSMS 153 (Cambridge: Cambridge University Press, 2012), 181–83; Bruce G. Schuchard, *1–3 John*, ConC (Saint Louis: Concordia, 2012), 530–32. Jensen (*Affirming the Resurrection*, 180nn20–26) lists scholars who advocate each of the various interpretations of this text. But it should be noted that some who take this view think that there is also reference to baptism and the Eucharist in 5:6, just as they think there is also in John 19:34.

and water[118] but also seek a further, symbolic meaning. The most popular and plausible is that blood symbolizes Jesus's sacrificial death (or his life poured out in death), and water the Spirit of life (connecting especially with 7:37–39).[119] Some scholars, accepting this as the secondary meaning, add reference to the Eucharist and baptism as a third level of meaning,[120] while others opt for only two levels of meaning, of which the sacramental forms the second.[121]

That the blood signifies sacrificial death and the water (as a proleptic sign) signifies the Spirit that flows from Jesus's redemptive death ties in well with the unambiguous meaning of other parts of the Gospel, as well as the Passover theme of 19:31–36. This is the point in the Gospel's narrative at which John the Baptist's witness to Jesus at the beginning of the story (1:29: "the Lamb of God who takes away the sin of the world") comes to fulfillment and is therefore appropriately witnessed by the Beloved Disciple (19:35). But a reference to the sacraments will seem plausible probably only to interpreters who find clear and strong references to baptism in 3:5 and to the Eucharist in 6:53–56. While the context of 3:5 might well suggest an association of "water" with baptism to Christian readers accustomed to connect baptism with regeneration, there is nothing in the context of "water" in 19:34 that would bring baptism to mind. For an allusion to the Eucharist simply by means of the word "blood" not even a eucharistic reading of 6:53–56 would prepare readers. Moreover, there is little evidence in the New Testament that Christians were accustomed to thinking of baptism and the Eucharist as a pair, especially since they evidently had no word (meaning "sacraments") with which to categorize them as two of the same sort of thing. The pairing of the two may seem natural in later periods, but we may not simply assume that it would have seemed so in the late first century. Elsewhere in the New Testament, probably only 1 Cor. 10:1–4 suggests a linking of the two rites as a pair, unless, of course, 1 John 5:6–7 is read in this way. But there the interpretative issues parallel those at John 19:34. The case for any level of allusion to the Eucharist and baptism in John 19:34 is very weak.

Conclusion

Johannine soteriology is overwhelmingly concerned with the fundamental aspects: faith in Jesus the Savior and reception of eternal life, which comes

118. Those who are content include Ridderbos, *John*, 619–20; Kruse, *John*, 372.

119. For example, Westcott, *St. John*, 279; Carson, *John*, 623–24; Beasley-Murray, *John*, 357–58; Lincoln, *Saint John*, 479; Keener, *John*, 1153; cf. Witherington, *John's Wisdom*, 311.

120. For example, Barrett, *John*, 557.

121. For example, Schnelle, *Antidocetic Christology*, 209; Smith, *John*, 363.

from God and through participation in the life of Jesus himself. These re-alities are represented in the church's liturgical practice by baptism and the Eucharist, and it is not surprising that various passages in the Gospel of John, whose imagery resembles the material elements of these sacramental rites, have frequently been understood to refer to them. My own conclusion from this study of the three passages in John where a sacramental overtone is most plausible is that this Gospel's contribution to a theology of the sacraments is to prioritize the soteriological realities that are focused in the sacraments but always exceed the sacraments. There is no reason to see this prioritization as polemical. John is not opposing sacraments or an overemphasis on sacraments or a mistaken reliance on the outward rite as such. That the Gospel refers to sacraments only in secondary overtones, if at all, should be attributed to its genre as a narrative of the history of Jesus and to its topical selectivity, its concentration on key themes to the exclusion of much that might otherwise be judged important. That it has nevertheless funded sacramental liturgies and spirituality with words and images is not problematic, because the sac-raments represent those central realities of salvation in Christ to which this Gospel gives memorable expression.

6

Dualisms

By common consent the Gospel of John is "the most dualistic of the New Testament literature."[1] But "dualism," as we shall see, is a slippery term, and this Gospel has been much misunderstood by interpreters who have too hastily assimilated the various kinds of dualism or duality that are undoubtedly a major feature of Johannine thought and expression. In this chapter I hope particularly to bring some clarity to this subject by analyzing more precisely than has usually been done the variety of dualisms and dualities in the Gospel and the ways in which they function in the narrative and theology of the Gospel. I shall begin, however, with the work of Rudolf Bultmann, since probably no one has grappled more strenuously with the problem of Johannine dualism, in terms both of historical explanation and of theological interpretation, than he did.

Rudolf Bultmann on Johannine Theology

Reading Bultmann's interpretation of the Gospel of John,[2] even in the light of the kinds of critique that must be applied to it at the present day, is still

1. Robert Kysar, *John, the Maverick Gospel* (Atlanta: John Knox, 1976), 48–49.
2. In *Theology of the New Testament*, Bultmann treats Johannine theology as the theology of the Gospel and the Epistles of John considered as a coherent unity. However, because the

an exhilarating experience. As an attempt at a truly theological interpretation of the Gospel it has few rivals in more recent writing. This is because of
Bultmann's thoroughgoing attempt to penetrate to what is really going on
theologically in the evangelist's work. Though primarily a historical exegete,
trained in the history-of-religions school with its commitment to history un-
encumbered by dogma, Bultmann had the express aim of uniting exegesis and
theology. He did this most successfully in the case of the Gospel of John, both
in his *Theology of the New Testament* and in his remarkable commentary on
the Gospel,[3] because he believed that, among the New Testament writers, the
Johannine evangelist himself grasped most clearly the essential core and character of the Christian message, the kerygma of the early Christian movement,
and presented it in a way that most readily enabled the modern interpreter to
distinguish this essential core from the "mythological" forms of expression
that the evangelist deployed. In other words, this early Christian writer had
already carried out, to a large extent, the program of "demythologizing" the
kerygma that Bultmann held to be essential if Western people in the second
half of the twentieth century were to be able to hear it aright. Bultmann's
attempt to get inside the dynamic of the Johannine evangelist's thinking was
at the same time his attempt to locate and to express the Gospel message for
his own contemporaries. This means that it is certainly not a "purely historical" report of the thought of the Gospel (unlike many more recent accounts
of Johannine theology), but it is an interpretation that is importantly rooted
in Bultmann's historical reconstruction of the background and development
of the Gospel.

Three key factors give Bultmann's interpretation of Johannine theology
its distinctive character. One is the source analysis by which he isolated the
sources that the evangelist incorporated in his Gospel and the later redaction
of the evangelist's work by an editor who, by adding material, brought the
Gospel more into line with conventional Christian teaching. Second, behind the
Gospel, according to Bultmann, lies the Gnostic myth of the Revealer, which
the evangelist found in one of his main sources, the "revelation-discourses,"
and which Bultmann reconstructed from Mandean literature. According to
Bultmann, it is the Johannine evangelist's use of this pre-Christian, Gnostic
myth that explains the distinctiveness of the Johannine literature as compared
with the other main theological trends in early Christianity. It is important for

---

weight of his interpretation rests on the Gospel and because subsequently it has become much
more usual to treat the theology of the Gospel independently of that of the Epistles, this chapter
will focus especially on the Gospel, though with some reference to the Epistles.

3. Rudolf Bultmann, *The Gospel of John*, trans. George R. Beasley-Murray (Oxford: Blackwell, 1971).

Bultmann's interpretation of Johannine theology that the evangelist took over this already existing mythological framework for his Christology and soteriology, but also that he adapted it considerably to suit his own purposes. Third, the philosophical resource that Bultmann brought to his work of identifying and expressing the core message of the Gospel was the existential analysis of Martin Heidegger. This enabled him to understand the Christian kerygma not as a propositional statement belonging to myth or dogma, but rather as an understanding of human existence. Just as the Johannine evangelist himself formulated the kerygma as essentially a radical challenge to decide for a new possibility of human existence, using the Gnostic mythology merely as a framework for expressing this, so Bultmann was able to demythologize the Gospel's message by reexpressing it in the conceptual framework of a Heideggerian distinction between authentic and inauthentic existence. It may need to be stressed that Bultmann did not suppose that he drew the message itself from Heidegger, any more than the evangelist derived the kerygma itself from Gnosticism; rather, Heidegger provided the conceptual tools for expressing the message.

From Gnosticism, then, the Johannine evangelist took over the idea of the Redeemer who came from heaven into the world and returned to heaven, a Redeemer who came in order to reveal and only to reveal. The evangelist was also indebted to the cosmological dualism that provides the framework for this Gnostic soteriology of revelation, a dualism expressed by the opposing pairs of light and darkness, truth and falsehood, life and death, freedom and bondage. This myth of the Revealer and this dualistic picture of reality are what give this Gospel its peculiarity. But the Johannine evangelist did not in fact share the Gnostic view of reality. Crucially, what the Johannine Jesus reveals is not some secret about the true nature and destiny of a predetermined category of people, whom he thus frees from their bondage to demonic powers in this world. The "mythological statements have lost their mythological meaning."[4] The Johannine Jesus in fact "reveals nothing but that he is the Revealer,"[5] that he has come from beyond the human world of thought as the authoritative word of the Creator confronting his hearers with the necessity for the decision of faith.

That the Gospel's use of the Gnostic myth is in service of a non-Gnostic theology is nowhere clearer than in its claim that the Word became flesh (1:14), which is coherent with its view of the world as God's creation. Accordingly,

4. Rudolf Bultmann, *Theology of the New Testament*, trans. Kendrick Grobel (London: SCM, 1955), 2:62.

5. Bultmann, *Theology*, 2:66.

the dualistic terminology that the evangelist has taken over from Gnosticism no longer expresses a cosmological dualism that would explain the origin of evil by a myth of cosmic origins. Rather, these terms "take on their specifically Johannine meaning only in relation to the idea of creation,"[6] by which Bultmann means that they represent the two possibilities of human self-understanding: either understanding oneself as a creature, dependent on and open to the transcendent reality of God, or understanding oneself as autonomous and shutting oneself against the reality of the Creator. The world is in darkness in that the second form of self-understanding is prevalent in human society until the Light comes to open up the possibility of an authentic form of existence in relation to God. Jesus as the Light confronts humanity with the life-or-death decision for or against this possibility of existence—the decision to believe or to reject. Thus, the dualism of the Gospel is not a cosmological one,[7] but rather "the dualism of decision." It does not describe some extrahuman cosmic reality, nor a predetermined division of humanity into two categories, but expresses the significance of the existential decision with which God's Word, incarnate as Jesus, confronts all people.

Bultmann's understanding of the Johannine dualism requires a little more explanation. "The world" (*kosmos*) or "this world," which means primarily the human world, has appropriated darkness and falsehood (the terms are equivalent) and made them its own essence—that is, its way of being (which Bultmann distinguishes from nature).[8] Darkness and falsehood thus comprise a power to which the world is in bondage. That is to say, it is in the grip of an illusory self-understanding. It is this "illusion about itself, not some immoral conduct, that is the lie."[9] A self-understanding of oneself as sovereign, in revolt against God, cannot but issue in evil conduct. In turning away from the reality of God ("the truth"), the world "turns itself into a specious reality, which, being a lie, is simultaneously death."[10]

The two possibilities of existence open to humans are to live out of an origin in the world (to be "of the world," "of the earth," "of the devil," or "from below"), repudiating their true origin in God, or to live out of their origin in God (to be "of God," "of the truth," or "born of God," or "born from above"). The latter is to know the truth (that God is the Creator and

6. Bultmann, *Theology*, 2:17.

7. Bultmann writes, "Is the devil a reality for John in the mythical sense? That is very doubtful, to say the least" (*Theology*, 2:17).

8. In Gnostic cosmological dualism there is a distinction of nature between the children of light and the children of darkness, arising from the primeval cosmic fall.

9. Bultmann, *Theology*, 2:18.

10. Bultmann, *Theology*, 2:19.

thus the only true reality), while the correlative Johannine term "life" means "simply openness to God and to him who makes God manifest [Jesus]."[11] Only in acknowledging their creatureliness can humans acquire a true self-understanding and thus an authentic existence. In the face of the liberating revelation of truth in Jesus Christ, humans have only the two possibilities: to receive it in faith or to opt for self-delusion.

Bultmann acknowledges that there is much in the Gospel that makes it seem that the two categories of humanity are determined from the outset, but he explains this by supposing that in the Gnostic myth from which the Gospel's dualistic language came it did indeed refer to a predetermined division of humanity. In the Gospel, however, the language has been refunctioned to express the "dualism of decision": "John's predestinatory formulations mean that the decision of faith is not a choice between possibilities in this world that arise from inner-worldly impulses, and also that the believer in the presence of God cannot rely on his own faith."[12] Since faith is precisely a renunciation of self-assertion, it has to be understood as God's gift.

The Johannine Jesus says that it is only in rejecting the light he brings, by opting to remain in darkness, that people become sinners under judgment, because in "his decision between faith and un-faith a man's being definitively constitutes itself, and from then on his Whence becomes clear."[13] Thenceforth the two groups become recognizable by whether they follow the new commandment of love for one another. Because they effect this decisive division, the coming and going of Jesus are the eschatological event in which the judgment of the world takes place.

Salvation is the encounter with God that can be had only by faith. Bultmann is at pains to deny that the Gospel envisages a "mystical relationship,"[14] by which he seems to mean a kind of unmediated union with the divine—the Hellenistic religious mysticism that others in the history-of-religions school had identified in this Gospel. The believer's "eschatological existence" is a reality "only in faith . . . *not in any direct relationship to Jesus or to God*."[15] Here the traditional Lutheran insistence on "faith alone" meets a Heideggerian philosophy of existence. Nor is the new form of existence a new nature. The believer's freedom from sin should not be understood as "a new nature . . . to which sinlessness belongs as a natural quality [as in Gnosticism]. Sinlessness, rather, is inherent to faith"—that is, "the overcoming of the world that

11. Bultmann, *Theology*, 2:19.
12. Bultmann, *Theology*, 2:23.
13. Bultmann, *Theology*, 2:25.
14. Bultmann, *Theology*, 2:84.
15. Bultmann, *Theology*, 2:85.

must be done over and over again."[16] Here the emphasis on faith serves also to complete Bultmann's account of how Johannine theology, despite its use of Gnostic mythological categories, actually distinguishes itself sharply from everything that is distinctively Gnostic.

There is a final point of special interest in Bultmann's exposition of Johannine soteriology. The language of truth and life with which the Gospel speaks of salvation corresponds to the world's quest for reality and life. Since the world, despite its rebellion against God, cannot cease to be God's creation, it longs for what it must have in order truly to exist, even though it does not know what this is until it encounters the light.[17] When Jesus presents himself as the bread and water of life, the light of the world, or the good shepherd, he "is presenting himself as that for which the world is seeking."[18] He "assumes such a preliminary understanding as is expressed in mythology."[19] In this way Bultmann is able to acknowledge the broad resonance of the Gospel's images of salvation without deriving the Gospel's kerygma itself from the world of Hellenistic religion.

Assessment

There is much to appreciate in this interpretation of Johannine theology. In particular, in my view, Bultmann's account of "the dualism of decision" is an indispensable insight into the way Johannine dualism functions. But the three key factors that comprise Bultmann's approach to the interpretation of the Johannine Gospel have not fared well in subsequent study. The second factor—Bultmann's reconstruction of the Gnostic myth of the Revealer and the claim that this Gospel owes its distinctive character to its dependence on this myth—carries conviction with very few scholars today.[20] Reconstructing such a myth from Mandean sources seems a dubious enterprise, while it is extremely debatable what there was that might be called "Gnosticism" or "Gnosis" prior to the writings we now know from the Nag Hammadi library. Above all, perhaps, later scholars have not found the need for such a speculative hypothesis in order to explain the Gospel we have. This is partly because, for many scholars, the Qumran

16. Bultmann, *Theology*, 2:79.
17. Bultmann, *Theology*, 2:26, 65.
18. Bultmann, *Theology*, 2:26.
19. Bultmann, *Theology*, 2:27.
20. For a brief survey of views on the relationship of the Gospel of John to Gnosticism, see Raymond E. Brown, *An Introduction to the Gospel of John*, ed. Francis J. Moloney (New York: Doubleday, 2003), 116–26.

writings provide a more plausible parallel to at least one of the features of the Gospel that Bultmann thought needed a particular sort of history-of-religions background to account for it, namely, its dualism (see below). More generally, Judaism in forms not influenced by "Gnosis" is now very widely regarded as the only kind of "background" to the Gospel that we need to postulate. Another major trend has been to introduce sociological factors—the history and situation of the "Johannine community"—into the explanation of this Gospel's distinctiveness.

Many would also say that Bultmann exaggerated the difference between Johannine theology and other currents of early Christian thought. He did so because of the first of the three factors that made up his approach: his particular theory of sources and redaction. Bultmann excised, as due to the ecclesiastical redactor, those parts of the Gospel that especially make it less eccentric as compared with the other writings of the New Testament. For example, he was able to characterize the evangelist's eschatology as wholly realized or actually atemporal (i.e., demythologized) by attributing expressions of future eschatology to the redactor. This looks like resorting to a source-critical explanation too quickly, where a more patient attempt to understand and appreciate the patterns of thought and expression that the Gospel as we have it exhibits might conclude that the evangelist put a strong emphasis on the present experience of eternal life without excluding a still future dimension. It seems to be a feature of the way this Gospel is written that it sets such seemingly contrasting themes as eternal life in the present and resurrection in the future side by side so that readers can see them as complementary dimensions of the matter.

Finally, Bultmann's use of a philosophical analysis of human existence to express the kind of self-understanding that he found in the kerygma of the Gospel has attracted few followers in recent writing on John, though this is not to say that some of the exegetical insights that were facilitated or sharpened by Bultmann's use of Heideggerian analysis have not been appreciated and influential. Many scholars are simply not interested in a contemporary theological appropriation of Johannine theology, preferring to explore the thought world of the Gospel in other ways, especially social-scientific ones. Those who do have a serious theological concern tend to work with conceptual tools from the Christian theological tradition without seeing the need for anything so radical as Bultmann's demythologization. Indeed, it must be said that Bultmann's theological approach is reductionist in the sense that it deliberately leaves aside any information content, focusing exclusively on the divine word that challenges humans to faith—that is, to a self-understanding of the human being as creature dependent on and open to the transcendent

Creator. Penetrating as this focus for reading the Gospel can be, is it really all there is to say about Johannine soteriology?

That said, one may also wonder whether, after Bultmann, something important has not been lost. If Bultmann could be accused of reducing theology to existential self-understanding, a theological assessment of recent Johannine scholarship might highlight a danger of reducing theology to sociology.[21] There certainly are many who resist that danger, but is there anything comparable with Bultmann's attempt to enter the dynamic of Johannine thought with such a thoroughgoing, though necessarily risky, determination to let it speak to contemporary people?[22] I merely pose the question. Of course, there are some who would say that, whereas Bultmann found John the most theologically congenial of the New Testament writings, it now poses almost insuperable problems for contemporary appreciation and appropriation.[23] The Gospel's dualism is certainly a key factor in such reactions.

Dualism in Qumran Texts and in John

For many Johannine scholars, the place vacated by the Gnostic background to the Gospel postulated by Bultmann has been occupied instead by the Dead Sea Scrolls. It was the early publication of some of these (especially the *Community Rule* [1QS] and the *War Scroll* [1QM]) that convinced many scholars that one did not need to seek the background to the Johannine Gospel and letters outside first-century Judaism. Although a range of similarities have been observed between the Gospel and the Qumran literature,[24] Raymond Brown

21. I do not mean to deny that there is an essential social dimension to Johannine theology, which Bultmann particularly neglected, but I doubt if speculative reconstructions of the Johannine community and the dynamics of its allegedly very particular situation are the way to access it.

22. It is invidious to suggest particular candidates for consideration, but among other books from the last two decades that one might commend for their ambition and theological seriousness, are (in chronological order): Thomas L. Brodie, *The Gospel according to John: A Literary and Theological Commentary* (New York: Oxford University Press, 1993); Andrew T. Lincoln, *Truth on Trial: The Lawsuit Motif in the Fourth Gospel* (Peabody, MA: Hendrickson, 2000); Dorothy A. Lee, *Flesh and Glory: Symbol, Gender, and Theology in the Gospel of John* (New York: Crossroad, 2002). See also a collection of essays whose aim was to be programmatic for the enterprise of theological interpretation of John: Richard Bauckham and Carl Mosser, eds., *The Gospel of John and Christian Theology* (Grand Rapids: Eerdmans, 2008).

23. See, for example, Fernando F. Segovia, "Inclusion and Exclusion in John 17: An Intercultural Reading," in *Literary and Social Readings of the Fourth Gospel*, vol. 2 of *What Is John?*, ed. Fernando F. Segovia, SBLSymS 7 (Atlanta: Scholars Press, 1998), 183–209. A very different obstacle for some is the long-standing problem of the relationship between the Johannine Jesus and the historical Jesus. See, for example, Maurice Casey, *Is John's Gospel True?* (London: Routledge, 1996).

24. See especially the essays in James H. Charlesworth, ed., *John and Qumran* (London: Geoffrey Chapman, 1972); Mary L. Coloe and Tom Thatcher, eds., *John, Qumran, and the*

speaks for many when he claims that "there is only one area of relatively precise similarity," which is "dualism and its corollaries."[25] With a focus especially on the "Treatise of the Two Spirits" (1QS 3.13–4.26), a series of scholars have claimed that there is such a close correspondence in both concepts and terminology that there must be a close historical connection (or even direct literary dependence) between the two bodies of literature, especially since the dualism of the Qumran texts has been characterized as unique within ancient Judaism.[26] Other scholars, however, have found the contrasts more considerable than the resemblances.[27]

I myself have argued that the resemblances can be explained as independent developments from scriptural texts and traditional Jewish imagery. With reference to the use of light/darkness imagery, the terminological correspondences are negligible compared with the key terminology present in each text and missing in the other. The theological significance of the imagery also differs decisively in ways that can be better explained from other sources in Scripture and late Second Temple literature than as some kind of adaptation of the Qumran usage. Moreover, the Johannine dualism is expressed not only in

Dead Sea Scrolls: Sixty Years of Discovery and Debate, SBLEJL 32 (Atlanta: Society of Biblical Literature, 2011).

25. Raymond E. Brown, "John, Gospel and Letters of," in *Encyclopedia of the Dead Sea Scrolls*, ed. Lawrence H. Schiffman and James C. VanderKam (Oxford: Oxford University Press, 2000), 1:414–17, here 415.

26. Raymond E. Brown, "The Qumran Scrolls and the Johannine Gospel and Epistles," *CBQ* 17 (1955): 403–19, 559–74; James H. Charlesworth, "A Critical Comparison of the Dualism in 1QS 3.13–4.26 and the 'Dualism' Contained in the Gospel of John," in Charlesworth, *John and Qumran*, 76–106; Brown, "John"; Joseph A. Fitzmyer, "Qumran Literature and the Johannine Writings," in *Life in Abundance: Studies in Tribute to Raymond E. Brown*, ed. John R. Donahue (Collegeville, MN: Liturgical Press, 2005), 117–33; James H. Charlesworth, "The Fourth Evangelist and the Dead Sea Scrolls: Assessing Trends over Nearly Sixty Years," in Coloe and Thatcher, *John, Qumran*, 161–82, esp. 165–72; John Ashton, *Understanding the Fourth Gospel* (Oxford: Clarendon, 1991), chap. 6 (he thinks that John was most likely an Essene convert to Christianity).

27. Howard M. Teeple, "Qumran and the Origin of the Fourth Gospel," *NovT* 4 (1960–61): 6–25, reprinted in *The Composition of John's Gospel: Selected Studies from Novum Testamentum*, ed. David E. Orton, BRBS 2 (Leiden: Brill, 1999), 1–20; David E. Aune, "Dualism in the Fourth Gospel and the Dead Sea Scrolls: A Reassessment of the Problem," in *Neotestamentica et Philonica: Studies in Honor of Peder Borgen*, ed. David E. Aune, Torrey Seland, and Jarl Henning Ulrichsen, NovTSup 106 (Leiden: Brill, 2003), 281–303; Jörg Frey, "Licht aus den Höhlen? Der 'johanneische Dualismus' und die Texte von Qumran," in *Kontexte des Johannesevangeliums: Das vierte Evangelium in religions- und traditionsgeschichtlicher Perspektive*, ed. Jörg Frey and Udo Schnelle, WUNT 175 (Tübingen: Mohr Siebeck, 2004), 117–203; Frey, "Recent Perspectives on Johannine Dualism and Its Background," in *Text, Thought, and Practice in Qumran and Early Christianity: Proceedings of the Ninth International Symposium of the Orion Center for the Study of the Dead Sea Scrolls and Associated Literature*, ed. Ruth A. Clements and Daniel R. Schwartz, STDJ 84 (Leiden: Brill, 2009), 127–57.

the light/darkness imagery, which it shares with the Qumran texts, but also in the spatial contrast between above and below and in the related contrast between God and the world. These are not shared with Qumran, and yet they certainly are as formative of the Gospel's dualistic worldview as the light/darkness imagery is.[28] My case has been supported, in greater detail, by Jörg Frey.[29] It should be noticed also that, whereas the case for a close connection between the Qumran texts and the Johannine literature worked with a simple account of "Qumran dualism," based mainly on 1QS 3.3–4.26 and supposed to have belonged to the central ideology of the Qumran sect, recent studies of dualism in the Qumran texts have considerably problematized this topic, arguing for a range of forms of dualism even in the texts usually attributed to the community itself and highlighting the exceptional character of 1QS 3.13–4.26.[30] Any fresh attempt to compare dualism in the Qumran texts with dualism in the Johannine literature will need to take full account of that discussion.

In the present context it is especially important to note that those who have strongly supported a close historical connection between Qumran dualism and that of the Gospel of John have also insisted that John has made highly distinctive use of the concepts and images that he shares with Qumran, focusing them on Christology and soteriology in a way quite unparalleled at Qumran and thereby shifting their meaning considerably. James Charlesworth speaks

28. Richard Bauckham, "The Qumran Community and the Gospel of John," in *The Testimony of the Beloved Disciple: Narrative, History, and Theology in the Gospel of John* (Grand Rapids: Baker Academic, 2007), 125–36. This essay was published previously in two somewhat differing forms: "Qumran and the Gospel of John: Is There a Connection?," in *The Scrolls and the Scriptures: Qumran Fifty Years After*, ed. Stanley E. Porter and Craig E. Evans, JSPSup 26 (Sheffield: Sheffield Academic Press, 1997), 267–79; and "The Qumran Community and the Gospel of John," in *The Dead Sea Scrolls Fifty Years after Their Discovery: Proceedings of the Jerusalem Congress, July 20–25, 1997*, ed. Lawrence H. Schiffman, Emmanuel Tov, and James C. VanderKam (Jerusalem: Israel Exploration Society, 2000), 105–15.

29. Frey, "Licht aus den Höhlen?"

30. Jörg Frey, "Different Patterns of Dualistic Thought in the Qumran Library: Reflections on Their Background and History," in *Legal Texts and Legal Issues: Proceedings of the Second Meeting of the International Organization for Qumran Studies, Cambridge, 1995; Published in Honour of Joseph M. Baumgarten*, ed. Moshe Bernstein, Florentino García Martínez, and John Kampen, STDJ 23 (Leiden: Brill, 1997), 275–335; Klaus Koch, "History as a Battlefield of Two Antagonistic Powers in the Apocalypse of Weeks and in the Rule of the Community," in *Enoch and Qumran Origins: New Light on a Forgotten Connection*, ed. Gabriele Boccaccini (Grand Rapids: Eerdmans, 2005), 185–99; Géza G. Xeravits, ed., *Dualism in Qumran*, LSTS 76 (London: T&T Clark, 2010); Loren T. Stuckenbruck, "The Interiorization of Dualism within the Human Being in Second Temple Judaism: The Treatise of the Two Spirits (1QS III:13–IV:26) in Its Tradition-Historical Context," in *Light against Darkness: Dualism in Ancient Mediterranean Religion and the Contemporary World*, ed. Armin Lange et al., JAJS 2 (Göttingen: Vandenhoeck & Ruprecht, 2011), 145–68.

of John's "amazing creativity,"[31] while, more prosaically, Joseph Fitzmyer asks, "Why should one expect the light/darkness imagery to function in the same way in both bodies of literature?"[32] While intending a response to my critique, both scholars have failed to take account of my argument that the distinctively Johannine use of the light/darkness imagery has much better precedent in Jewish literature other than the Qumran texts.[33] There is indeed no reason why we should expect the light/darkness imagery to function in the same way in various different bodies of literature, but if we find plausible sources for the distinctive ways in which John uses the imagery, the hypothesis of John's dependence on the texts or traditions of Qumran becomes redundant. However, the most important point, in the present context, is that the more the distinctiveness of John's use of the light/darkness imagery is stressed, the less relevant the hypothesis of a relationship with the Qumran texts becomes for understanding the theology of the Gospel. Of course, Bultmann argued, rather similarly, that John radically refunctioned the Gnostic myth of the Redeemer, but the dualism of this (hypothesized) myth was already closely connected with a redeemer figure who came from the divine world in order to save people from this world. It had the christological and soteriological focus that the dualism of the Gospel has, and this gave it real explanatory power in Bultmann's interpretation of the Gospel. The Qumran dualism, on the other hand, entirely lacks any such christological and soteriological focus. Thus, it must be concluded that the Dead Sea Scrolls have failed to fill the place vacated by the Gnostic background to the Gospel that Bultmann postulated.

Types of Dualism and Duality in John

In discussions of "dualism" in the ancient world the term is used in narrower and broader senses. It can be usefully defined as "a mode of thought that separates reality into two opposing forces."[34] But when John Gammie lists a variety of kinds of dualism that scholars have identified in apocalyptic literature, it is clear that the term "dualism" embraces a wider range of contrasting pairs of concepts. He lists the following:

1. *Cosmic dualism*, in which the cosmos is divided into two opposing forces of good and evil (though in Jewish thought this always takes the form

---

31. Charlesworth, "Fourth Evangelist," 171.
32. Fitzmyer, "Qumran Literature," 123.
33. Bauckham, "Qumran Community," 132–35.
34. Eric M. Meyers, "From Myth to Apocalyptic: Dualism in the Hebrew Bible," in Lange et al., *Light against Darkness*, 92–106, here 94.

of a "modified dualism" in which God is ultimately sovereign and the opposition is not absolute).

2. *Temporal, or eschatological, dualism*, in which the contrast is between the present age and the age to come.

3. *Ethical dualism*, in which two categories of humans, the righteous and the wicked, are contrasted.

4. *Psychological dualism*, in which the contest between good and evil takes place within individual humans.

5. *Spatial dualism*, in which a contrast is drawn between heaven and earth.

6. *Theological dualism*, which entails a radical distinction between God and humanity, Creator and creation.

In other discussions of dualism he identifies four more types:

7. *Physical dualism*, which draws an absolute distinction between spirit and matter.

8. *Metaphysical dualism*, which refers to the opposition between God and Satan.

9. *Soteriological dualism*, in which humanity is divided into two categories by people's acceptance or rejection of a savior.

10. *Cosmological, or ontological, dualism*, in which (in contrast to 1) the dualism of opposing cosmic principles is original and absolute.[35]

It is clear that only some of these kinds of "dualism" qualify as "a mode of thought that separates reality into two opposing forces." Types 1, 3, 4, 8, 9, and 10 are all forms of the fundamental polarity of good and evil, while 2 can be classified with them because it distinguishes the two ages as that in which evil is dominant and the coming age in which good will no longer be opposed by evil. But 5, 6, and 7 do not necessarily posit opposing categories, but merely contrasting ones. In 6 God is radically distinguished from, but not opposed to, his creation in the way that he is to evil. In Platonism, a version of 7, spirit and matter are radically different, superior and inferior, but not opposed to each other as good and evil are. Gnosticism, on the other hand, tended to assimilate its dualism of distinction between spirit and matter to a dualism of good and evil. Finally, dualism 5, the spatial contrast between heaven and earth, may signify a relationship of radical difference or a hierarchical

35. John G. Gammie, "Spatial and Ethical Dualism in Jewish Wisdom and Apocalyptic Literature," *JBL* 93 (1974): 356–85, here 356–59.

Table 6.1 Dualisms and Dualities in the Gospel of John

I. Creation and Creator

this world	the Father	13:1; 16:28; 17:11
earth	heaven	3:31
earthly things	heavenly things	3:12
from the earth	from above/heaven	3:31
flesh	Spirit	6:63
born of flesh	born from above/of Spirit	3:3–8
born of blood, will of flesh, and will of man	born of God	1:13
life (*psychē*) in this world	life (*psychē*) for eternal life	12:25
perish	have eternal life	3:16; 10:28
die	live forever	6:50–51, 58
die	never taste death	8:51–53
food that perishes	food that endures to eternal life	6:27
this water (and thirst again)	living water (and never thirst again)	4:10–15

II. Evil and Good

darkness	light	1:3–9; 3:19–21; 8:12; 9:5; 11:9–10; 12:35–36, 46
walk in darkness	walk while you have light	12:35
night	day	9:4; 11:9–10
walk in the night	walk in the day	11:9–10
blind	seeing	9:26, 39
lies	truth	8:44
to do evil	to do truth	3:21
to do evil	to do good	5:29
from this world	not from this world	8:23
from what is below	from what is above	8:23
from the devil	from God	8:44–47; 7:29
glory from humans	glory from God	5:41, 44; 7:18; 12:43
ruler of this world	kingdom not from this world	12:31; 14:30; 18:36
father of lies	Spirit of truth	8:44; 14:17; 16:13
children of the devil	children of God	1:12; 8:44
thief and bandit	shepherd	10:1–2
in his own name	in my Father's name	5:43
do not know God	know God	7:28–29; 8:55
do not believe	believe	3:18, 36
disobey the Son	believe in the Son	3:36
slavery to sin	freedom	8:33–36
the world	Jesus	17:25
the world	those chosen from the world	15:19; 17:6–9
from the world	not from the world	15:18–19
the world	those whom you gave me	17:9
the world	you (the disciples)	14:17–19, 22; 16:20
do not love Jesus	love Jesus	14:23–24
do not keep his words	keep his words	14:23–24
in the world	in me (Jesus)	16:33

III. Provisional Good and Eschatological Good

grace	grace	1:16
law	grace and truth	1:17
Moses	Jesus Christ	1:17; 5:45; 9:28–29
what Moses wrote	what I say	5:47
worship in Jerusalem	worship in Spirit and truth	4:21–24
my Father's house (temple)	my Father's house	2:16; 14:2
inferior wine	best wine	2:10
manna	true bread from heaven	6:31–32
vine	true vine	15:1

IV. Miscellaneous Dualities

baptize with water	baptize with the Holy Spirit	1:26, 33
destroy	raise up	2:19
needed no one to testify	he himself knew	2:25
ascended into heaven	descended from heaven	3:13
judge the world	save the world	3:17; 12:47
resurrection of judgment	resurrection of life	5:29
increase	decrease	3:31
on this mountain	in Jerusalem	4:20
worship what you do not know	worship what we know	4:22
hour is coming	is now	4:23; 5:25
sow, labor	reap	4:37–38
what you said	for ourselves	4:42
on his own	what he sees the Father do	5:19
on my own	as the Father taught me	8:28; 12:49
my own will	the will of him who sent me	5:30; 6:38
on his own	prophesied	11:51
lose	raise up	6:39–40
openly	in secret	7:4, 10
from God	on my own	7:17
come on my own	sent	7:28; 8:42
slave does not remain	son remains	8:35
have the poor	have me	12:8
at first	when Jesus was glorified	12:16
love life—lose it	hate life—keep it	12:25
for your sake	for my sake	12:30
not understand now	understand later	13:7
servants do not know	friends know	15:15
you did not choose me	I chose you	15:16
speak on his own	speak what he hears	16:13
rejoice	weep and mourn	16:20
joy	pain	16:20–21
plainly	in figures	16:25, 29
come from the Father	go to the Father	16:28
come into the world	leave the world	16:28
in the world	no longer in the world	17:11
see—believe	not see—believe	20:29
were younger	grow old	21:18

difference of superior and inferior, though it too can be assimilated to a dualism of good and evil if the earth is regarded as the sphere of creation in which evil is dominant. In most Jewish cases this is allied to dualism 2, that of eschatology, such that in this age the earth is subject to the powers of evil, but in the age to come, as God's good creation, it will be liberated from evil.

It may be useful to reserve the term "dualism" for the various forms that the polarity of good and evil takes in Jewish and Christian literature and to use the term "duality" for forms of thinking that divide reality into two contrasting, but not opposed, categories, such as Creator and creation. In fact, if we use this distinction, all versions of Jewish and Christian monotheism entail both some form of dualism (the good God is opposed to all evil) and some form of duality (the Creator is ontologically distinguished from creation). Since all versions of Jewish and Christian monotheism also hold that God's good creation has been in some way and to some degree corrupted by evil, there is also a correlation between the dualism (God against evil) and the duality (God and creation). However, this correlation is not identity. Indeed, any form of belief that God is rescuing or will rescue his creation from evil requires that the dualism and the duality are distinguished, as well as correlated. Were creation and evil identified, there could be no salvation.

These remarks may serve to suggest that generalizing about "dualism" in the Gospel of John is potentially misleading. We need to make careful distinctions between kinds of dualism and duality. In table 6.1 I have divided the terms and expressions that the Gospel of John uses in contrasting pairs into several categories.[36] (In most cases both components of the pair occur in the same context, but I have included some cases, such as "ruler of this world" and "kingdom not from this world," where the two components are in obvious contrast, even though they occur in widely separated contexts.) In addition to the major categories I–III, I have also listed, in IV, a large number of "Miscellaneous Dualities" (the list could doubtless be extended). In these cases the contrasting terms or phrases cannot easily be aligned with the major categories. Some compare good and bad alternatives, others superior and inferior, others temporal differences. In some cases of the pairing of a negative and a positive (e.g., "You did not choose me but I chose you"), the negative is purely hypothetical and serves merely to underline the positive. In some cases, the contrast belongs to the style of an epigram (e.g., 4:37; 8:35; 12:25). Indeed, this author has a strong tendency to express himself in a quasi-epigrammatic style, which may in part account for the prevalence of

---

36. Relevant material in 1 John is given in table 6.2 for comparison. It falls into a much simpler pattern of usage.

contrastive ways of speaking throughout the Gospel. More generally, what the examples listed in IV show is that the use of contrasting pairs of terms or phrases is a dominant habit of thought and expression in this Gospel. It is a way of formulating thought that is to some extent universal and seems to come naturally to the human mind. That the author of this Gospel is particularly fond of it may be part of the reason for the fact that the dualism that can be found to some degree throughout early Christian literature comes to unusual prominence in this Gospel. Perhaps this is less of a theological choice than a habit of mind.

Most of what is usually called "Johannine dualism" I have included in category II, but it is too often confused with some or all of the material

Table 6.2 Dualisms and Dualities in 1 John

I. Evil and Good

darkness	light	1:5–7; 2:8–9
walk in darkness	walk in light	1:6–7
is in/walks in darkness	remains in the light	2:9–11
hate	love	2:9–11; 3:14–15; 4:20
the world	those who do the will of God	2:17
passes away	remains forever	2:17
lie	truth	2:4, 21–22, 27
lie	do the truth	1:6
not from us	from us	2:19
denies the Son	confesses the Son	2:23
the world	we	3:2
children of the devil	children of God	3:1–2, 10
from the devil/the evil one	from God/born of God	2:29; 3:8–10, 12
from the world	from the Father/God	2:16; 4:2–6
do sin	do righteousness	3:4–10
evil deeds	righteous deeds	3:12
remains in death	passed from death to life	3:14
the one who is in the world	the One who is in you	4:4
spirit of error	spirit of truth	4:6
does not believe	believes	5:10
does not have the Son	has the Son	5:12
does not have life	has life	5:12
the evil one	the One who was born of God	5:18

II. Miscellaneous Dualities

old commandment	new commandment	1:7–8
word or speech	deed and truth	3:18
we loved God	he loved us	4:10

that I have put into category I. In category II occur the various forms of the fundamental polarity of good and evil. Here light is opposed to darkness, God to the devil, truth to lies, Jesus to religious imposters, his disciples to the world, faith and obedience to unbelief and disobedience, freedom to slavery. The category combines what Gammie lists as 1 (cosmic dualism), 3 (ethical dualism), 8 (metaphysical dualism [not a very helpful term]), and 9 (soteriological dualism). In category I, on the other hand, I have placed expressions of kinds of "dualism" from Gammie's list that are not forms of the opposition of good and evil and that I have suggested we might therefore call "dualities." These are 5 (spatial dualism) and 6 (theological dualism).

The spatial contrast between heaven and earth, "above" and "below," functions in the Gospel largely to make the contrast between God and creation. There is no interest in a heavenly world of angelic beings. Heaven is where God is, where the Father and the Son are united in glory, and where Jesus's own will go to be with him in the place he has prepared for them. Heaven is the space that represents transcendence. The distinction between Creator and creation is also the basis for the contrast between flesh and Spirit, mortal life and eternal life, which is integral to the Gospel's soteriology. "Flesh" is created human existence,[37] naturally mortal, while life from the Spirit or from above or eternal life is the gift of participation in the divine life that transcends death. While flesh left to itself dies, its true destiny in God's purpose is to be united with the divine life. The Son, who has eternal life in himself, becomes flesh in order to give flesh eternal life. Thus, flesh is not evil, even in its weakness and mortality, but its natural mortality means that if humans reject the Savior, who can give them eternal life, then they must die. At this point, it could be said, the contrast between creaturely, mortal life and eternal life converges with the ethical dualism of good and evil and the soteriological dualism that is created by human acceptance or rejection of the Savior. Those who choose to remain in their sins die in their sins. Death, the natural fate of creaturely life left to itself, becomes the actual fate only of sinners, because it is they who reject the Savior, who brings eternal life from God.

There is one key Johannine term that bridges categories I and II: "this world" or "the world" (the two are used synonymously). On the one hand, the world is the "all things" that God, through the Word, created and is the created sphere into which the Word came in incarnation. On the other hand, the world is the sphere of darkness, the human world under the dominion of "the ruler of this world," ignorant of God and practicing evil. Since the latter is the actual condition of the world into which Jesus comes, the transition

37. The best recent discussion of this topic is Lee, *Flesh and Glory*, chap. 2.

from one sense to the other is easily made, as in 1:10, which introduces the negative usage of "world": "He was in the world, and the world came into being through him, yet the world did not know him." Thus, "the world" or "this world" becomes a key term in expressions of ethical dualism and also of soteriological dualism, in that those who reject Jesus are "from the world," while his disciples are those whom he has "chosen from the world." The world that Jesus comes to save (3:16, 17; 4:42; 6:33, 51) is at the same time God's good creation, which he loves (3:16), and also that creation subject to evil and in need of salvation. Once again it is soteriology that requires the evangelist to work with both the duality of category I and the dualism of category II. For the Gospel's soteriology to make sense, the two must converge but remain different.

In category III I have brought together contrasts that relate the provisional good of the Mosaic covenant to the eschatological good that arrives with Jesus. It is important to distinguish these as a distinct category of duality because some interpreters tend to assimilate them to the true dualism of good and evil. When the Jewish leaders of Jesus's day reject Jesus, they do not represent the old covenant but betray it.

Dynamic Dualism

What holds together the various dualisms and dualities that I have grouped and distinguished in categories I, II, and III is soteriology. Without soteriology, the complexity that I have highlighted might seem merely confusion. Johannine soteriology, however, requires just this complexity. The Gospel does not oppose one world of reality to another in order merely to separate eternally what have always been distinct. As C. K. Barrett observed, "The distinguishing feature of John's dualism is its mobility; it is dualism in motion, in becoming."[38] The dualism is essentially a framework for portraying how the divine Son became mortal flesh in this world in order both to overcome the world and to save the world.

We can illustrate this briefly in terms of each of the two most prominent ways in which the dualism is expressed: the opposition of light and darkness, and the opposition of Jesus and the world. The generative sources of the light and darkness imagery in the Gospel are not Qumranic but scriptural: the opening verses of Genesis (Gen. 1:3–5) and the Isaianic prophecies of messianic light shining in the darkness of the world (Isa. 9:2; 42:6–7;

---

38. C. Kingsley Barrett, *Essays on John* (London: SPCK, 1982), 106.

60:1–3).[39] Conspicuously opening his Gospel at the same "beginning" that opens the Torah, the evangelist joins a Jewish tradition of speculation about the primordial light that inaugurated creation, identifying both the divine Word in the beginning and the primordial light that preexisted the universe with the eternal Son. The point is to claim that the light that illuminated creation in its pristine state and persisted in spite of the darkness that opposed it (whose origin is not explained) is the same light that has come into the world with the incarnation of the Word. The exposition of Genesis therefore prepares for the central and dominant focus of the Gospel's use of light/darkness imagery: a great light coming into the world, shining in the darkness of the world, giving light to all people, so that they may come out of the darkness into the light and be able to walk in the light instead of stumbling in the darkness (1:5, 9; 3:19; 8:12; 11:9–10; 12:35–36, 46). It is notable that the imagery of light and darkness is confined to chapters 1–12, and, just as it is prominent in the prologue, so it is prominent at the very end of Jesus's period of public ministry (12:35–36; cf. 12:40) and in his summation of his mission: "I have come as light into the world, so that everyone who believes in me should not remain in the darkness" (12:46).

Except for the hint in 1:5, the imagery of light and darkness in the Gospel is not used to describe a perennial conflict between light and darkness. Rather it is inspired by the prophetic picture of a messianic light with its overtones of eschatological novelty. The picture is of a world in darkness[40] whose situation is changed when the light comes into it, floods it with light, and requires people either to live in it and walk by it, or to stay in the darkness. This is what Bultmann's existential insight valuably called a "dualism of decision." It is all about the challenge of the new situation created by the incarnation and mission of Jesus. After chapter 12 Jesus no longer calls the world into the light (12:36). (Later his disciples, inspired by the Paraclete, will witness to the world, but the Gospel does not portray this in the language of light and darkness.)

Expressions of dualism that use the terms "the world" or "this world" function rather differently from those that use the imagery of light and darkness.

39. Bauckham, "Qumran Community," 132–35. The "Treatise of the Two Spirits" (1QS 3.13–4.26) also has scriptural sources, perhaps including Gen. 1:1–3, but if so, its reading of Genesis is controlled by Isa. 47:5 and thus is very different from the Gospel's. While both texts draw to some extent on the dualism of the sapiential literature, only 1QS portrays the destiny of the righteous and the wicked as light and darkness, perhaps in dependence on Prov. 4:17–18. Messianic light has no place in 1QS.

40. This is a hyperbolic picture that should not be read literally to mean that there was no light in the world before Jesus (cf. 5:35), but the hyperbole functions to highlight the new situation into which Jesus puts humanity.

As we have noticed, these terms are frequently used to refer to the world that the divine Son created, entered, and came to save. It is sinful and in need of salvation, but in a large majority of the occurrences of these terms the world is not explicitly portrayed as an entity opposed to God or to Jesus. The antagonism, when it occurs, is a consequence of the Son's coming into the world. It is how the world and its ruler respond to the salvific mission of the Son. So once again we are concerned with a dualism "in motion," a dualism that comes about and develops along with the eschatological divine invasion of the world. The opposition of the world to Jesus (and his disciples) emerges only gradually in the story, after its initial adumbration in the prologue (1:10). As opposition to Jesus, it is found in chapters 1–12 only at 7:7; 8:23; 9:39. It really comes into its own, when the light/darkness imagery has disappeared from the Gospel, in the Last Supper Discourse (chaps. 14–16) and the prayer of Jesus in chapter 17. In these chapters we find that Jesus's disciples, who are "not from the world" and "chosen from the world," become, along with Jesus, one of the two components of a dualistic contrast between them and the world. The coming of the Son into the world has divided the world into those who are born from above and so are no longer "from the world" and those who reject the one who comes from above and so become the world in this pejorative and dualistic sense.

Thus, we discover that these two fields of dualistic discourse—the light/darkness imagery and the world/Jesus antinomy—function differently. The former is a "dualism of decision," calling people to live in and by the light that has come into the world. The latter is a "dualism of opposition," portraying the antipathy of those who reject Jesus to him and to those who accept him. Appropriately, the former predominates in chapters 1–12, the latter in chapters 14–18. With characteristic Johannine irony, the apparent victory of the powers of this world over the king whose royal authority is not from this world is in fact his "conquest" of the world (16:33) and the proclamation of his rule (19:19–22). Thus, the "dualism of opposition" proves to be not only the consequence of the Son's salvific mission but also the very means by which he brings eternal life into the world. The Gospel therefore uses its "dualism of opposition" in a much more theologically profound way than simply to bolster the identity of a sectarian group at odds with its social context.

Conclusion

This discussion has focused on dualism and on soteriology insofar as it relates to dualism. I have concluded that soteriology is the central concern in the Gospel's prominent use of both dualisms and dualities. In the Gospel's narrative of salvation the coming of the divine Son into flesh sets its dualistic categories in motion. Light dispels darkness, requiring decision, while the world that rejects Jesus is conquered and saved by him through its very rejection of him.

7

Dimensions of Meaning
in the Gospel's First Week

You put two things together that have not been put together before. And the world is changed.[1]

The writer of John's Gospel is constantly putting two things together. He deploys the power of metaphor, symbol, and allegory, which illumine something by referring to it as something else. He creates correspondences between different parts of his narrative. He tells stories such that they have more meanings than the literal one. He is a master of irony who constantly has his characters say more than or even the opposite of what they mean. What Jesus says in metaphor and symbol the characters misunderstand, thereby foregrounding the question of its true meaning. Moreover, the Gospel has many intertexts in the Hebrew Bible that expand the meaning of the Gospel text when they are observed and pondered.

Despite such multiple meanings, the Gospel would make adequate sense to a first-time reader, especially one who already knows the story of Jesus from some other source. Many of its symbols appeal to common knowledge and experience of the world. Its stories are skillfully told to involve the reader

1. Julian Barnes, *Levels of Life*, 2nd ed. (London: Vintage, 2014), 3.

with convincingly portrayed characters. But clearly it was written not only to make some sense to first- (or second- or third- . . .) time readers but also to be studied and to yield its full cornucopia of meanings only to the most attentive of students. To this end, its frequently riddling character is not meant, as some scholars think, to enable informed readers to feel superior to characters in the Gospel who do not understand the riddles, but rather to tease the intelligence and to entice its readers into its world of multidimensional meaning. It is a text that constantly creates the impression that more is going on than immediately meets the eye. It is also a closely integrated whole, so that the more familiar readers become with the whole Gospel, the better they will understand its parts.

Unlike other chapters in this volume, this chapter does not focus on a particular theological theme but instead explores a section of the Gospel (the first main section after the prologue) in which several of the Gospel's main themes are introduced. The intention is not to provide a complete exegesis of the text but rather to show how multiple meaning is generated in a wide variety of ways. One aim is to show that the literal meaning—the meaning on the level of the events narrated in their chronological placement within a developing narrative—has its own integrity that is not manipulated or disrupted by other levels of meaning. Interpretation of this Gospel sometimes misses that. But equally important is to recognize that further meaning is generated in a variety of different ways. The search for symbolism in this Gospel has sometimes been pursued with more enthusiasm and imagination than attention to the carefully crafted structure of the text and to its often quite precise indications of further meaning. Attention to the detail of the relevant texts of the Hebrew Bible (often neglected because of an unjustified assumption that only the Septuagint Greek is relevant), along with an understanding of Jewish techniques of exegesis, is also required.

The Momentous First Week

Following the prologue (1:1–18), the Gospel of John's narrative begins with a series of events that are carefully assigned to a series of successive days (1:19–2:11). The last of these events is the wedding and miracle at Cana, after which the indications of time become more vague (2:12–13). The sequence of days is for the most part clearly indicated by three occurrences of the phrase "the next day" (1:29, 35, 43) and one occurrence of the phrase "on the third day" (2:1) (see table 7.1). But exegetes differ as to whether the events described in 1:40–42 should be assigned to a distinct day and consequently as to whether the whole sequence comprises six or seven days.[2] In my view, the latter is more probable. According to 1:39, the man subsequently named as Andrew and his anonymous companion stayed with Jesus "that day," which means for the rest of the day until evening (when, in Jewish reckoning, the next day began). This makes it quite clear that what Andrew then does (according to 1:41) must take place on the following day. John does not have to specify "the next day" in this case because he has already made clear (in a spare narrative in which details are reduced to what is strictly necessary) that the previous day has ended.

This point seems to me to stand whatever we make of "first" in 1:41. The most probable reading here is *prōton*, although some manuscripts have *prōtos* and a few manuscripts of the Old Latin have *mane* ("in the morning"). This may reflect a Greek text that had *prōi* ("early in the morning" [cf. 18:28; 20:1]), or the translator may have taken *prōton* to mean this. No extant Greek manuscript actually has *prōi*, and so, although it probably would make the best sense in the context, it is unlikely to be the original reading.[3] The latter is most likely *prōton*, which would mean that the first thing Andrew did was to find his brother. A plausible general meaning is that the first thing Andrew did the next day, once it was light, was to go to find his brother. Then he brought him to Jesus (1:42).

If the argument that the events of 1:40–42 take place on a distinct day is accepted, then the whole narrative (1:19–2:11) covers precisely a week. Given the biblical and Jewish significance of the week as a period of time, established by the Creator at the beginning (Gen. 1:1–2:4), there is an obvious appropriateness in beginning the Gospel's narrative of new creation with a week. But we should notice that there is one other week whose seven days are carefully enumerated by the writer of the Gospel, a week that is almost (though not quite) at the end of the narrative. This is the week that begins six days before the last Passover in the Gospel (12:1) and ends with the day of Jesus's resurrection on "the first day of the week" (20:1) (see table 7.1). Careful comparison can show that these two momentous weeks in the Gospel's narrative correspond to each other in some key respects, though it is not the case that the sequence of events in either week is controlled by the other.

2. Those who reckon seven days include John Henry Bernard, *A Critical and Exegetical Commentary on the Gospel according to St. John*, ICC (Edinburgh: T&T Clark, 1928), 1:33–34; Marie-Émile Boismard, *Du baptême à Cana (Jean, 1,19—2,11)*, LD 18 (Paris: Cerf, 1956); Donald A. Carson, *The Gospel according to John* (Leicester: Inter-Varsity; Grand Rapids: Eerdmans, 1991), 167–68; Andreas J. Köstenberger, *John*, BECNT (Grand Rapids: Baker Academic, 2004), 56.

3. This reading is defended by Bernard, *St. John*, 1:58; Boismard, *Du baptême*, 82–84.

Table 7.1 The Gospel's Two Momentous Weeks

	First Week	Passion Week
	Week of John the Baptist's Witness	Week of John the Beloved Disciple's Witness
	Week of the First Sign	Week of the Seventh Sign
Day 1	1:19–28 *In "Bethany beyond Jordan" (1:28)* John responds to the delegation from Jerusalem	12:1–11 *"Six days before the Passover Jesus came to Bethany" (12:1)* dinner at Bethany
Day 2	1:29–34 *"the next day" (1:29)* John's witness to Jesus	12:12–36 *"the next day" (12:12)* Jesus rides into Jerusalem
Day 3	1:35–39 (Sabbath?) *"the next day" (1:35)* Anonymous (Beloved Disciple) and Andrew meet Jesus	 Jesus in hiding (12:36)
Day 4	1:40–42 Andrew brings Simon to meet Jesus	 Jesus in hiding (12:36)
Day 5	1:43–51 *"the next day" (1:43)* Jesus leaves for Galilee after meeting Philip and Nathanael	13:1–19:42 *"the day of Preparation" (19:31, 42)* Last Supper (after sunset) arrest and trials of Jesus crucifixion and burial
Day 6	(traveling to Cana)	Passover/Sabbath (19:31)
Day 7	2:1–11 (fourth day of the week?) *"on the third day" (2:1)* Wedding at Cana	20:1–23 *"the first day of the week" (20:1)* events at the empty tomb appearance of Jesus in the house (before sunset)

Correspondences: The Two Key Witnesses

Day 1	John's witness	
Day 2	John's witness	
Day 3	Beloved Disciple hears John's witness (Jesus as Passover Lamb)	
Day 4		
Day 5		Beloved Disciple's witness at the Last Supper Beloved Disciple witnesses fulfillment of John's witness (19:32–35) (Jesus as Passover Lamb)
Day 6		
Day 7		Beloved Disciple witnesses the empty tomb

	First Week	Passion Week
Correspondences: Christological Themes		
Day 1		
Day 2		Jesus as king of Israel (12:13, 15)
		Jesus speaks about "this hour" (12:27)
Day 3		
Day 4		
Day 5		*Jesus's hour has come (13:1; 17:1)*
	"You are the king of Israel" (1:49)	Jesus as king of the Jews (18:33–19:21)
	first "Son of Man" saying (1:51)	last "Son of Man" saying (13:31)
	first prediction of Jesus's exaltation (1:51)	predictions of Jesus's exaltation fulfilled
Day 6		
Day 7	*Jesus's hour has not yet come (2:4)*	
	first sign: provision of wine (2:11)	seventh sign: resurrection (2:18–19; cf. 20:30)

These correspondences will be explained in the following sections. They are one of the ways in which the writer has achieved such a remarkable density of meaning in his narrative of the first week.

Geography and Chronology

John's Gospel is notable for its chronological and geographical precision. I have argued elsewhere that, since this kind of precision was expected of good historiography in the ancient world, John's Gospel would have seemed to its first readers or hearers more like historiography than the Synoptic Gospels would.[4] Of course, this runs counter to the general opinion that John's narrative is symbolic or theological *rather than* historical. But, while it is true that John often gives more than matter-of-fact significance to his notices of time and place, it is also the case that many of these resist all attempts to give them symbolic significance. For example, that Herod's temple had been in construction for forty-six years (2:20), that the lame man had been so for thirty-eight years (5:5), that Jesus was in "the portico of Solomon" in the temple (10:23), or that Pilate's seat of judgment was in a place called

4. Richard Bauckham, "Historiographical Characteristics of the Gospel of John," in *The Testimony of the Beloved Disciple: Narrative, History, and Theology in the Gospel of John* (Grand Rapids: Baker Academic, 2007), 93–112.

"Gabbatha" (19:13) are not plausibly symbolic. So when chronological or topographical features of the narrative do appear to have additional significance, sometimes explicitly indicated by the author, we should not suppose that this is alternative to their role as literal features of the narrative. This is not to claim that they can necessarily be shown to be historically accurate, although, when John's topography can be checked, it has usually proved an accurate account of places in pre-70 CE Jewish Palestine.[5]

The important point is that John's topography and geography are plausible at the literal level of a historical narrative. Even if he writes historical fiction, John evidently takes the trouble to write a narrative that works on the level of a narrative about a specific past. Whether or not he achieves historical *accuracy*, at the literary level he certainly aims at historical *realism*, a feature of this Gospel that is too rarely recognized, probably because interpreters assume it to be incompatible with the Gospel's richly symbolic dimension. In fact, it is not incompatible, as can be seen whenever the text is studied with careful attention to its realistic features. In the case of the temporal and geographical features of the narrative, we should expect them always to have a literal dimension, whether or not they also have additional significance.

There is nothing especially implausible in the sequence of seven days in itself. A lot can happen in a week! But the narrative also contains three geographical indications (1:28, 43; 2:1, 11) that have often been regarded as incompatible with the chronology. The events of the first four days of the narrative are localized in "Bethany across the Jordan, where John was baptizing" (1:28 [cf. 3:26; 10:40]). On the fifth day Jesus leaves for Galilee (1:43), and on the seventh day he is in "Cana of Galilee" (2:1, 11). It should be noted that this last reference to a place is a knowledgeable one, since this Cana is called "of Galilee" to distinguish it from another Cana near Tyre (Josh. 19:28: Kanah). It is certainly to be identified as Khirbet Qana, some nine kilometers due north of Nazareth. But where was "Bethany beyond Jordan" (*Bēthania*[6] *peran tou Iordanou*), and could Cana have been reached in only two days' travel from it?

Apart from some very implausible identifications, Bethany beyond Jordan has usually been sought on the eastern side of the Jordan in the lower Jordan Valley.[7] In this area the most likely site is on the Wadi el-Kharrer, opposite

5. For example, Ingo Broer, "Knowledge of Palestine in the Fourth Gospel?," in *Jesus in Johannine Tradition*, ed. Robert T. Fortna and Tom Thatcher (Louisville: Westminster John Knox, 2001), 83–90.

6. The variant reading *Bēthabara*, though it appears to refer to a place that in the time of Origen was regarded as a place where John baptized, is unlikely to be original. Probably because it was known to be a place where John baptized, scribes substituted it for the unknown *Bēthania*.

7. See the discussion of all suggestions in Rainer Riesner, "Bethany beyond the Jordan (John 1:28): Topography, Theology and History in the Fourth Gospel," *TynBul* 38 (1987): 29–64,

Jericho.[8] The attempt to locate Bethany beyond Jordan in this area has no doubt been influenced by the fact that, according to the Synoptic Gospels, John appeared in the wilderness of Judea (Matt. 3:1; cf. Mark 1:4; Luke 3:2) and baptized people, including Jesus, in the river Jordan nearby (Matt. 3:6, 13; Mark 1:5–9), though it is worth noticing that Luke indicates a quite wide geographical area for John's ministry (Luke 3:3: "all the region around the Jordan"). However, the Synoptic data need not determine the location of Bethany beyond Jordan in John.[9] This Gospel does not recount the baptism of Jesus, but has John describe later his vision of the Spirit descending on Jesus (John 1:32–33). The evangelist deliberately dates the beginning of his Gospel narrative at a later date than the baptism of Jesus, which he certainly knew from Mark's Gospel and probably expected his readers also to know from Mark's Gospel.[10] The events narrated in the first week of John's Gospel could take place a considerable time after the baptism of Jesus, when John had moved to a different part of the country, in order to reach the people there and perhaps to be out of reach of Herod Antipas. Wherever Bethany beyond Jordan was, John's Gospel has John move his ministry of baptism from there to another place that cannot be certainly identified (3:23). This Gospel portrays John as an itinerant prophet.

A few scholars in the past have suggested that Bethany beyond Jordan is the region (not a town or village) known in the first century CE as Batanaea (Greek *Batanaia, Batanea, Bataneias, Batanis*),[11] and relatively recently this identification has been advocated, defended, and discussed at length by Rainer Riesner.[12] I am persuaded by his case, though not by all the speculation that he associates with it,[13] and need not repeat the case at length

here 34–43; Riesner, *Bethanien jenseits des Jordan: Topographie und Theologie in Johannes-Evangelium*, SBAZ 12 (Giessen: Brunnen, 2002), 43–56.

8. See, most recently, John F. McHugh, *A Critical and Exegetical Commentary on John 1–4*, ICC (London: T&T Clark, 2009), 144–47; Jerome Murphy-O'Connor, "Place-Names in the Fourth Gospel (II): Bethany (John 1:28; 11:18) and Ephraim (John 11:54)," *RB* 120 (2013): 85–98, here 90–94.

9. The phrase *to prōton* in 10:40 need not mean that John began his ministry in Bethany beyond Jordan. It may mean only that it was the first place in the Gospel's narrative where John baptized, distinguishing it from Aenon (3:23).

10. Richard Bauckham, "John for Readers of Mark," in *The Gospels for All Christians: Rethinking the Gospel Audiences*, ed. Richard Bauckham (Grand Rapids: Eerdmans; Edinburgh: T&T Clark, 1997), 147–71.

11. Josephus, *Ant.* 4.173; 9.159; 12.136; 15.343; 17.25, 189, 319; 20.138; *J.W.* 1.398; 2.95, 247, 482; 3.56; *Life* 54, 183.

12. Rainer Riesner, "Bethany beyond the Jordan," *ABD* 1:703–5; Riesner, "Bethany beyond the Jordan (John 1:28)"; Riesner, *Bethanien*.

13. Douglas S. Earl also accepts the identification with Batanaea and develops possible symbolic associations of Bashan and "across the Jordan" ("'[Bethany] beyond the Jordan':

here.[14] Batanaea, lying to the east of the Lake of Galilee, is called "Bashan" (*bāšān*) in the Hebrew Bible. In the time of Jesus it was in the territory of the tetrarch Philip. The Greek forms of the name derive from the Aramaic version of "Bashan," variously attested as *bôtenayyê, bôtenāyyim, bôteneyîn, bûtenan, bātenayyāy'*, and *bêtenayyā'*. Modern Arabic versions are "el-Bottein" and "el-Betheneyeh."[15] John's *Bēthania* is a plausible Greek transliteration (Semitic ת can be represented by either τ or θ in Greek). The fact that precisely this form is not otherwise attested is not a problem, because John will have chosen to transliterate the Aramaic name in this way in order to correspond with the other Bethany in his Gospel, the one near Jerusalem (11:1), which he takes the trouble to say was fifteen stadia (about two miles) from Jerusalem (11:18). He calls Batanaea "Bethany beyond the Jordan"[16] in order both to parallel it with and to distinguish it from the Bethany near Jerusalem.

The reason for creating the parallel is not, as Donald Carson suggests, to indicate that Jesus's ministry began in a Bethany and ended in a Bethany.[17] In fact, Jesus's ministry ended in Jerusalem (12:12–36), on the second day of the passion week. Rather the parallel means that the first week and the passion week both begin in a Bethany (see table 7.1). The place name signals that we are to look for further parallels between the two weeks. Between the two weeks there is also a transition from one Bethany to the other in 10:40–11:18, where Jesus is first in Bethany beyond Jordan (10:40–41) and then in Bethany near Jerusalem, to which he goes in order to bring his friend Lazarus back from death, but thereby walks into danger that will prove mortal for himself. In this sequence John avoids naming Bethany beyond Jordan but calls it "the place [*topos*][18] where John had been baptizing earlier" (10:40), whereas Bethany near

---

The Significance of a Johannine Motif," *NTS* 55 [2009]: 279–94). I am not convinced that such associations can really be found in the Gospel. Geography in this Gospel is symbolic only to a limited extent, and in this case the significance of "Bethany beyond Jordan" is sufficiently explained by genuine historical reminiscence along with the parallel and contrast with Bethany near Jerusalem. Had John wished to make connections with prophecies naming Bashan in the Hebrew Bible, he could have used the term *Basan* (LXX) or made some other verbal allusion to the prophecies, as he does elsewhere to other prophecies.

14. Riesner's case is accepted by Carson, *John*, 146–47.

15. William H. Brownlee, "Whence the Gospel according to John?," in *John and Qumran*, ed. James H. Charlesworth (London: Geoffrey Chapman, 1972), 166–94, here 169.

16. For the appropriateness of referring to Batanaea as "beyond Jordan," see Riesner, *Bethanien*, 43–70. He shows that it does not have to refer to Perea, the area to the east of the Jordan that belonged to Herod Antipas's tetrarchy.

17. Carson, *John*, 147.

18. Craig R. Koester argues that Bethany beyond Jordan cannot be Batanaea because elsewhere John uses *topos* of very specific places ("Topography and Theology in the Gospel of John," in *Fortunate the Eyes That See: Essays in Honor of David Noel Freedman in Celebration*

Jerusalem he calls "the village [kōmē] of Mary and her sister Martha" (11:1). The former, under Philip's tolerant authority, is a place of safety for Jesus (as it would have been for John the Baptist). Jesus was escaping there from threats to his life in Jerusalem (10:31, 39), whereas the village of Bethany, in its proximity to Jerusalem, represents a return to the sphere of serious danger (11:16). The two Bethanys thus present a contrast between the two weeks: the first week, when Jesus's ministry was just beginning and there was as yet no antagonism towards him, and the passion week, when he walks deliberately into mortal danger, ends his ministry, and is executed.

If Bethany beyond Jordan, in Philip's tetrarchy, was a place of safety for John the Baptist, it was also a place of opportunity. Though within a larger area of predominantly Gentile habitation, Batanaea itself had a Jewish population that had recently settled there.[19] Moreover, while Galilee, on the other side of the lake, was in Herod Antipas's territory and thus dangerous for John, Batanaea was within easy reach of Galilee, with its large Jewish population. But more precisely where within Batanaea was John baptizing? Batanaea did not border the lake. Between it and the southern part of the eastern shore of the lake lay the Decapolis city of Hippos, while between Batanaea and the northeastern shore of the lake lay Gaulanitis, which also extended far to the north. Bethsaida, from which Andrew, Peter, and Philip came (John 1:44), was on the shore of the lake, just east of where the Jordan River entered the lake and marked the boundary between Antipas's Galilee and Philip's territory, and thus within Gaulanitis.[20] William Brownlee, who preceded Riesner in identifying Bethany beyond the Jordan as Batanaea, proposed that John was baptizing in the Jordan River north of the lake. He argues that Bashan in the Hebrew Bible included Golan, so that a "person with a biblical perspective would claim Gaulanitis as simply a subdistrict of Batanaea."[21] However, it is not necessary to stretch the terminology in this way. Riesner thinks that the area where John was baptizing, according to John 1, was around the lower reaches of the Yarmuk River[22]—that is, somewhere to the southeast or east of Hippos. He argues that this (rather than a more northerly location) is

of His Seventieth Birthday, ed. Astrid B. Beck et al. [Grand Rapids: Eerdmans, 1995], 436–45, here 446). But since the word is a vague one, John was free to use it variously. Even if Bethany beyond Jordan were a village, topos would be a unique use of the term within John's Gospel. It is also possible that in 10:40 John does not refer to Batanaea as such but more precisely to the location within Batanaea where John baptized.

19. Josephus, Ant. 17.23–31; Life 54–57. See also Shimon Applebaum, Judaea in Hellenistic and Roman Times: Historical and Archaeological Essays, SJLA 40 (Leiden: Brill, 1989), chap. 4.

20. In John 12:21 it is loosely called "Bethsaida in Galilee."

21. Brownlee, "Whence the Gospel according to John?," 170.

22. Riesner, Bethanien, 122.

indicated by the narrative of John 11, where Jesus evidently takes three to four days to travel from Bethany beyond Jordan to Bethany near Jerusalem (see 11:11–14, 39). We should note that the area around the Yarmuk River was also the area that had been settled by Jews in the time of Herod the Great.

That the Gospel of John envisages John the Baptist baptizing in the Yarmuk Valley seems very plausible, but it creates difficulties for another part of Riesner's argument: his interpretation of Jesus's movements on day 5 of the first week (John 1:43–51). He understands the passage to mean that Jesus sets out for Galilee and travels through Bethsaida to Cana, meeting Philip in Bethsaida and Nathanael in Cana (which was Nathanael's home, according to 21:2). Then day 6, which is ignored in the narrative, he takes to have been a Sabbath, on which Jews could not travel.[23] This interpretation requires Jesus to walk from Batanaea to Cana in Galilee in just one day, hardly a practical possibility.[24] Even if we modify the scheme to allow Jesus to meet Nathanael not in Cana but somewhere closer to Bethsaida and then to complete the journey to Cana after the Sabbath, on day 7, arriving at the wedding late in the day, the time frame is probably still too compressed. It is better, as I shall argue below, to read 1:43–51 as meaning that Jesus decides to leave for Galilee (1:43a), then, still in Batanaea, meets Philip and Nathanael and only then actually sets out for Galilee. He then has most of day 5 and the whole of day 6 (and, if necessary, even part of day 7) to walk from Batanaea to Cana. Such a journey presents no difficulty. In that case, day 6 cannot be a Sabbath. Of course, the week must have included a Sabbath, but it could be any of the first three days (or day 4, if Andrew is not understood to have to travel back to Bethsaida to find his brother). According to the Mishnah, the Jewish custom was for the wedding of a virgin to take place on the fourth day of the week, the wedding of a widow on the fifth (*m. Ketub.* 1.1). If this custom goes back to the time of Jesus and the wedding at Cana was of a virgin, then day 7 would be the fourth day of the week and day 3 the Sabbath.[25]

If day 6 in this first week is not the Sabbath, then the days of the week in this first week of the Gospel do not correspond to the days in the passion week, where the Sabbath is undoubtedly day 6. However, the fact that in the first week we are not explicitly told that anything happened on day 6 (we have to assume that Jesus is traveling) could be a deliberate parallel to the fact that, similarly, in the passion week nothing at all is said to happen on day 6.

23. Riesner, "Bethany beyond the Jordan (John 1:28)," 45–47; Riesner, *Bethanien*, 73–76.
24. Crossing the lake by boat would be quicker, but in that case Jesus would not pass through Bethsaida, as Riesner envisages.
25. Bernard, *St. John*, 1:72.

Thus getting the geography right does make the chronology plausible. Jesus can get from Bethany beyond Jordan to Cana in two days (as chaps. 1–2 require) and from Bethany beyond Jordan to the other Bethany within four days (as chap. 11 requires).

As well as the reckoning of days, there is one other temporal indication in the narrative: "It was about the tenth hour" (1:39). This is one of John's many narrative "asides" and indicates the time at which Jesus and his two guests reached his lodgings. Attempts to see symbolic significance in this notice[26] have been patently unsuccessful, as most recent commentators recognize. Comparable notices of the hour of the day later in the Gospel (4:6, 52; 19:14) have rather more obvious narrative functions. In this case we might have expected a time that would have given Andrew and his companion a longer period with Jesus "that day" than just two or three hours[27] (though perhaps it is implied that they continued to talk after sunset). That the reference to the tenth hour is no more than "a typical vivid touch of the storyteller's art"[28] also seems unlikely, for this is a peculiarly spare narrative that confines itself to essentials. Even in John's many more expansively told narratives, it is surprisingly hard to find details that do not have some identifiable narrative function (which is not the same as symbolic meaning, which may or may not be attached to them). In this case, it seems most probable that the notice of the hour is a deliberate hint of eyewitness testimony,[29] connected with the identity of the anonymous companion of Andrew (to be discussed further below).

Discipleship: Levels of Meaning in 1:35–46

It is widely recognized that among literary devices characteristic of the Gospel of John is *double entendre*—words (or larger semantic units) that have two different levels of meaning. But this general phenomenon varies considerably in character and use, and we should be cautious of generalizations about

26. For example, Rudolf Bultmann, *The Gospel of John: A Commentary*, trans. G. R. Beasley-Murray (Oxford: Blackwell, 1971), 100–101n9.

27. The ancients divided the daylight period from sunrise to sunset into twelve hours, whatever the time of year. Thus, the length of an hour varied according to the length of the day, but this made it easy to reckon hours approximately from the position of the sun. That the hours in John's Gospel are always said to be approximate ("about the *n*th hour") is realistic.

28. Barnabas Lindars, *The Gospel of John*, NCB (London: Marshall, Morgan & Scott, 1972), 114. He adds that "it is simply a narrative device to get the disciples into Jesus's entourage, so that they are with him when he goes to Galilee (vv. 43; 2.2)," but it is not clear to me why a particular hour of the day is required for this purpose. "They remained with him that day" would surely be sufficient.

29. Köstenberger, *John*, 75.

it.[30] One well-recognized category is that of misunderstanding. Typically, a character misunderstands what Jesus says, taking in a literal or material sense what Jesus means in a metaphorical or spiritual sense.[31] There are also many examples of irony.[32] Typically, a character says something that the reader sees or should see is untrue in the most obvious sense, the sense that the character intends, but is really true at another level. In irony, the meaning at the higher level, the true meaning, is "contradictory, incongruous, or incompatible with" the meaning at the lower level, the apparent meaning.[33] We shall later observe examples of irony in 1:37–46. Both misunderstanding and irony involve two levels of meaning, one of which the reader (following what the implied author explicitly or implicitly indicates) should *reject* as untrue or misleading.

The phenomenon to which I want to draw attention in this section does not involve opposition between the two levels of meaning. There is one meaning that is correct at the level of the narrative and another level of further meaning that does not contradict or cancel the literal level but adds an additional dimension of meaning for the perceptive reader. The relationship between the two levels is one not of contrast, but of analogy. Nevertheless, this phenomenon is more like irony than it is like allegory or symbol, where one thing stands for something else. In the phenomenon that we shall observe in 1:35–46 the same words have two levels of meaning, as they do in irony, but without incompatibility. I also need to distinguish this phenomenon from the "two-level" reading of the Gospel that J. Louis Martyn introduced into Johannine studies, according to which at one level the narrative tells the story of Jesus during his earthly lifetime while at another level it tells the story of the "Johannine community" at (or up to and including) the time when the Gospel was written.[34] Ostensibly at least, on this kind of reading of the Gospel as portraying the history and situation of the Johannine community, each level of the narrative has its own integrity, though interpreters tend to assume that the history of the community is really the controlling narrative

---

30. See Frédéric Manns, "Les mots à double entente: Antécédents et fonction herméneutique d'un procédé johannique," *Liber Annuus* 38 (1988): 39–57, here 56.

31. On misunderstandings, see R. Alan Culpepper, *Anatomy of the Fourth Gospel: A Study in Literary Design* (Philadelphia: Fortress, 1983), 152–65.

32. Paul D. Duke, *Irony in the Fourth Gospel* (Atlanta: John Knox, 1985), is a masterly study; see also Culpepper, *Anatomy*, 165–80; Gail R. O'Day, *Revelation in the Fourth Gospel: Narrative Mode and Theological Claim* (Philadelphia: Fortress, 1986), chap. 1.

33. Culpepper, *Anatomy*, 167; compare Duke, *Irony*, 14–16.

34. J. Louis Martyn, *History and Theology in the Fourth Gospel*, rev. ed. (Nashville: Abingdon, 1979), 29. Martyn actually uses the term "Johannine church," but in subsequent studies along these lines it has become more common to refer to the "Johannine community."

that has generated this particular version of the story of Jesus as a kind of epiphenomenon. In the "Johannine community" reading of parts of the Gospel, the relationship between the two levels of the Gospel can be quite literalistic (e.g., the Samaritans who believe in Jesus in chap. 4 represent a stage of the community's history when Samaritans were converted and the community was located in Samaria) but in an inevitably very partial way. This "community reading" has been cogently criticized.[35] I mention it only to distinguish it from the way I propose reading 1:35–46.

Here is a reading of the story at the literal level: The two disciples of John the Baptist hear him identify Jesus as the expected figure about whom he had been speaking on the preceding day. They naturally want to know more about him and so follow Jesus—in the ordinary sense of walking behind him. Disciples of Jewish teachers did walk behind their master (according to rabbinic evidence), and the two men may already be thinking of transferring their allegiance from John to Jesus, but they certainly do not mean to make themselves disciples of Jesus by walking behind him. They could not be disciples of Jesus until asked by him to be disciples, and in any case they do not yet know enough about him. Jesus, seeing them walking up behind him, asks the very natural question "What do you want?" (The same Greek phrase, when it appears again in 4:27, there means no more than this.) They address him, in the respectful way one would expect, as "Rabbi," and ask a question ("Where are you staying?") that amounts to a polite way of asking if they may visit him in his lodgings. Jesus invites them to do so: "Come and see!" (literally, "Come and you will see!"). They stay two or three hours, until sunset, and, since one would hardly expect guests to return home after dark, it is probably implied that they stay the night.

Next morning, Andrew, evidently now convinced that Jesus really is the Messiah, brings his brother to Jesus. Jesus's immediate recognition of him as "Simon son of John" may indicate paranormal knowledge. He predicts that Simon will be known not by his patronymic, but rather by a nickname meaning "Rock."

The next day, Jesus decides to leave for Galilee, but before doing so he finds Philip. The aside in which we are told that Philip was from the same town as Andrew and Simon probably functions to explain how he already knows who Jesus is. He has been with them (perhaps also a disciple of John) and has heard about Jesus from them. When Jesus says, "Follow me!" the meaning on the literal level need be no more than that Jesus asks Philip to accompany

35. See especially Edward W. Klink, *The Sheep of the Fold: The Audience and Origin of the Gospel of John*, SNTSMS 141 (Cambridge: Cambridge University Press, 2007).

him to Galilee. Conventional requirements of rank would require Philip to let Jesus lead the way while he walked behind.

However, it is Jesus's summons to Philip to follow him that, more than any other part of this narrative, demands to be read also at another level: as a summons to follow him *as a disciple*. John's first readers would very probably have known the stories in Mark's Gospel, where the phrase "Follow me!" is used repeatedly by Jesus to call people to be his disciples (1:17; 2:14).[36] In these Markan stories the physical act of following Jesus entails leaving their homes and occupations and devoting themselves wholly to Jesus. Moreover, in the Johannine narrative the encounters between the five men and Jesus, along with their professions of faith in him, evidently do make them his disciples, transferring them from John the Baptist's company to form the nucleus of a group around Jesus. John calls them "disciples" at 2:2, 11–12, and thereafter throughout the Gospel.

The verb "to follow" occurs four times in 1:37–43. The first three occurrences refer to the merely physical following of Jesus by Andrew and his anonymous companion. The remarkable emphasis on this must mean that, at a level additional to the literal, we are to hear a reference to the following that constitutes discipleship. With Jesus's summons to Philip, the fourth occurrence of the verb, it may be that the literal and the additional level come together, since in Philip's case we could suppose that, even at the literal level, a call to discipleship is intended. But we may ask, why has John not told a story in which Jesus actually calls the first three men he encounters—the anonymous, Andrew, and Simon—to discipleship? Why, in their case, is the following that constitutes discipleship present not at the literal level but only as an overtone at the additional level in regard to the first two, and not at all in regard to Simon?

I think that there are probably two, not incompatible answers. If John knew Mark's Gospel and expected his readers to do so, he will not be intending to replace the rather different narrative of the call of Andrew and Simon Peter in Mark 1:16–18. John records only their initial meeting with Jesus. They join his company, but they have not yet received the call to take the radical step of leaving relatives, home, and occupation. In fact, Mark's narrative cannot mean that Jesus then met Simon and Andrew for the first time: he already knows who they are (how else could he select them to become "fishers of people"?), and they know him (how else could they opt to obey his call?).[37]

---

36. In 1:17 the words are *deute opisō mou*, but in 2:14 *akolouthei moi*, as in John 1:43.
37. Among commentators who make this point is Rudolf Schnackenburg, *The Gospel according to St. John*, trans. Kevin Smyth (London: Burns & Oates, 1968), 1:306.

John in fact leaves implicit room for Mark's story when he says that, on leaving Cana, Jesus, with his mother, brothers, and disciples, went to Capernaum and stayed there a short time before setting off for the Passover in Jerusalem (2:12). Leaving room for Mark's stories within his own is something that John does elsewhere (7:1; 18:24, 28).

The second reason is that, if we look carefully at John's use of the verb "to follow" (*akolouthein*) throughout the Gospel, we gain the strong impression that, for John, truly to follow Jesus was something that became possible for the disciples only after Jesus's death and resurrection. This is because it entails following Jesus's way to the cross (a perspective already found in Mark 8:34). The following exchange between Jesus and Simon Peter at the Last Supper is instructive:

> Simon Peter said to him, "Lord, where are you going?" Jesus answered, "Where I am going, you cannot follow me now; but you will follow me afterward." Peter said to him, "Lord, why can I not follow you now? I will lay down my life for you." Jesus answered, "Will you lay down your life for me? Very truly, I tell you, before the cock crows, you will have denied me three times." (John 13:36–38)

Other uses of the verb *akolouthein* in the Gospel accord with this indication that true following of Jesus is really possible only after his death and resurrection. In some cases the meaning is simply the literal one (6:2; 11:31; 18:15; 20:6). In some cases the word occurs in parabolic sayings where it functions allegorically: in its literal meaning, at the level of the parable's story, it stands for discipleship at the implied level (8:12; 10:4, 5, 27). In these cases the reference could be to post-Easter discipleship.

In 12:26a Jesus says, "Whoever serves me must follow me, and where I am, there will my servant be also." The context (12:23–25) gives this a clearly post-Easter reference. John has put several short sayings of Jesus together. In the little parable of the grain of wheat (12:24) Jesus speaks of his death and the "fruit" it will bear. Then comes the saying, which occurs in the Synoptics several times (Matt. 10:39; 16:25; Mark 8:35; Luke 9:24; 17:33), about losing life and keeping life. While Jesus himself, in his death and resurrection, exemplifies the meaning of this saying, its epigrammatic form means that it also applies to his followers. The lesson for his disciples is then made explicit in 12:26. This verse means that the disciple of Jesus must follow him on the way of the cross. (Compare the parallel saying in Mark 8:34, which is connected with the saying about losing life and saving life [8:35], just as the saying about discipleship is in John.) Only by following in this way can the disciple finally arrive where Jesus is—in his Father's heavenly house (cf. 14:3;

17:24). Here it is very clear that "to follow" means to follow Jesus on his way through the cross to glory.

As well as these occurrences of *akolouthein*, there is at least one place where its absence is notable. According to 6:66, "many of his disciples turned back and no longer went about [*periepatoun*] with him." John prefers to say that the disciples "went about" with Jesus rather than "followed" him (cf. 2:12; 11:16; contrast, e.g., Mark 10:52; Luke 22:39). During his ministry Jesus's disciples believe in him (2:11; 6:64), accompany him, and presumably (since this is the meaning of "disciple," *mathētēs*) are taught by him. But, in John's chosen vocabulary, they do not really follow him, except in the literal sense that the verb has at the literal level of the narrative of 1:37–43. But at this narrative's additional level of further meaning, the literal following prefigures the true following that is possible only after the passion week. The two momentous weeks correspond in that the disciples become disciples of Jesus in the first week, but only in the passion week are they taught what it will mean for them truly to follow Jesus on the way through the cross to glory that he himself takes in that week (e.g., 14:18–25).

The prefigurement in 1:37–43 is finally fulfilled on the literal level in the epilogue to the Gospel, where the words Jesus spoke to Philip in 1:43 recur and are repeated, addressed now to Peter: "Follow me!" (21:19, 22). This is what Jesus had told Peter he could not do before the cross but would be able to do afterward (13:36). Significantly, the command is first addressed to Peter immediately following Jesus's prediction of Peter's martyrdom, when Peter's death will "glorify God" just as Jesus's death had done (21:18–19). To follow Jesus is to follow him on the way of the cross. (John surely does not mean that every true disciple must die a martyr's death, but rather that the nature of a true disciple's following of Jesus must be such that he or she would be willing to die, should the contingent circumstances that require this arise [cf. Mark 8:34].)

Not only is the command to Peter to follow Jesus an echo of 1:37–46. So too is the little incident that intervenes between the first and second times that Jesus says, "Follow me!" to Peter:

> Peter turned and saw the disciple whom Jesus loved following[38] [*Epistrapheis ho Petros blepei ton mathētēn hon ēgapa ho Iēsous akolouthounta*]. . . . When Peter saw him, he said to Jesus, "Lord, what about him?" (21:20a, 21)

---

38. Like most English versions, the NRSV adds "them" here (cf. KJV), but the fact that this has no equivalent in the Greek is significant. It allows the sense that it was really Jesus the Beloved Disciple was following, as in 1:37–38.

We should surely be reminded of this:

> The two disciples heard him [John] say this, and they followed Jesus. When Jesus turned and saw them following [*strapheis de ho Iēsous kai theasamenos autous akolouthountas*], he said to them, "What are you looking for?" (1:37–38a)

The vocabulary varies a little (according to John's habit of employing synonyms), but the action is strictly parallel: one person turns, sees the other(s) following, and asks a question. Who turns, who is following, and who asks the question—these are different in each case. But just as the charcoal fire that Jesus makes on the beach (21:9) is there to remind readers of the one that burned in the courtyard of the high priest (18:18) and so of Peter's denials, so the action of turning and seeing someone follow serves to remind readers of the very first occasion on which disciples-to-be appeared in the narrative.[39] Just as the two disciples' following in 1:37–38 is literal, but with an overtone of further meaning, so is the Beloved Disciple's in 21:20. In the next section I shall argue that the anonymous disciple in 1:35–40 is in fact the Beloved Disciple, and so the parallel is between his first and last appearances in the Gospel, in both cases following Jesus. But his is to be a different manner of following from Peter's. Peter is to shepherd Jesus's flock and to die a martyr's death; the Beloved Disciple is to "remain," in order to be the witness par excellence to Jesus and to write the Gospel.

"To follow" (*akolouthein*) is one of the repeated keywords in 1:37–46, but it is not the only one (see table 7.2). The others also have an ordinary meaning at the literal level, but, at the additional level of meaning, they prefigure something about true discipleship. Jesus's invitation "Come and see" (1:39),[40] repeated by Philip in 1:46, suggests that discipleship begins by "coming" to Jesus (3:21; 5:40; 6:35, 37, 44, 65; 7:37) and "seeing" Jesus (6:40; 14:9; cf. 12:21).

The claim, made both by Andrew and by Philip, that "we have found" the Messiah (1:41, 45)[41] corresponds to Jesus's question "What do you seek?" (as these words can be translated). Initially, they may not really know what they are seeking, but it is the Messiah they find when they get to know Jesus. This successful seeking and finding contrasts with what Jesus says later to

---

39. For this and other literary links between 1:35–50 and 21:15–23, see M. Franzmann and M. Klinger, "The Call Stories of John 1 and John 21," *SVTQ* 36 (1992): 7–15.

40. I am not at all convinced by the argument that this phrase portrays Jesus as the divine Wisdom (e.g., McHugh, *John 1–4*, 151–52).

41. I do not agree with those exegetes who take this claim to be misguided because truly it is Jesus who finds people (as in 1:43), not they who find him (e.g., Francis J. Moloney, *Belief in the Word: Reading the Fourth Gospel, John 1–4* [Minneapolis: Fortress, 1993], 68–69). There is no reason why both perspectives cannot be valid.

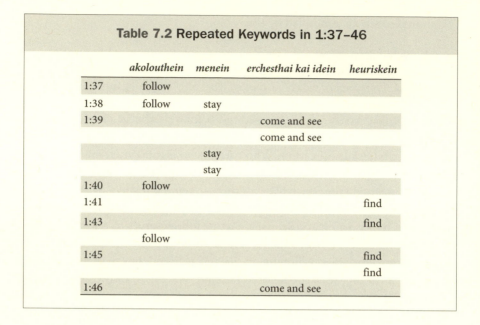

	akolouthein	menein	erchesthai kai idein	heuriskein
1:37	follow			
1:38	follow	stay		
1:39			come and see	
			come and see	
		stay		
		stay		
1:40	follow			
1:41				find
1:43				find
	follow			
1:45				find
				find
1:46			come and see	

Table 7.2 Repeated Keywords in 1:37–46

the Jewish leaders: "You will search for me but you will not find me" (7:34, 36 [cf. 8:21; 13:33]). The word *zētein* ("to seek") is a favorite of John's,[42] but most examples of people seeking Jesus in the Gospel show them doing so for wrong or inadequate reasons (6:24, 26; 7:1, 11, 19, 20, 25, 30, 34, 36; 8:21, 37, 40; 10:39; 11:8, 56; 18:4, 7, 8; 19:12).[43] Only the last occurrence of the verb corresponds to the first in 1:38. There Jesus asks "What do you seek?" (*ti zēteite*);[44] in 20:15 he asks Mary Magdalene, "Whom do you seek?" (*tina zēteis*). The two disciples-to-be, on day 3 of the first week, scarcely know what they are seeking; Mary, on day 7 of the passion week, knows that she is seeking Jesus, but she expects only to find his corpse. In both cases, what is found exceeds what is sought.

In three of the occurrences of "to find" (*heuriskein*) in 1:37–46 it is not Jesus who is found, but one of the disciples-to-be: Andrew finds Simon (1:41), Jesus finds Philip (1:43), and Philip finds Nathanael (1:45). This is another aspect of this early narrative that is echoed in the Gospel's epilogue. The first occurrence of *heuriskein* in the Gospel refers to Andrew finding Simon Peter (1:41); the last is in Jesus's promise to the disciples in the fishing boat that if

42. Thirty-four times in John; cf. Matt. 14×; Mark 10×; Luke 26×.
43. These examples include both people seeking Jesus and people seeking to do something to Jesus (e.g., to kill him).
44. These are the first words of Jesus in the Gospel.

they cast their net on the right side they "will find" (fish is the implied object of the verb, which is left without an object in the Greek text) (21:6). This is by no means an insignificant occurrence of the verb, because the great catch of fish in chapter 21 prefigures the disciples' mission to the world. The fish represent "those who will believe in [Jesus] through their word" (17:20). In the implicit background lies Jesus's promise to Andrew and Peter in Mark's Gospel that he will make them "fishers of people" (1:17). (John himself never tells his readers that Peter was a fisherman before becoming a disciple of Jesus, but this is presupposed in 21:3.) Thus 1:41, 45 already prefigure the disciples' post-Easter mission to bring other disciples to Jesus.

The last of the repeated keywords in 1:37–46 is *menein* ("to remain, to abide, to stay, to dwell"). Once again this is a favorite Johannine word,[45] used in a variety of ways. As we have seen, its occurrences in 1:38–39 seem quite ordinary (as in 2:12; 4:40; 7:9; 10:40; 11:6, 54), but its threefold occurrence in these two verses suggests that there is more going on than the literal references to the place where Jesus was lodging and to the disciples-to-be spending some time with him there. Discipleship leads to staying permanently with Jesus where he stays—in his Father's heavenly home. This promise is made in 14:1–3, using not *menein* but the related noun *monai* ("dwelling places" [cf. 14:23; see also 17:24]). Other ways of speaking that do use the word *menein* are rather more distant from the literal usage in 1:38–39: disciples will "abide" in Jesus and he in them (6:56; 15:4–7), or they are to "abide" in his love (15:9–10) as he "abides" in his Father's love (15:10).

As we have already noticed, discipleship is a theme that links the first week and the passion week. Between these weeks the theme occurs only in 6:60–71. But chapter 12 brings to an end Jesus's public ministry to the people, and from 13:1 onwards he focuses solely on "his own," the disciples. The theme that is adumbrated in the first week becomes a dominant feature of the passion week. The correlation may be even closer: the days on which Jesus meets and recruits his first disciples are days 3–5 of the first week, and it is on the fifth day of the passion week that he instructs them and prepares them for the true following of him that will begin to be possible for them only after this week. Once this relationship between the two weeks is recognized, it is clear that it would be going too far to say that 1:35–39 "contain a Johannine paradigm of discipleship."[46] The passage does no more than prefigure what discipleship

45. Forty times in John; cf. Matt. 3; Mark 2; Luke 7.
46. Raymond F. Collins, *These Things Have Been Written: Studies on the Fourth Gospel*, LTPM 2 (Louvain: Peeters; Grand Rapids: Eerdmans, 1990), 100. Collins's discussion of this passage (pp. 99–103) is helpful, but he does not explain why discipleship is present only at "the level of Johannine meaning" and not at "the level of event."

means in a dimension of meaning that becomes fully meaningful only in the light of the rest of the Gospel, especially chapters 13–21. Finally, we should note also that, while the relationship with the passion week is important, there are also clear links with chapter 21. In this, as in other respects, the Gospel narrative requires the epilogue to complete what it commences.[47]

Two Weeks of Witness

John the Baptist (whom the Gospel always calls simply "John") is the primary witness to Jesus in this Gospel. This is already abundantly clear in the prologue: [John] "came as a witness to testify to the light, so that all might believe through him" (1:7). Just as it is insisted that he was not the light itself, so his indispensable role as witness to the light is underlined by repetition (1:8).[48] Even some of the words of his testimony are interjected into the prologue at a later stage (1:15, repeated in 1:30), perhaps significantly words in which he indicates Jesus's preexistence. This parenthetical citation of John in the prologue probably functions literarily to form a "chain-link" construction that binds the prologue together with the opening narrative of the Gospel, a common stylistic feature of ancient literature.[49] But how can the prologue's remarkably large claim that John "came as a witness . . . so that all might believe through him" (1:7) be justified? John the Baptist himself says that he "came baptizing with water for this reason, that he might be revealed to Israel" (1:31). In accordance with the Jewish tradition that it was not for the Messiah to claim for himself his messianic role and status, a primary witness is required, one who could testify to God's own anointing of the Messiah, which took place in John's vision of the descent of the Spirit on Jesus (1:32–34).[50]

This testimony of John is the basis for the belief of the first disciples, though it had to be confirmed by their direct experience of Jesus, especially the first of Jesus's signs (cf. 2:11). But these men would never have got to know Jesus had the first two of them not been initially disciples of John who

---

47. For chap. 21 as integral to the design of the Gospel, see Bauckham, *Testimony*, chap. 13.

48. Although John was not *the* light, as a witness to the light he was "a burning and shining lamp" that gave light (5:35).

49. See Bruce W. Longenecker, *Art at the Boundaries: The Art and Theology of New Testament Chain-Link Transitions* (Waco: Baylor University Press, 2005).

50. John's testimony begins on the first day of the Gospel's first week, when he testifies to the emissaries of the Jerusalem authorities by denying that he himself was any of three expected eschatological figures (1:19–21; cf. 3:28) but rather is one who goes ahead of a greater figure to come (1:23–27). On 1:19–21, see Bauckham, *Testimony*, 209–12. It is not necessarily implied that Jesus fulfills all three roles.

heard John's testimony pointing out Jesus as the man of whom he had been speaking (1:35–36).[51] John's testimony remains primary even for readers of the Gospel, which is why the prologue speaks of it in the present tense: "John testifies [*martyrei*] about him and has cried out, saying . . ." (1:15). In the pages of the Gospel, he still testifies, just as the Beloved Disciple does (21:24: "This is the disciple who is testifying [*martyrōn*] about these things and has written these things"). Indeed, it is the Beloved Disciple's testimony that includes John's testimony and enables him still to testify, just as the Beloved Disciple's testimony includes, by recording them in the Gospel, all the other testimonies to Jesus to which the Gospel refers.[52]

But this is not the only link between the Beloved Disciple's testimony and John's. John's testimony is remarkable not only for its primacy, but also for its far-reaching content. He does not just reveal Jesus to be the Messiah, though this is all that the first five disciples seem to recognize in Jesus. He recognizes him as the one who is to baptize with the Holy Spirit, something that Jesus does not do until after his glorification (7:39; 20:22), and something that no one else within the narrative foresees. He also recognizes Jesus as "the Lamb of God who takes away the sin of the world" (1:29 [cf. 1:36]), again something that no one else within the narrative foresees. In other words, John's testimony to Jesus in the first three days of the Gospel's first week looks ahead to its fulfillment in the last three days of the passion week. Those are precisely the days on which the Beloved Disciple first enters the Gospel's narrative as a witness (13:23–30; 19:31–37; 20:3–10). On those days the Beloved Disciple witnesses the fulfillment of John's witness (see table 7.1). This gives added significance to the fact that it is only on these occasions and in chapter 21 that the Gospel draws attention to the Beloved Disciple's presence as a witness within the narrative.

But we have still not grasped the full extent to which John's witness and that of the Beloved Disciple are connected. In my view, the anonymous companion of Andrew in 1:35–40 must be the Beloved Disciple. In the first place, the anonymity of this figure, who presumably becomes one of the initial group of disciples of Jesus to which 2:2, 11–12 refer, is strange. The other four are named and feature by name later in the Gospel (though Nathanael only at 21:2). On first reading of 1:35–2:13, this anonymous disciple may be sufficiently unobtrusive to escape the reader's focused attention. At 1:40 the narrative moves on and he is seemingly forgotten. But on further

---

51. For the importance of John's testimony in John's Gospel, see also 5:33–36; 10:40–41.

52. For these various witnesses, see Andrew T. Lincoln, *Truth on Trial: The Lawsuit Motif in the Fourth Gospel* (Peabody, MA: Hendrickson, 2000), 23 (he counts seven within the narrative).

reflection—and the Gospel undoubtedly was written for further reflection as well as for initial reading—the fact that one of the first two disciples to get to know Jesus is unnamed must arouse curiosity. We should also note that in 15:27 Jesus says to his disciples that, after his glorification, they are "to testify because you have been with me from the beginning."[53] The Gospel presents the Beloved Disciple as *the* witness to Jesus, the one who "remained" (21:22–23) so that he could continue to bear witness to Jesus and embody that witness in the Gospel (21:24).[54] The qualification for witness stated by Jesus—to "have been with me from the beginning"—must apply to the Beloved Disciple. In retrospect, readers realize that he was there "at the beginning"—one of the first two who had the opportunity to get to know Jesus and to recognize him as the Messiah. It is, in effect, the Beloved Disciple and Andrew who say to Simon Peter, "We have found the Messiah" (1:41), just as it is the Beloved Disciple who, in the epilogue, points out to Peter, "It is the Lord!" (21:7).

Of course, the Beloved Disciple cannot, on first acquaintance with Jesus, be called "the disciple whom Jesus loved," but his anonymity is sufficient link, given other indications, with the Beloved Disciple in his later appearances in the narrative. I have already pointed out that the reference to the hour of the day (1:39), which has no other narrative function, does make good sense as a deliberate hint of eyewitness testimony. That the disciple had this opportunity to spend time with Jesus at the beginning is important for his role as the witness whose testimony is embodied in the whole Gospel. This detail is the same kind of precise observation as the one made about disposition of the grave clothes in the empty tomb (20:7). I have also already pointed out the parallel between 1:38–39 and 21:20–21. This too makes most sense if it is the same disciple whom Jesus sees following him in both cases. The parallel makes a subtle *inclusio* between the Beloved Disciple's first appearance in the Gospel's narrative and his last.[55] As the ideal witness, he was there at the beginning, and he is there at the end. He appears in the Gospel just before Peter does, and he remains just for a moment after Peter. Jesus's last words in the Gospel are addressed to Peter (21:22), but the words excerpted from

53. On this qualification for witness, see Richard Bauckham, *Jesus and the Eyewitnesses: The Gospels as Eyewitness Testimony* (Grand Rapids: Eerdmans, 2006), chap. 6.

54. On the Beloved Disciple as "ideal witness," see Bauckham, *Testimony*, chap. 3.

55. Note also that precisely the same phrase, "two of his disciples" (*ek tōn mathētōn autou dyo*), appears in 1:35 and 21:2. In the latter case, the Beloved Disciple is one of the two (cf. 21:7). The parallel may suggest that the other unnamed disciple in 21:2 is Andrew, who is otherwise rather surprisingly not included in the group of seven disciples who go fishing. It may be that the evangelist has left him unnamed in order to be able to use the phrase that recalls 1:35.

them in the next verse, "If it is my will that he remains until I come,"[56] are about the Beloved Disciple.[57]

What is probably the most important link between John's witness and the Beloved Disciple's can now be appreciated. He is one of the two disciples who, on the third day of the Gospel's first week, hear John identify Jesus as "the Lamb of God" (1:36)—that is, the figure he has more fully described, on the previous day, as "the Lamb of God who takes away the sin of the world" (1:29). This testimony of John is fulfilled when, at the time when the Passover lambs were being slaughtered, a soldier pierced the side of Jesus with a spear and "at once blood and water came out" (19:34). The minimal significance of this[58] is that Jesus's death was sacrificial. For a sacrifice to be valid, blood must flow. For this occurrence, the Beloved Disciple's witness is emphatically adduced, in words that anticipate the summary statements at 20:31 and 21:24: "He who saw this has testified[59] so that you may believe. His testimony is true, and he knows that he tells the truth" (19:35).

John came as a witness "so that all might believe through him" (1:9). The Beloved Disciple heard John's testimony that Jesus is the Lamb of God (1:35–36). The Beloved Disciple himself witnessed the fulfillment of this testimony and testified to it "so that you also may believe" (19:35). Thus it is through the Beloved Disciple's witness in the Gospel to the events at which he was present that the witness of John remains—"so that all might believe through him."

The Scriptural Sources of John's Testimony

So far we have given attention especially to the way in which further dimensions of meaning open up when the narrative of the Gospel's first week is read in relation to other parts of the Gospel and in particular when the correspondences between the first week and the passion week are observed. But the text of the Gospel is also frequently in intertextual relationship with the Jewish Scriptures or Hebrew Bible, which is often cited in the Septuagint Greek

56. In 21:23 the reading that lacks *ti pros se* ("what is it to you?") is to be preferred because it is the harder reading. The absence of those words leaves an incomplete sentence that scribes will have completed in conformity with 21:22. The author surely left the sentence incomplete in order to make the words "until I come" the last words of Jesus in the Gospel.

57. There is a kind of one-upmanship in the Gospel's portrayal of the Beloved Disciple in comparison with Peter. In my view, this is not at all intended to denigrate Peter, but rather is meant to establish the Gospel's claim to bear witness to Jesus in a way that goes further and deeper than Peter's witness as it is embodied in the Gospel of Mark.

58. For possible further meanings, see chap. 5, "Sacraments?"

59. Note the parallel with John the Baptist: "I myself have seen and have testified" (1:34).

version but whose Hebrew text often accounts for the Gospel's allusions more adequately than the Greek.

John the Baptist's testimony to Jesus in 1:29–34 is a good example of the way exegesis of the Hebrew Bible lies behind the text of the Gospel, such that the text becomes more meaningful when the full range of its biblical allusions is recognized (see table 7.3). An important key to understanding the exegesis of Scripture in this passage is the Jewish exegetical principle that the rabbis later called *gezerah shavah* (which might be translated "equal category"). It is a principle that most of the New Testament writers used. It means that passages from different parts of Scripture that use the same words or phrases can be brought together and interpreted in relation to each other.

John's reference to Jesus as "the Lamb of God who is to take away[60] the sin of the world" (1:29) has evoked much discussion, especially with regard to its scriptural or Jewish background. Probably a majority of recent commentators agree that there is allusion both to the Passover lamb (especially as Jesus's death seems to be aligned with the sacrifice of the Passover lamb in 19:31–36)[61] and to the Suffering Servant of chapter 53 of Isaiah, who is compared with a lamb (53:7)[62] and of whom it is said that "he bore the sin of many" (53:12) (see table 7.3).[63] The latter allusion makes it certain that the Gospel is here dependent on the Hebrew text of Isaiah, for the Greek has the plural "the sins of many."[64] The singular "the sin" of this verse in the Hebrew is echoed in John's "the sin of the world." Probably John has understood "many" in the Hebrew text in the fullest possible way, taking the reference to be to "the

60. McHugh (*John 1–4*, 130) correctly notes that the present participle (*airōn*) "is best understood as a futural present."

61. Though the commentators do not usually recognize it, the scriptural quotation in 19:36 itself is an instance of *gezerah shavah*, dependent on the coincidence of words between Ps. 34:20 and Num. 9:12 (cf. also Exod. 12:46). It identifies Jesus both with the righteous sufferer of the psalms of David and with the Passover lamb. The common attempt to limit the allusion to only one of these is misguided.

62. In my view, the slaughtered lamb of Rev. 5:6 is also based on both the Passover lamb and Isa. 53:7.

63. For example, Lindars, *John*, 109; Andrew T. Lincoln, *The Gospel according to Saint John*, BNTC (Peabody, MA: Hendrickson; London: Continuum, 2005), 113; Craig S. Keener, *The Gospel of John: A Commentary* (Peabody, MA: Hendrickson, 2003), 452–54. The notion of a tradition of an "apocalyptic lamb," supposed to be a military leader, on the basis of *1 En.* 90.38, has lost support because the context in *1 Enoch* is a long allegorical history in which all kinds of animals represent different historical figures and peoples. Nor can *T. Jos.* 19.8 any longer be reliably cited as a pre-Christian Jewish text. The Lamb (representing Christ) in Revelation derives from the Passover lamb and Isa. 53:7 and acquires his martial role from being incorporated in an extended metaphor of messianic war. There is no need to postulate dependence on a military lamb figure already existing in apocalyptic tradition.

64. This probably is assimilation to the plurals in Isa. 53:4, 11.

Table 7.3 The Scriptural Sources of John's Testimony (1:29–34)

The Lamb of God who is to take away [*ho airōn*] the sin of the world

Gen. 22:8: Abraham said, "**God** himself will provide [*yir'eh*] **the lamb** [*haśśeh*] for a burnt offering."

Exod. 12:3: Tell the whole congregation of Israel that on the tenth of this month they are to take a **lamb** [*śeh*] for each family, a **lamb** [*śeh*] for each household.

Isa. 53:7b, 11b, 12c:
     like a **lamb** [*śeh*] that is led to the slaughter,
     and like a sheep that before its shearers is silent,
     so he did not open his mouth. . . .
     The righteous one, my servant [*'abdî*], shall make many righteous,
     and he shall bear [*yisbōl*] their iniquities. . . .
     Yet he **bore** [*nāśā'*] **the sin** [*ḥēṭĕ'*] of many,
     and made intercession for the transgressors.

I saw the Spirit descending from heaven . . . and it remained [*emeinen*] on him. . . . He on whom you see the Spirit descend and remain [*menon*]

Isa. 11:1–2a:
     A shoot shall come out from the stump of Jesse,
     and a branch shall grow out of his roots.
     The Spirit of the LORD **shall rest on him** [*nāḥâ 'ālāyw rûaḥ YHWH*].

I myself have seen and have testified that this is the Chosen One of God

Isa. 42:1:
     Here is my servant [*'abdî*], whom I uphold,
     my chosen [*bĕḥîrî*], in whom my soul delights;
     I have put **my Spirit upon him** [*rûḥî 'ālāyw*];
     He will bring forth justice to the nations.

Link words
    Gen. 22:8 — Exod. 12:3 — Isa. 53:7: **lamb** (*śeh*)
              Isa. 11:2 — Isa. 42:1: **Spirit upon him** (*'ālāyw rûaḥ / rûḥî 'ālāyw*)
         Isa. 53:11 — Isa. 42:1: **my servant** (*'abdî*)

sin of the world."[65] Commentators note the difficulty of supposing that "the Lamb of God" in John derives only from Isa. 53, in that there the reference to a lamb is only in a simile: Isaiah compares the Servant of the Lord with a lamb. On the other hand, the Passover lamb was not understood in Judaism as a sacrifice for sin, and so it fails to explain John's statement that the Lamb of God "is to take away the sin of the world." But if we recognize that Exod. 12 (about the Passover lamb) is linked to Isa. 53 by means of the link word "lamb" (*śeh*), according to the principle of *gezerah shavah*, then we can explain not only the combination of the two passages in the background to John, but also the highlighting of what might seem a minor feature of Isa. 53: the comparison of the Servant with a lamb. By means of the link word *śeh*, Jesus as the Passover Lamb of the new exodus can be understood also as the Suffering Servant, whose death is depicted in Isaiah as a sacrifice for sin.

It may be, as has been suggested, that the phrase "the Lamb of God" has been formed by analogy with the title "the Servant of the Lord" in Isaiah.[66] But it is also possible that it echoes yet another passage that uses the link word *śeh* to refer to a sacrificial offering. When Abraham, on his way to sacrifice Isaac, is asked by his son where the lamb for the offering is, he tells him, "God himself will provide a lamb [*śeh*] for a burnt offering" (Gen. 22:8 [see table 7.3]). A different word (*'ayil*, "ram") is used later in the narrative for the animal that Abraham actually sacrifices in place of Isaac (Gen. 22:13), but 22:8, where *śeh* is used, is the point where it is actually said that God will provide the animal. This provision of the sacrificial victim by God is underlined by Abraham's subsequent naming of the place "The-LORD-Will-Provide" (*yhwh yir'eh* [22:14, echoing 22:8]). This is what John means by calling Jesus "the Lamb of God"—the Lamb that God is providing. Jesus is not a lamb taken from the flocks of Israelites who bring it as an offering; he is the lamb that has come from God, the lamb that God gives for the salvation of the world (cf. 3:16). Only one lamb in the Hebrew Bible is said to be provided by God: the lamb of Gen. 22:8. Given the importance that undoubtedly was attached to the narrative of Abraham's offering of Isaac (whatever the precise significance given to it at this period),[67] it seems likely that John 1:29 alludes to it, as well as to the Passover lamb and the Suffering Servant. The thought might be that Jesus is the ultimate substitute for Isaac on the altar.

John has chosen the Greek verb *airein* to translate the Hebrew verb *nāśā'* in Isa. 53:12, whereas the Septuagint uses *anapherein*. The verbs *airein* and

65. McHugh, *John 1–4*, 131–32. Note also (especially in view of the allusion to Isa. 42:1 in John 1:34 [see below]) the universal scope of the Servant's work according to Isa. 42:1, 4.

66. So, for example, Schnackenburg, *John*, 1:300.

67. Note the possible allusion in John 3:16.

nāśā' are well matched; both can mean either "to lift up" or "to take away." It is likely that John intends both meanings. The most obvious meaning is that the Lamb of God will take away—remove—the sin of the world. This is how the word is used in 1 John 3:5: "he was revealed to take away [*arēi*] sins." (Note that this verse seems to echo John 1:29–31 in using the word "revealed" [*ephanerōthē*; cf. John 1:31: *phanerōthē*] as well as "to take away sins.") But John will have noticed that the verb *nāśā'* is used also in Isa. 52:13: "my servant shall be exalted and shall be lifted up [*niśśā'*] and shall be very high." This introduction to the Suffering Servant passage was very important for John's Gospel,[68] not least in being the basis for the cryptic sayings in which Jesus predicts that he will be "lifted up" (3:14; 8:28; 12:32–34) (the Greek verb is *hypsoun*), meaning both that he will be lifted up literally on the cross and that at the same time he will be exalted to heavenly glory. By using *airein* to translate *nāśā'*, John surely is exploiting the range of meaning of both verbs to suggest that the Lamb of God will remove the sin of the world by lifting it up with him when he is lifted up on the cross. His lifting up will be his exaltation to heaven; the lifting up of the sin of the world will be its removal from the world.

It is remarkable how many commentators miss the allusion to Isa. 11:2 in John 1:32–33 ("the Spirit . . . remained on him"; "he on whom you see the Spirit . . . remain"), perhaps because John is once again independent of the Septuagint version. He has used a favorite verb, *menein*, which he uses frequently (forty times in all) but in a wide variety of ways. But it is quite appropriate for rendering the Hebrew verb *nûaḥ*, used in Isa. 11:2 and here transposed into the context of John the Baptist's vision.[69] The Hebrew verb can mean "to settle upon," "to come to rest on," and can be used of birds (2 Sam. 21:10) as well as of the divine Spirit (Num. 11:25–26; 2 Kings 2:15; Isa. 11:2). In the Isaianic words, "The Spirit of the LORD shall rest on him" (11:2), John could easily see the image of the vision: the Spirit descending from heaven and settling upon Jesus. Isaiah 11:1–5 was one of the most commonly cited prophecies of the royal Messiah from the house of David. Typically, John makes a strikingly original application of it to Jesus by finding in 11:2 a prophecy of the anointing of Jesus with the Spirit at his baptism.

The last of the scriptural allusions in this passage requires some discussion of the textual variants. At the end of John 1:34 the overwhelming majority of the Greek manuscripts have *ho huios tou theou* ("the Son of God"), and this

---

68. See chap. 3, "Glory."

69. The verb *menein* is never used to translate *nûaḥ* in the LXX, and so John's use of it must be attributed to his particular fondness for the verb.

is the reading preferred by all modern editions of the Greek Testament. But there is just a little evidence for an alternative reading: *ho eklektos tou theou* ("the Chosen One of God"). Many scholars have judged this the original,[70] on the grounds that it is easy to see why a scribe should have changed *eklektos* to *huios* but very difficult to see why the opposite change should have been made. "The Son of God" is a familiar title for Jesus in the New Testament and would most naturally have been associated with his baptism (Matt. 3:17; Mark 1:11; Luke 3:22). "The Chosen One of God," on the other hand, occurs elsewhere as a title for Jesus only in Luke 23:35 (where it is the Jewish leaders who use it as a title for the Messiah).

If John wrote "the Chosen One of God," he was alluding to Isa. 42:1 (where the LXX also has *ho eklektos mou* for the Hebrew *běhîrî* but identifies the figure as Israel, which the Hebrew does not). This verse has a clear link with Isa. 11:2 in its reference to the Spirit ("I have put my Spirit upon him") as well as with Isa. 53 (for the figure is also called "my Servant"). Moreover, Isa. 42 was already connected with the vision at Jesus's baptism in Mark, where the heavenly voice says, "You are my Son, the Beloved; with you I am well pleased" (Mark 1:11). "You are my Son" alludes to Ps. 2:7, but "with you I am well pleased" to Isa. 42:1. ("The Beloved" [*ho agapētos*] has been understood as a translation of *běhîrî* in Isa. 42:1, but it more likely belongs closely with "my Son" and echoes Gen. 22:2.) Another advantage in reading "Chosen One" in John 1:34 is that it is a title that does not recur in the confessions of the first disciples in John 1:41–49, whereas "the Son of God" accompanies "the King of Israel" on the lips of Nathanael (John 1:49). In every other respect John the Baptist's insight into the identity of Jesus is distinctive and more perceptive than the confessions of the disciples, who merely apply to Jesus the most obvious titles for the Davidic Messiah. "Chosen One" fits this pattern much better than "Son of God."

By means of *gezerah shavah* John has collected a series of scriptural texts that are all connected with each other by link words. The interesting result is that John is undoubtedly speaking of the Davidic Messiah (Isa. 11) but is identifying this royal Messiah with the Servant of Isa. 42 and Isa. 53, as well as with the Passover Lamb of the new exodus and probably also the substitute for Isaac as a sacrifice that God himself will provide. This is the kind of radical interpretation of what it meant for Jesus to be the messianic king that we find also and more fully developed in John's passion narrative. There too Jesus is the Isaianic Servant (12:32, 34, 38) and the Passover lamb (19:36), as well as the suffering king of the royal psalms (13:18; 19:24, 28, 31),

70. For lists, see Schnackenburg, *John*, 1:306n72; McHugh, *John 1–4*, 141.

the lowly and peaceable king of Zechariah (12:15), and Zechariah's crucified Messiah (19:37).

What the First Disciples First Believed about Jesus

John the Baptist's testimony reflects studied exegesis of Scripture and paints a picture of the Messiah very different from the usual expectation at the time. The same cannot be said of the confessions of faith expressed by the first disciples of Jesus in 1:41–49. They voice no more than a conventional view of the expected Davidic Messiah:

> Andrew: "We have found the Messiah." (1:41)
>
> Philip: "We have found him about whom Moses in the law and also the prophets wrote." (1:45)
>
> Nathanael: "Rabbi, you are the Son of God! You are the King of Israel!" (1:49)

Philip's comment can refer only to the Davidic Messiah,[71] who was widely thought to be predicted in Gen. 49:8–12 and Num. 24:17–19, as well as in various passages in the prophets such as Isa. 11:1–5 and Jer. 23:5–6.[72] "The Son of God" (especially as Nathanael correlates it with "the King of Israel") is probably here no more than a title for the human Messiah of David, used on the basis of 2 Sam. 7:14; Ps. 2:7; Ps. 89:26–27. Evidence for the use of this title for the Messiah in late Second Temple Judaism is not plentiful, but it is sufficient to indicate that it was sometimes, if not very often, used.[73] "The King of Israel," an obvious way to describe the expected new David, was also in Jewish use.[74]

It is worth noting that this title is no different in meaning from the title "the King of the Jews" that is used later in the Gospel (see table 7.4). The verbal difference reflects no more than a standard difference of usage between Palestinian Jews and Gentiles.[75] Gentiles called the inhabitants of Jewish Palestine "Jews" (as Pilate does in this Gospel) but Palestinian Jews speaking to or writing for each other called themselves "Israelites" (as in John 1:47) and

---

71. On the term "Messiah" ("Christ") in John, see Bauckham, *Testimony*, 225–28.

72. Philip cannot be referring to the prophet like Moses, predicted in Deut. 18:18–19, because this figure does not appear in the prophecies of the prophets.

73. Bauckham, *Testimony*, 229.

74. Bauckham, *Testimony*, 230.

75. See Bauckham, *Testimony*, 230–31, with the literature cited there.

their nation "Israel" (as in John 1:31; 3:10; 12:13). However, when speaking to or writing for non-Jews, they followed the Gentile practice and called themselves "Jews" (as the evangelist does in this Gospel).[76] "King of the Jews" is therefore just "King of Israel" put into Gentile or Gentile-friendly terms. There is no theological distinction to be discerned.

It is a mistake to see the term "Rabbi" (used by Andrew and the anonymous disciple in v. 38 and Nathanael in v. 49) as a title to be compared with the others in this passage, as though the disciples start with a very "low Christology" (Jesus as merely a teacher) and progress to seeing Jesus in more exalted terms. The disciples continue to address Jesus as "Rabbi" up to 11:8, and Mary Magdalene uses the variant "Rabbouni"[77] in 20:16 (see table 7.4). The alternative form of address "Lord" (*kyrie*), which the disciples use more often, beginning in 6:68 and continuing to the end of the Gospel (21:21, the last words of a disciple to Jesus in the Gospel), is not necessarily a more elevated term, since it can mean no more than "Sir" and is used as a polite form of address even by people who do not know who Jesus is (4:11; 5:7) and even by the Greeks addressing Philip (12:21). When it means more (as in 13:13–14, where "Teacher" [i.e., Rabbi][78] and "Lord" are used together), it is more or less equivalent to "Rabbi," designating the relationship of "Master" and "disciples." Only in Thomas's address to the risen Jesus does "my Lord" gain the significance that its use here in parallel with "my God" demonstrates (20:28). In fact, John consistently avoids attributing to the disciples before the resurrection the christological insight that came about only after it.

Nor is there a progression of understanding from "Messiah" to "Son of God" and "King of Israel." There is no basis for Raymond Brown's claim, "On each day there is a gradual deepening of insight and a profounder realization of who it is that the disciples are following."[79] All of these disciples express no more than a conventional Jewish understanding of the Davidic Messiah. Evidently, this is all they had understood John the Baptist to mean when he

76. Similarly, Jesus and the Samaritan woman, both of whom would have called themselves Israelites, distinguish between each other by using the terms "Jew" (i.e., Judean) and "Samaritan" (John 4:9, 22).

77. According to Jean-Claude Moreau, the difference is that the "designation *Rabbî* acknowledges the authority of a teacher; the designation *Rabbûnî* evokes someone in command" ("Rabbouni," *RB* 199 [2012]: 403–20, here 403). This suggests that in John it is the Aramaic equivalent of the Greek *kyrios* (cf. 20:13).

78. John uses "Rabbi" only as an address to Jesus; otherwise he translates it as "the Teacher" (11:28).

79. Raymond E. Brown, *The Gospel according to John (I–XII): Introduction, Translation, and Notes*, AB 29 (New York: Doubleday 1966), 77.

Table 7.4 Designations of Jesus

Christological Titles

Word	1:1 (2x), 14
God	1:1, 18; 20:28 ("my Lord and my God")
Only Son (*monogenēs*)	1:14, 18; 3:16, 18
Christ (*Christos*)	1:17; (1:20, 25); 1:41; (3:28);[a] 4:25, 29; 7:26, 27, 31, 41 (2x), 42; 9:22; 10:24; 11:27; 12:34; 17:3; 20:31
Messiah (*Messias*)	1:41; 4:25
Lord (implying divinity)	1:23; 20:28 ("my Lord and my God")
Lamb of God	1:29, 36
Chosen One of God	1:34
Son of God	1:49; 5:25; 10:36; 11:4, 27; 19:7; 20:31
Son	3:17, 35, 36 (2x); 5:19 (2x), 20, 21, 22, 23 (2x), 26; 6:40; 8:36; 14:13; 17:1
your Son	17:1
King of Israel	1:49; 12:13
King of the Jews[b]	18:33, 39; 19:3, 19, 21 (2x)
your [Zion's] king	12:15
your [Jews'] king	19:14, 15
Savior of the world	4:42
the Prophet[c]	(1:21, 25);[d] 6:14; 7:40
Holy One of God	6:69

Non-Messianic Designations

Rabbi	1:38; 3:2; 4:31; 6:25; 9:2; 11:8
Rabbouni	20:16
Teacher	1:38; 11:28; 13:13, 14; 20:16
Lord (not implying divinity)	4:11, 15, 19, 49; 5:7; 6:23, 34, 68; 9:36, 38; 11:2, 3, 12, 21, 27, 32, 34, 39; 13:6, 9, 13, 25, 36, 37; 14:5, 8, 22; 20:2, 13, 15, 18, 20, 25; 21:7 (2x), 15, 16, 17, 20, 21

Self-Designation

Son of Man	1:51; 3:13, 14; 5:27;[e] 6:27, 53, 62; 8:28; 9:35; 12:23, 34 (2x); 13:31

[a]In the verses in parentheses John denies that he is the Christ.
[b]This is no more than a Gentile's version of "the King of Israel."
[c]Not including references to Jesus as "a prophet."
[d]In the verses in parentheses John denies that he is the Prophet.
[e]The phrase is anarthrous in this case only.

identified Jesus as the one he had been speaking about. They have not taken in the subtler aspects of John the Baptist's testimony.

Commentators often point out that 1:29–51 introduces a series of seven christological titles: Lamb of God, Chosen One of God (if this reading is adopted), Rabbi, Messiah, Son of God, King of Israel, and Son of Man. But this obscures the clear distinctions among these "titles." As I have pointed out, "Rabbi" is not a title in the same sense as most of the others. It is a respectful form of address to a religious teacher (cf. 3:2). But neither is "Son of Man," which in John is not a title but rather an enigmatic form of self-reference that Jesus uses to refer to himself in sayings about his future destiny (see below). Furthermore, we should not obscure the distinction between John the Baptist's far-reaching insight into the nature of Jesus's identity and mission, on the one hand, and, on the other hand, the merely conventional notion of a royal Messiah that the disciples express.

John the Baptist's titles for Jesus are never used again in the Gospel. They encapsulate his unique testimony. But the titles used by the disciples in 1:41–49 do recur (see table 7.4). The theme of Jesus's sonship to God his Father recurs frequently throughout the Gospel, mostly on his own lips (the only exception before 20:31 is in Martha's confession in 11:27). The theme of Jesus as King of Israel does not appear after 1:49 until the passion week, where, beginning with Jesus's entry into Jerusalem (12:12–16), it becomes a major part of John's understanding of Jesus's way to the cross. The title "King of the Jews" is highlighted here considerably more than in the other Gospels. Then, in the first part of the Gospel's two-stage conclusion, readers are told that the narrative of the signs has been written "so that you may believe that Jesus is the Messiah, the Son of God, and that through believing you may have life in his name" (20:31). Clearly, the three titles "Messiah," "Son of God," and "King of Israel" are of key importance in this Gospel. But that does not mean that already in chapter 1 the disciples "believe" and "have life in his name" in the sense intended in 20:31. Rather, the titles are introduced in chapter 1 as no more than expressions of common messianic expectation. It takes the rest of the Gospel narrative to transform their significance and fill them with the full meaning that the Gospel finally gives them.

Thus, readers of the first chapter can recognize that the first disciples at first believe no more about Jesus than could easily be expected of them at this stage of the narrative. At the same time, readers who are not reading for the first time can recognize the messianic titles that, they know, the rest of the Gospel will fill with distinctive meaning. They will also see that the disciples themselves take a small step toward this fuller meaning when, on the last day of the first week, they "believed in him" (2:11).

Can Anything Good Come out of Nazareth?

Nathanael's incredulous retort to Philip's claim that "Jesus son of Joseph from Nazareth" was the Messiah—"Can anything good come out of Nazareth?" (1:46)—would no doubt be read by a first-time reader to indicate simply that Nazareth was an insignificant place. Many commentators take this view. It probably makes adequate sense of the words, and it is true that Nazareth was insignificant, like many other villages in Galilee. It probably had only between two and four hundred inhabitants.[80] It goes unmentioned in the Hebrew Bible (which may be because it was a recent settlement, founded only in the wake of the Hasmonean conquest of Galilee), as well as by Josephus and early rabbinic literature.[81] However, the information that the Gospel divulges only at 21:2, that Nathanael's home village was Cana,[82] permits us to see that, as is often the case with this Gospel's topographical information, Nathanael's comment about Nazareth evinces, for a really well-informed reader, rather precise geographical and historical realism. Cana (undoubtedly the modern Khirbet Qana) was nine miles north of Nazareth, and, as we now know from excavations, a larger (about one thousand inhabitants) and certainly more prosperous place than Nazareth.[83] Nathanael's comment expresses the disdain of a prosperous community for its smaller and poorer neighbor. The tone of the remark is probably "more flippant than hostile."[84]

In the broad context of the whole Gospel, Nathanael's question has another level of meaning, a level of which Nathanael and Philip within the story could have no awareness. It is the first of a series of questions about Jesus's origins that runs through the Gospel (see table 7.5). There are also statements on the subject, some made by Jesus himself. In the background to all of these is the Gospel's claim, of which readers were already made very aware in the prologue, that Jesus comes from God—in the sense that he was with God eternally and

---

80. John Dominic Crossan and Jonathan L. Reed, *Excavating Jesus: Beneath the Stones, behind the Texts* (London: SPCK 2001), 34; Jonathan L. Reed, *Archaeology and the Galilean Jesus: A Re-examination of the Evidence* (Harrisburg, PA: Trinity, 2000), 131.

81. Against the highly implausible claim that Nazareth did not exist in the first century (made by some who deny that Jesus himself existed), see Maurice Casey, *Jesus of Nazareth: An Independent Historian's Account of His Life and Teaching* (London: T&T Clark, 2010), 128–31.

82. This surely relates to the prominence of Cana in John's Gospel compared with its complete absence from the other Gospels. The only traditions about the Galilean ministry that John adds to those in Mark (apart from chap. 21) are set in Cana (2:1–11; 4:46–54).

83. C. Thomas McCollough, "City and Village in Lower Galilee: The Import of the Archeological Excavations at Sepphoris and Khirbet Qana (Cana) for Framing the Economic Context of Jesus," in *The Galilean Economy in the Time of Jesus*, ed. David A. Fiensy and Ralph K. Hawkins, SBLECL 11 (Atlanta: Society of Biblical Literature, 2013), 49–74, here 57–74.

84. Keener, *John*, 483.

Table 7.5 Whence Jesus?

Can anything good come from [*ek*] Nazareth? (1:46)

Then the Jews began to complain about him because he said, "I am the bread that came down from [*ek*] heaven." They were saying, "Is this not Jesus, the son of Joseph, whose father and mother we know? How can he now say, 'I have come down from [*ek*] heaven'?" (6:41–42)

[The people said] "Can it be that the authorities know that this is the Messiah? Yet we know where this man is from [*pothen estin*]; but when the Messiah comes, no one will know where he is from [*pothen estin*]." Then Jesus cried out as he was teaching in the temple, "You know me, and you know where I am from [*pothen eimi*]. I have not come on my own. But the one who sent me is true, and you do not know him. I know him, because I am from him [*par' autou*], and he sent me." (7:26b–29)

Others said, "This is the Messiah?" But some asked, "Surely the Messiah does not come from [*ek*] Galilee, does he? Has not the Scripture said that the Messiah is descended from [*ek*] David and comes from [*apo*] Bethlehem, the village where David lived?" (7:41–42)

They [the Jewish leaders] replied [to Nicodemus], "Surely you are not also from [*ek*] Galilee, are you? Search and you will see that no prophet is to arise from [*ek*] Galilee." (7:52)

came into the world from God. So when people say that they "know where this man is from" (7:27) or assume that he comes "from Galilee" (7:41), the irony is that they are ignorant of his true origin beyond this world (cf. 8:23). In 7:41–42, 52, there is very likely another level of irony. John would hardly cite the scriptural expectation that the Messiah would come from Bethlehem (7:42) if he did not believe that it had been fulfilled. He must know, and expect his readers to know, the tradition that Jesus was actually born in Bethlehem, though he grew up in Nazareth and was known as "Jesus of Nazareth." So the characters in the Gospel who think that he comes from Galilee do not even know his human place of birth, let alone his divine origin.

Nathanael, on the fifth day of the first week, is the first person in the Gospel to ask a question about Jesus's origins.[85] Pilate, on the fifth day of the passion

85. John the Baptist alludes to Jesus's preexistence in a riddling way in 1:15, 30, but he does not ask a question.

Jesus answered and said to them [the Pharisees], "Even if I testify on my own behalf, my testimony is valid because I know where I have come from [*pothen ēlthon*] and where I am going, but you do not know where I have come from [*pothen erchomai*] or where I am going." (8:14)

He [Jesus] said to [the Jewish leaders], "You are from [*ek*] below, I am from [*ek*] above; you are of [*ek*] this world, I am not of [*ek*] this world." (8:23)

[The Pharisees said to the man who had been blind] "We know that God has spoken to Moses, but as for this man, we do not know where he comes from [*pothen estin*]." The man answered and said to them, "Here is an astonishing thing! You do not know where he comes from [*pothen estin*], and yet he opened my eyes. . . . If this man were not from God [*para theou*], he could do nothing." (9:29–30, 33)

He [Pilate] entered his headquarters again and asked Jesus, "Where are you from [*pothen ei sy*]?" But Jesus gave him no answer. (19:9)

Compare

[Jesus said] "The wind blows where it chooses, and you hear the sound of it, but you do not know where it comes from [*pothen erchetai*] or where it goes. So it is with everyone who is born of the Spirit." (3:8)

week, is the last person in the Gospel to do so (19:9). Both know that Jesus was supposed to have come from Nazareth (see 19:19). Nathanael's question, unlike those of other Jewish questioners in the Gospel, is not one that presupposes a Jewish belief about where the Messiah will come from. It is simply whether "anything good" can come from Nazareth. The irony is that Jesus is not just "something good," but is the supreme Good (cf. John 7:12; Mark 10:17–18),[86] along with the fact that he does not really come from Nazareth. At a level of which Nathanael is quite unaware, he is right to question whether anything truly good can come from Nazareth—or from any human place. The truly good must come from God. It is perhaps because, in this sense, Nathanael is right, that his dismissive attitude toward Nazareth evidently does not impede Jesus's high assessment of his character (1:47).

Only Pilate, who asks the last question about Jesus's origins, asks Jesus himself the direct question, "Where are you from?" (19:9). This is not a question

---

86. Like the rich man in Mark 10:17–18, those who say of Jesus "he is good" (John 7:12) say more than they realize.

about Jesus's human origins. Pilate is following up the information he has just acquired, that Jesus not only claims to be a king, but also "claimed to be the Son of God" (19:7). Here at last the questions about Jesus's origins, which Nathanael was the first to ask, give way to a knowing question about his more-than-human origins, though Pilate doubtless thinks in pagan terms. Jesus does not answer the question, because he has already said all that Pilate should need to hear (18:37). But readers are reminded, just before Jesus is handed over to be crucified, that he is the Son of God, who came into the world from God. This is the Johannine equivalent of the centurion's confession in Mark (15:39).

Nathanael, Representative of the Renewed Israel (1:45–51)

Like the rest of this narrative of the first week, the story of Nathanael's encounter with Jesus makes good sense purely at the literal level. Jesus greets him with a comment that shows supernatural insight into his character (such as is attributed to Jesus elsewhere in this Gospel [2:23–25; 6:70–71]) (1:47), and Nathanael is, naturally, surprised: "Where did you get your knowledge of me from?" (1:48). Jesus's reply, "I saw you under the fig tree before Philip spoke to you," provides Nathanael with the basis for concluding for himself that Jesus is, as Philip had claimed, indeed the Messiah (1:48–49), even if he does come from Nazareth. It is sometimes said that Jesus's words "I saw you under the fig tree" must be more significant than at first appears, since Nathanael can hardly base his confession of faith on such a trivial instance of supernatural knowledge. But the case is similar to that of the Samaritan woman, who is so impressed that Jesus knows she has had five husbands that she not only concludes he must be a prophet (4:17–19) but also wonders, "He cannot be the Messiah, can he?" (4:29 [cf. 16:30]). It is important to note that, as Barnabas Lindars points out, Nathanael's

> belief has been evoked by Jesus's insight, but the content of it is not derived from it, but from Philip's announcement. From the outset only two alternatives have been open to him—either to believe that Jesus is the Messiah, or to deny it. There is no mediating position, as that Jesus might be a holy man or a prophet.[87]

The next words of Jesus—"Do you believe because I told you that I saw you under the fig tree?"—acknowledge that Nathanael's belief has only a slender

---

87. Lindars, *John*, 119. It is also possible that John's narrative presupposes a Jewish tradition of interpretation of Isa. 11:4, according to which the Messiah was expected to have clairvoyant powers, and which may lie behind Mark 14:65; Luke 22:64; Matt. 26:68.

foundation. Therefore, at the literal level of the story, there is no need to give Nathanael's sitting under the fig tree any more significance than a matter-of-fact observation. All that Nathanael sees in Jesus's insight is that he knows something about him that he could know only by supernatural means.

Later rabbinic references to people studying Torah under fig trees, as well as other trees,[88] are no basis for supposing that this is what Nathanael was doing under the fig tree. In the Palestinian climate, people would doubtless take advantage of the shade of a fig tree to rest or to talk or even to sleep, as well as to read. On the literal level, a fig tree is specified merely because there had to be some specific scene to which Jesus could refer.

I suggest that there is an additional dimension of meaning to the fig tree, but this is plausible only because it can be seen as a coherent part of a pattern of additional meaning to be found also in verses 47, 51, tying together the whole story of Jesus's encounter with Nathanael in a common more-than-literal theme, much as verses 37–45 are unified by the theme of discipleship. In this case the theme is the renewed Israel of the last days, of which Nathanael is here treated as a representative. The most obvious scriptural resonance of "under the fig tree" is with a phrase that occurs several times in the Hebrew Bible: "every man under his vine and his fig tree." Some commentators mention this, correctly observing that it serves as a picture of peace and security (as in the idealistic portrayal of Israel during the golden age of Solomon's rule [1 Kings 4:25]), but they fail to notice that in Micah 4:4 it is used to characterize the messianic age (as also, in a slightly variant form, in Zech. 3:10 [see table 7.6]).[89] It is one way of expressing a common expectation that in the messianic age Israel will have peace and security (e.g., Isa. 65:21–22; Jer. 30:10; 46:27; Ezek. 34:27–28; Zeph. 3:13). Another recurrent expression of this is the standard expression "no one shall make them afraid" (Jer. 30:10; 46:27; Ezek. 34:28; Mic. 4:4; Zeph. 3:13).

Of these texts, the two that are crucial for understanding John 1:47–50 are Zeph. 3:12–13 and Mic. 4:4 (see table 7.6). These two texts are linked not only by the common theme of peace and security in the messianic age, but also by their common use of the expression "no one shall make them afraid"—that is, by the exegetical principle of *gezerah shavah*. These two prophecies account for both Jesus's description of Nathanael ("truly an Israelite in whom there is no deceit") and his sight of Nathanael under the fig tree. The latter corresponds to Mic. 4:4 ("they shall sit, every man under his vine and his fig

88. References in Keener, *John*, 486.
89. In 1 Macc. 14:11–12 Simon Maccabeus is portrayed as a messianic figure who brought about the fulfillment of Mic. 4:4.

tree"), the former to Zeph. 3:13 ("nor shall a deceitful tongue be found in their mouths"), a text that is also echoed in order to characterize the Messiah's followers in Rev. 14:5.[90]

There is no significance (despite most of the commentators) in the fact that Jesus calls Nathanael an Israelite. A Palestinian Jew, speaking of another Jew, would never use the term "Jew." This is a rule of linguistic practice that John always observes, along with the other evangelists, as we have already noted. But it is, of course, significant that Jesus calls Nathanael "truly an Israelite." This use of the adverb *alēthōs* links this description of Nathanael with descriptions of Jesus himself elsewhere: "truly the Savior of the world" (4:42), "truly the prophet that is to come into the world" (6:14), "truly the prophet" (7:40).[91] It indicates that Nathanael really deserves the name "Israelite." This is because he exemplifies the faithful remnant of Israel described by the prophet: "They shall do no wrong and utter no lies, nor shall a deceitful tongue be found in their mouths" (Zeph. 3:13).

Probably the theme that can be said to characterize the whole of this first week of the Gospel is that of messianic fulfillment. John the Baptist's testimony effects, for the first time, the revelation of the Messiah to Israel (1:31). As we shall see, the great event of the last day of this week, Jesus's first sign, signifies the arrival of the messianic age by alluding to the feast of vintage wine that the Lord will make for all peoples, according to Isaiah (25:6). It is not itself yet the abundant life of the messianic age, but it prefigures its proximate coming with the Messiah Jesus. The image of Nathanael under the fig tree is another image of messianic fulfillment, alluding to Micah's prophecy. As the Israelite without guile, he enjoys the peace and security of the people of God in the messianic age. Of course, he does so only symbolically (his actual session under the fig tree was merely a transient feature of entirely ordinary life), but this is why the significance of the fig tree must be understood only as an additional level of its meaning, not as something that Nathanael would have understood on the literal level of the story, which has its own integrity without reference to symbolism.

While the commentators have missed the significance of Zeph. 3:13 for our passage, they have often noted that Nathanael, an Israelite in whom there is no deceit, forms a contrast to the ancestor of the people, Jacob, who famously employed deceit to acquire the paternal blessing that should have been given to his brother Esau.[92] That this contrast is intended seems very likely because, as

90. Here the method of *gezerah shavah* is used to connect Zeph. 3:13 and Isa. 53:9.

91. Note also 8:31 ("truly my disciples").

92. The way in which Jacob bought his brother's birthright (Gen. 25:29–34) cannot be called deceitful. Jacob takes advantage of Esau's extreme hunger, but he does not deceive him. The narrative blames Esau for selling the birthright rather than Jacob for buying it.

Table 7.6 No Deceit under the Fig Tree

For I will leave in the midst of you a people humble and lowly.
They shall seek refuge in the name of the LORD—the remnant of
	Israel;
they shall do no wrong and utter no lies,
nor shall a **deceitful** tongue [*lĕšôn tarmît*] be found in their mouths.
Then they will pasture and lie down,
and **no one shall make them afraid** [*'ên mahărîd*]. . . .
The king of Israel, the LORD, is in your midst;
you shall fear disaster no more. (Zeph. 3:12–13, 15b)

But they shall sit, every man under his vine and under his fig tree,
and **no one shall make them afraid** [*'ên mahărîd*],
for the mouth of the LORD of hosts has spoken. (Mic. 4:4 NRSV
	altered)

But he [Isaac] said [to Esau], "Your brother came **deceitfully** [*bĕmirmâ*],
and he has taken away your blessing." (Gen. 27:35)

Compare

During Solomon's lifetime the people lived (literally, *sat*) in safety, from Dan
even to Beersheba, *every man under his vine and under his fig tree*. (1 Kings
4:25 NRSV altered)

On that day, says the LORD of hosts, every man of you shall invite his neighbor
under his vine and under his fig tree. (Zech. 3:10 NRSV altered)

He [Simon Maccabeus] established peace in the land,
and Israel rejoiced with great joy.
And *each one sat under his vine and his fig tree*,
and **there was none to make them afraid**. (1 Macc. 4:11–12 NRSV
	altered)

But as for you, have no fear, my servant Jacob, says the LORD,
and do not be dismayed, O Israel;
for I am going to save you from far away,
and your offspring from the land of their captivity.
Jacob shall return and have quiet and ease,
and **no one shall make him afraid**. (Jer. 30:10 = 46:27)

we shall see, John 1:51 alludes to Jacob's vision at Bethel, which in the Genesis narrative follows immediately his act of deceit.[93] In fact, the exegetical principle of *gezerah shavah* can be used to link Zeph. 3:13 with the verse in Genesis (27:35) that refers to Jacob's deceit (see table 7.6). The Hebrew word for "deceit" is not the same in the two passages, but both words derive from the same Hebrew root and would be readily recognized as cognate. Thus Scripture itself could be understood to draw the contrast between Jacob the deceiver and the faithful remnant of Israel in whom will be found no deceit. Of course, Jacob deceived his father when he was still Jacob ("the supplanter"), before he was given the name "Israel." The true ancestor of faithful Israel is not Jacob the deceiver, but rather Israel, for whom the covenant promises of descendants and land were renewed after his name was changed (Gen. 35:9–12).

We probably should not conclude that John portrays Nathanael as a new Jacob. Rather, he is a true descendant of Jacob-become-Israel. While sinful Israel in the days of its apostasy might be compared with Jacob, the faithful Israel of the messianic promises corresponds to Jacob-become-Israel (cf. Hosea 12:2–6). It is this people of Israel (not Jacob) that Nathanael represents. He does not do so uniquely, but as one among others, for when Jesus promises him a vision comparable with Jacob's at Bethel, he speaks to all the disciples ("you" is plural in v. 51), not only to Nathanael. John has used the story of this one disciple, Nathanael, to suggest that the disciples of Jesus, already portrayed as his followers in the preceding verses, are also to be the nucleus of the messianic people of God. But just as true discipleship will be possible only after Jesus's death-and-exaltation, so the disciples can really begin to be the Messiah's people only after his death-and-exaltation.

We should now be able to appreciate the parallelism between 1:29, 32 and 1:47–48 (see table 7.7).[94] As in the case of 1:37–38 and 21:20–21, discussed above, the evangelist has used parallel wording to indicate a connection of meaning. In the former passage John fulfills his mission to reveal the Messiah to Israel (1:31) by announcing that Jesus is he, and he authenticates this testimony by recounting a vision that symbolizes Jesus's anointing with the Spirit. In the latter passage Jesus announces that Nathanael is representative of the Israel to whom the Messiah is revealed, the Israel that is beginning to be reconstituted by the revelation of the Messiah, and he authenticates this

93. It is also likely that there is already an allusion to this part of the story of Jacob in 1:31, 33, where John the Baptist says, "I did not know him." Compare Gen. 28:16, where Jacob says, "Surely the LORD is in this place—and I did not know it [or "him"]!" This is suggested by Anthony Tyrrell Hanson, *The Prophetic Gospel: A Study of John and the Old Testament* (Edinburgh: T&T Clark, 1991), 36–37.

94. See Boismard, *Du baptême*, 97–98.

Table 7.7 Israel's Messiah and the Messiah's Israel

John 1:29	John 1:47
The next day	
he [John] sees Jesus	Jesus saw Nathanael
coming towards him	coming towards him
and says,	and says,
"Behold, the Lamb of God,	"Behold, an Israelite indeed,
who takes away	in whom
the sin of the world!"	there is no deceit!"
Tēi epaurion	
blepei ton Iēsoun	*Eiden ho Iēsous ton Nathanaēl*
erchomenon pros auton	*erchomenon pros auton*
kai legei	*kai legei*
Ide ho amnos tou theou	*Ide alēthōs Israēlitēs*
ho airōn	*en hō*
tēn hamartian tou kosmou.	*dolos ouk estin.*
John 1:32	**John 1:48**
I saw the Spirit descending	I saw you under the fig tree
out of heaven like a dove. . . .	before Philip spoke to you.

Note: The translations are mine.

announcement by recounting a vision that symbolizes Nathanael's status as a member of the messianic people. Both visions allude to prophecy: John's to Isa. 11:2, Jesus's to Mic. 4:4. This is a good instance of how something that is not very clear on the surface of the texts, read individually, becomes clearer in the light of the way John creates correspondences between passages. It is a way of adding further dimensions to a text, quite similar to the way the larger scheme of correspondences between the first week and the passion does so.

Jesus as Jacob's Ladder

In 1:50–51 there is a transition in Jesus's words from addressing Nathanael ("you" singular in v. 50) to addressing the group of disciples ("you" plural).

Nathanael is promised a much more adequate basis of faith than the rather trivial example of clairvoyance Jesus provided in 1:48, but the content of the promise is directed to all the disciples in 1:51. This is the first teaching that Jesus gives in the Gospel. It is the first of the twenty-five sayings that are marked out for special attention by the opening formula "Amen, amen, I say to you," and it is the first of the "Son of Man" sayings in which Jesus speaks in an enigmatic, riddling way about his destiny. It is sometimes thought to be problematic because the promise is not fulfilled in the rest of the Gospel narrative. But in fact it is the first of the series of Jesus's prophecies of his coming death-and-exaltation. Only one member of this group of disciples, the Beloved Disciple, actually witnesses Jesus's death on the cross, but they all meet him risen from the dead, demonstrating that his death was his exaltation. The saying in 1:51 uses the language of vision ("heaven opened"), and so it refers not to mere physical sight of Jesus's death and resurrection, but rather to God-given perception of their significance.

That 1:51 alludes to Jacob's dream in Gen. 28:12 is obvious (see table 7.8): of the seventeen words of the saying (following "I say to you"), eight correspond exactly to the Genesis text ("the angels of God ascending and descending on"). Although the church Fathers before Augustine surprisingly missed the allusion,[95] virtually all modern exegetes have recognized it, though a few refuse to see it as decisive for the meaning of the Johannine saying.[96] The exact citation of eight words from the biblical text must mean that the Johannine saying is actually an interpretation of that text. But precisely how the Johannine saying relates to the text of Gen. 28:12–13 is not agreed upon and has been much discussed. In my view, the relationship is very straightforward. Jacob saw the angels ascending and descending on *the ladder* that reached from earth to heaven. Jesus promises the disciples they will see the angels ascending and descending on the *Son of Man*. In other words, "the ladder" in the biblical text is understood as a symbol of "the Son of Man."[97] Some interpreters point out the ambiguity of the word *bō* in the Hebrew text: it could mean "on it" (the ladder) or "on him" (Jacob). The latter interpretation is reported as the view of some rabbis in *Genesis Rabbah* 68.12.[98] These interpreters of John 1:51 conclude therefore that "the Son of Man" in the

95. Bernard, *St. John*, 1:70–72.

96. For example, Bernard, *St. John*, 1:67–69; J. Ramsey Michaels, *The Gospel of John*, NICNT (Grand Rapids: Eerdmans, 2010), 136–38.

97. Commentators who take this view include Herman N. Ridderbos, *The Gospel according to John: A Theological Commentary*, trans. John Vriend (Grand Rapids: Eerdmans, 1997), 93–94; Lincoln, *Saint John*, 122; Keener, *John*, 489–91.

98. Hugo Odeberg, *The Fourth Gospel: Interpreted in Its Relation to Contemporary Religious Currents in Palestine and the Hellenistic-Oriental World* (Amsterdam: Grüner, 1968), 33–34.

Table 7.8 Jesus as Jacob's Ladder

Amen, amen, I say to you, you will see heaven opened and the angels of God ascending and descending upon the Son of Man. (John 1:51 NRSV altered)

And he [Jacob] dreamed, and behold there was a ladder [*sullām*] set up [*muṣṣab*] on the earth ['*arṣâ*], the top of it reaching to heaven; and, behold, the angels of God were ascending and descending on it [*bō*]. And, behold, the LORD stood above it [or: beside him] ['*ālāyw*] and said, "I am the LORD, the God of Abraham your father and the God of Isaac. . . ."
  Then Jacob woke from his sleep and said, "Surely the LORD is in this place—and I did not know it!" And he was afraid, and said, "How awesome is this place! This is none other than the house of God, and this is the gate of heaven." (Gen. 28:12–13a, 16–17 NRSV altered)

And he [Jacob] dreamed and, behold, a ladder [*klimax*] set firmly on the earth, whose top reached into heaven, and the angels of God were ascending and descending on it [*ep' autēs*]. And the Lord rested on it [*epestērikto ep' autēs*] and said. . . . (Gen. 28:12–13a LXX [my translation])

And he [Jacob] dreamed on that night and behold a staircase was set up upon the earth and its head touched heaven. And behold, angels of the Lord were going up and down upon it. And, behold, the Lord was standing upon it. And he spoke with Jacob. . . . (*Jub.* 27.21–22a; trans. O. S. Wintermute, *OTP* 2:109)

Compare

> See, my servant shall prosper;
> he shall be exalted and lifted up [*yārûm wĕniśśā'*], and shall be very
>   high. (Isa. 52:13)

And just as Moses lifted up the serpent in the wilderness, so must the Son of Man be lifted up, that whoever believes in him may have eternal life. (John 3:14–15)

When you have lifted up the Son of Man, then you will realize that I am he. . . . (John 8:28)

[Jesus answered] And I, when I am lifted up from the earth, will draw all people to myself. . . . [The crowd answered] How can you say that the Son of Man must be lifted up? (John 12:32, 34)

Parallel Synoptic Sayings

Amen, I say to you, there are some standing here who will not taste death until they see that the kingdom of God has come with power. (Mark 9:1 NRSV altered)

Amen, I say to you, there are some standing here who will not taste death before they see the Son of Man coming in his kingdom. (Matt. 16:28)

I am, and you will see the Son of Man seated at the right hand of the Power and coming with the clouds of heaven. (Mark 14:62)

Isaianic "Highway" Prophecies

So there shall be a highway [*měsillâ*] from Assyria
for the remnant that is left of his people. . . . (Isa. 11:16a)

A highway [*maslûl*] shall be there, and it shall be called the Holy
Way,
the unclean shall not travel on it, but it shall be for God's people.
(Isa. 35:8)

In the wilderness prepare the way of the Lord,
make straight in the desert a highway [*měsillâ*] for our God. (Isa.
40:3)

And I will turn all my mountains into a road,
and my highways [*měsillōtay*] shall be raised up [for the return of
the exiles]. (Isa. 49:11)

Go through, go through the gates,
prepare the way for the people
build up, build up the highway [*měsillâ*],
clear it of stones,
lift up an ensign over the peoples. (Isa. 62:10)

Johannine text corresponds to Jacob in the Genesis text.[99] However, it is surely the disciples who correspond to Jacob. They are to see the angels ascending

99. For example, Donald A. Carson claims that "on Jacob" is "clearly how John understands Genesis 28:12" (*John*, 163). Unusually, he seems to think that this reading of Gen. 28:12 is correct—that is, the original meaning of the text. He also denies that John 1:51 "draws a

and descending, as Jacob does in Gen. 28:12. To suppose that both Jesus ("the Son of Man") and the disciples correspond to Jacob—Jesus as the one on whom the angels ascend and descend, the disciples as those who see the angels ascending and descending on him—introduces an unnecessary confusion into the postulated exegesis of Gen. 28:12. It is also worth mentioning that the earliest extant interpretations of Gen. 28:12 do not support reading *bō* as "on him." Both the Septuagint and *Jubilees* take the meaning to be "on it"—the ladder (see table 7.8). The alternative reading is not attested until long after the first century CE (in *Genesis Rabbah*), though this is not a decisive argument against the suggestion that John already read the Genesis text in that way.

Other problems attend another suggestion about how John 1:51 relates to Gen. 28:12–13—the suggestion that "the Son of Man' in John corresponds to YHWH in Gen. 28:13. There is a grammatical ambiguity in the Hebrew text here too. It could be read to mean that YHWH stood above the ladder or that he stood beside Jacob. But reading the text in the first of these ways does not facilitate identification of "the Son of Man" with YHWH. Whichever way we read the Hebrew text, it cannot be made to mean that the angels ascend and descend upon YHWH.

Jerome Neyrey, who argues for this interpretation, finds it plausible because he assumes that in the vision promised to the disciples heaven will be opened so that they can see into heaven and the glorious figure of "the Son of Man" in heaven. But this is not the function of the opening of heaven in John 1:51. Rather, it is opened so that the angels can ascend into it and descend from it, just as in Mark 1:10 heaven is opened so that the Spirit can descend from it, in Acts 10:11 it is opened so that the sheet can descend, in Rev. 4:1 it is opened so that John can ascend into heaven, and in Rev. 19:11 so that the Word of God can ride from heaven to earth.[100] Genesis 28:13 can be read (if YHWH stands above the ladder) as a theophany of YHWH in heaven, but John 1:51 does not take up this element of the dream. It confines itself to an interpretation of Gen. 28:12. Neyrey seems to take the words "ascending and descending upon the Son of Man" to mean that the angels "are heavenly courtiers who stream toward the throne of God," but this makes no sense of the movement up and down that is clearly ascribed to them. He further remarks, "They are not traveling to and from earth, for there is no ladder mentioned in 1:51."[101]

---

parallel between Jacob and the disciples," despite his own argument for a comparison between Nathanael and Jacob in 1:47 (pp. 160–61).

100. In Acts 7:55–56 heaven is opened so that Stephen can see into it.

101. Jerome Neyrey, "The Jacob Allusions in John 1:51," *CBQ* 44 (1982): 586–605, here 605. Neyrey writes, "But the ladder, which figures so prominently in Jacob's dream, is not mentioned

This misses the point entirely. The ladder is not mentioned in John 1:51 precisely because "the Son of Man" takes its place as the reality symbolized by the ladder in Jacob's dream.

That in John 1:51 the ladder in Jacob's dream, on which the angels ascend to heaven and descend to earth, is interpreted as a symbol of "the Son of Man" is such a simple and obvious way of understanding the text in relation to its biblical intertext that it is hard to comprehend why scholars have engaged in complex discussions of later Jewish traditions about Jacob and his dream in order to establish other interpretations.[102] Later Jewish traditions, used with care, can be illuminating in relation to the New Testament. They often open up ways in which a Jewish exegete possibly could interpret a text, so that we can consider whether a New Testament author might be adopting that interpretation, whether or not it already existed in an earlier tradition of exegesis. But in this case, the interpretations of Jacob's dream attested in the Targumim and rabbinic literature simply do not fit the New Testament text. But what I have called the obvious way of understanding John 1:51 in relation to Gen. 28:12 may perhaps be made more convincing to those who have dismissed it if we explore it a little further and see how well it coheres with other passages in the Gospel.

The Hebrew word for "ladder" in Gen. 28:12 (*sullām*)[103] is a *hapax legomenon* in the Hebrew Bible, but it derives from the root *sll*, "to lift up" (e.g., Job 19:12; Isa. 57:14) or "to exalt" (e.g., Ps. 68:5; 4Q177 3.10). This verb is more or less synonymous with the Greek verb *hypsoun* ("to lift up, to exalt"), which John uses in three riddling references to Jesus's death (3:14; 8:28; 12:32–34), all of which say that "the Son of Man" will "be lifted up." The ambiguity of the Greek verb enables John to refer at the same time to the physical manner of Jesus's death ("lifted up" on the cross) and to his exaltation to heavenly glory, which, theologically at least, he sees as coincident. In these verses *hypsoun* reflects the use of the Hebrew verbs *rwm* ("to be high, exalted") and *nś'* ("to

in John 1:51. The disciples look directly into heaven, so there is no need for a ladder to mediate between heaven and earth" (p. 589).

102. Because I consider them very unlikely to be relevant to John 1:51, I have not discussed traditions about Jacob's image on the throne of glory that appear in the Targumim with reference to his vision at Bethel. See Christopher Rowland, "John 1.51, Jewish Apocalyptic and Targumic Tradition," *NTS* 30 (1984): 498–507; Martin McNamara, *Targum and Testament: Aramaic Paraphrases of the Hebrew Bible; A Light on the New Testament* (Shannon: Irish University Press, 1968), 146–47; Michèle Morgen, "La promesse de Jésus à Nathanaël (Jn 1,51) éclairée par la haggadah de Jacob-Israël," *RevScRel* 67 (1993): 3–21, here 13–15; Neyrey, "Jacob Allusions," 598, 601–4.

103. It probably referred originally to a staircase rather than a ladder in the modern sense. But in CD 11.17 the word probably refers to a ladder. For possible meanings in Gen. 28:12, see *DCH* 6:163.

lift up") in Isa. 52:13. But John could readily connect these verbs with *sullām* in Gen. 28:12, which he also makes the basis of another saying about "the Son of Man." It follows that John has interpreted the ladder of Jacob's dream as Jesus lifted up on the cross. The ladder is set up on earth and reaches to heaven, which precisely fits John's understanding of the cross as lifting Jesus up from the earth (12:32) and exalting him to heaven.

The angels probably figure in John 1:51 mainly to identify an allusion to Genesis 28:12, but their movement up and down the ladder, between earth and heaven, may well indicate that the crucified-and-exalted Jesus is the way of communication between earth and heaven. It may well be relevant that a word closely related to *sullām* ("ladder") is *mĕsillâ*, which means a "raised highway" and is used in Isa. 40:3 for the highway, the way of the Lord, that John the Baptist, according to the Gospels (John 1:23), prepared, as well as in related Isaianic passages about the highway by which the exiles will return to Zion (Isa. 11:16; 49:11; 62:10; cf. 35:8: *maslûl*) (see table 7.8). These are the passages that probably lie behind Jesus's claim to be "the Way" (John 14:6)—that is, the way to the Father's house. Again, it is the crucified-and-exalted Jesus who is the Way. So it seems likely that John connected the *sullām* of Jacob's dream with the *mĕsillâ* of Isaiah's prophecies of restoration.

Among interpreters of John 1:51, more popular than the identification of "the Son of Man" with the ladder of Jacob's dream has been the identification of him with "the place" of Jacob's dream (Gen. 28:16–17), which Jacob calls "the house of God" and "the gate of heaven" (28:17). The implication, then, is that Jesus is the place of revelation or the place of God's presence.[104] That he is the place of God's presence, fulfilling the meaning of the temple, the house of God, is certainly a theme of the Gospel (cf. 2:19–22; cf. 4:23),[105] but it would be unnecessary and confusing to see it in 1:51 in addition to the identification of the Son of Man with the ladder. John 1:51 is strictly an interpretation of Gen. 28:12 and does not need any other aspects of Jacob's dream at Bethel for its meaning.

John 1:51 can now be understood, therefore, as the first of Jesus's many enigmatic references to his coming death-and-exaltation, and in particular of those in which he speaks of himself as "the Son of Man" (3:13–15; 8:28; 12:32–34; 13:31). Much discussion of 1:51 has been clouded by the assumption that "the Son of Man" in John is a title with specific theological meaning. This

104. For example, Ben Witherington, *John's Wisdom: A Commentary on the Fourth Gospel* (Louisville: Westminster John Knox, 1995), 72–73; D. Moody Smith, *John*, ANTC (Nashville: Abingdon, 1999), 77–78.

105. See Mary L. Coloe, *God Dwells with Us: Temple Symbolism in the Fourth Gospel* (Collegeville, MN: Liturgical Press, 2001). She refers only minimally to 1:51 (pp. 73, 215).

assumption is as much a mistake with regard to "the Son of Man" in John as it is with regard to "the Son of Man" in the Synoptics. It depends on the now untenable view that "the Son of Man" was a messianic title in Second Temple Judaism or on the linguistic fallacy that *what is said about* the Son of Man in a Gospel is what the "title" *means*. Instead, "the Son of Man" should be seen, in John as in the Synoptics, as a distinctive self-designation (meaning no more than "the man") that Jesus adopted when he spoke of his coming destiny.[106] John in particular makes it clear that it was not a recognized title (9:35–37; 12:34). To Jesus's hearers in the narrative and to readers of the Gospel it is enigmatic until we realize that it is a form of solemn self-reference. Only in one instance in John is there an allusion to Dan. 7:13, and in that case (5:27) John indicates this by using the anarthrous form of the expression (*huios anthrōpou*), which is not his usage in the twelve other occurrences of "the Son of Man" in the Gospel but which corresponds literally to Dan. 7:13.

There is one further argument that can confirm the conclusion that in 1:51 John has identified "the Son of Man" with the ladder in Jacob's dream. In addition to *gezerah shavah*, another Jewish exegetical procedure was the use of *gematria*. Hebrew letters also serve as numbers, and so for any Hebrew word it is possible to treat the letters as numbers, to add them up and thus to calculate the numerical value of the word. The use of *gematria* in exegesis then allows the exegete to substitute for a word or phrase in the text another word or phrase that has the same numerical value. I have argued elsewhere that John made use of this technique in the exegesis of Ezek. 47 that lies behind chapter 21 of his Gospel.[107] I see another instance in 1:51. The Hebrew phrase "a ladder set up on the earth" (*sullām muṣṣāb 'arṣâ*), occurring in Gen. 28:12, has the numerical value 558.[108] This is also the numerical value of the phrase "the Son of Man" in Aramaic, the language in which Jesus would have used this expression.[109] This helps to explain how John came to understand this biblical text as a prophecy of Jesus's death-and-exaltation.

106. I agree broadly with the view of Larry W. Hurtado on the use of "the Son of Man" in the Synoptics ("Summing Up and Concluding Observations," in *Who Is This Son of Man? Latest Scholarship on a Puzzling Expression of the Historical Jesus*, ed. Larry W. Hurtado and Paul L. Owen, LNTS 390 [London: T&T Clark International, 2011], 159–77) and think that the same is true of John's Gospel.

107. Bauckham, *Testimony*, 278–80.

108. ס = 60 + ל = 30 + מ = 40 + מ = 40 + צ = 90 + ב = 2 + א = 1 + ר = 200 + צ = 90 + ה = 5.

109. This requires that the phrase be written as בר אנשה, which is one acceptable spelling of the definite/emphatic form (in this period the Aramaic final א can also be written as ה). Thus ב = 2 + ר = 200 + א = 1 + נ = 50 + שׁ = 300 + ה = 5.

Just as John the Baptist's testimony to Jesus points right ahead to Jesus's death and its significance, so this first "saying" of Jesus himself in the Gospel points ahead to his death-and-exaltation. Throughout the continuing narrative the Gospel maintains this strong orientation toward its climax—at least for readers who understand the many enigmatic pointers to Jesus's coming death-and-exaltation. Everything that happens prior to that climax is preliminary and takes its meaning from what is still to come.

So in 1:51 Nathanael, who, along with the other disciples, represents the renewed Israel, is promised a vision comparable with that of his ancestor Jacob. Indeed, it will be the ultimate fulfillment of Jacob's dream and the promises made by God to Jacob at that time. What Nathanael will see—although of course he cannot be supposed to have any understanding of what Jesus means at this point in the narrative—is Jesus crucified-and-exalted, Jesus in the completion of his messianic work. Only then will Nathanael and the other disciples understand what it truly means for Jesus to be the Messiah. It will entail a transformation of what they currently understand by the titles that they attribute to Jesus: Messiah, Son of God, King of Israel. And only then will it also become apparent what it will mean to be the renewed Israel. It is Jesus's death-and-exaltation that will bring about the fulfillment of the biblical prophecies of the restoration of Israel. Nathanael's representative status will then come into its own. This is why, although he does not appear again in the Gospel narrative before chapter 21, it is highly appropriate that he does reappear in 21:2, where he takes part in netting the great catch of fish.

John 1:51 predicts what is elsewhere in the Gospel referred to as the glorification of Jesus—the event that reveals his glory, "glory as of the Father's only Son," as the prologue has already adumbrated (1:14). It is followed by Jesus's first sign, the miracle at Cana, in which Jesus "revealed his glory, and his disciples believed in him" (2:11). This is a kind of preliminary fulfillment of the promise in 1:51, a fulfillment only in the sense that the miracle at Cana, like all of Jesus's signs, itself points ahead to the climactic revelation of Jesus's glory in his death-and-exaltation.

The relationship between 1:51 and 2:1–11 in John's narrative closely resembles the relationship in Mark's narrative between Jesus's promise to the disciples in 9:1 and the narrative of the transfiguration that immediately follows (9:2–8). Like the saying in John 1:51, the saying of Jesus in Mark 9:1 is an "Amen, I say to you" saying,[110] and, like the saying in John 1:51, it promises that some of the disciples will "see": "Amen, I say to you, there are

---

110. The single "Amen" in the Synoptics' version of this formula is always doubled in John's usage, probably to underline its connection with the truth that Jesus speaks and is.

some standing here who will not taste death until they see the kingdom of God come with power" (NRSV altered).[111] This is a prophecy of the parousia, but its placement in the narrative sequence must mean that Mark would have his readers understand the transfiguration as a preliminary fulfillment of it, a foretaste of the glory in which Jesus will come at his parousia. Similarly, in John, the miracle at Cana is a preliminary fulfillment of the prophecy in 1:51, but only as a foretaste of future glory. It seems likely that John has modeled his narrative sequence here on Mark's. The reply of Jesus to the high priest in Mark 14:62 (and parallels) has often been proposed as a Synoptic parallel to the saying in John 1:51. However, in Mark 14:62 Jesus addresses the chief priests, not the disciples. Mark 9:1 corresponds more closely to John 1:51, which is certainly not to say that John 1:51 is a version of it. As an interpretation of Gen. 28:12, it is an entirely different saying, but in its narrative function it resembles Mark 9:1. A further difference is, of course, that whereas Mark 9:1 finds its true fulfillment in the parousia, John 1:51 finds its true fulfillment in Jesus's death-and-exaltation. This is not because John has abandoned the expectation of the parousia or gives it no theological significance (Jesus's last words in John's Gospel are "until I come" [21:23]) but because his focus is on the cross-resurrection-exaltation event, and he designs his entire narrative so that this climax is in view from the beginning and throughout.

The Beginning of the Signs (2:1–11)

A full discussion of this narrative is not possible here, but one common misunderstanding of the significance of the sign needs dispelling. The story has the form of a "pronouncement story" (to use the form-critical term), like those stories in the Synoptic Gospels that lead up to a significant saying of Jesus (e.g., Mark 2:1–12; 3:31–35). It is an unconventional pronouncement story in that the "pronouncement" is made not by Jesus but by the steward (2:10). This is in keeping with the fact that Jesus is not yet a public person and has performed the miracle without the knowledge of most people at the banquet, including the steward. The steward's humorous comment to the bridegroom is therefore ironic in the common Johannine sense. He says something that is not true in the sense in which he means it (the bridegroom has not reserved the best wine until last), but points to a higher truth. It is God who has "kept the good [i.e., the best] wine until now." The time for messianic fulfillment

111. Matthew's version of the saying is closer to John 1:51 in that it promises that the disciples will "see the Son of Man" (16:28), but it is less likely to have been known to John.

has arrived, and God's gift of eternal life, surpassing all his previous gifts to his people, is about to be given.

This saying of the steward is the surest indication readers are given of the significance that the sign has. It shows that the point does not lie in the conversion of water into wine. That is merely the mechanism of the miracle. The point lies in the fact that the wine that Jesus provides is better wine than what has preceded.[112] It follows that the story does not deliver a negative verdict on "Judaism" or the Mosaic dispensation of God's provision for his people (water contrasted with wine), but merely takes for granted what Jews believed about the messianic age: its blessings will surpass all the blessings of Israel's history. The message is that, with Jesus, the expected messianic age is dawning.

The misunderstanding of this story arises from finding symbolism in the wrong place. Expecting John's narratives to be full of symbolism, scholars have supposed that the "six stone water jars for the Jewish rites of purification" (2:6) must indicate that Jesus is replacing a religion of mere outward rites (water) with something very different (wine). But comparison with the other miracle stories in John (see table 3.3) shows that 2:6 is an example of a standard element in these stories. The important point about the jars is their number and capacity, which enable Jesus to provide a huge amount of wine (some 120 gallons), far in excess of the need. This detail emphasizes the marvelous nature of the act, something which is stressed in one way or another in all of the narratives of the signs, while also in this case suggesting the superabundance of God's provision in the messianic age (cf. 10:10). That the jars are "for the Jewish rites of purification" functions merely as an explanation of how there happened to be such large containers available. It is the kind of matter-of-fact point of information that John also makes elsewhere, such as in the narrative of Jesus's crucifixion, when he says that "a jar full of sour wine was standing there" (19:29a). This comment functions merely to explain how it was that someone was able to offer Jesus some sour wine. It has no symbolic value in itself. Similarly, the comment that the jars were "for the Jewish rites of purification" functions merely to explain how so much water could have been readily available for Jesus to transform into wine. (For similar notes of explanation, see 1:44; 3:23; 4:8, 9b; 13:29; 18:2; 19:23b.)

112. This also tells against the view of Judith M. Lieu that the contrast is between "dearth or absence and abundance" ("The Mother of the Son in the Fourth Gospel," *JBL* 117 [1998]: 61–77, here 70–71). It is true that the occasion for the miracle is that they have run out of wine, but there has been plenty of wine. The quality of the wine is the steward's point. But Lieu is right to reject the view that "the rites of purification" have anything to do with the message of the story.

Commentators correctly note that the wedding and the wine are images of the blessings and joy of the messianic age, according to Jewish traditions. But I should like to draw attention to the special relevance of Isa. 25:6–8a:

> On this mountain the LORD of hosts will make for all peoples
> a feast of rich food, a feast of well-aged wines,
> of rich food filled with marrow, of well-aged wines strained clear.
> And he will destroy on this mountain
> the shroud that is cast over all peoples,
> the sheet that is spread over all nations;
> he will swallow up death forever.[113]

Here the provision of the finest wine is linked with the abolition of death. The text provides a scriptural basis for connecting the miracle of Cana, the first of Jesus's signs, with the seventh sign, the resurrection of Jesus from the dead.

That connection is also made by the parallelism of the two weeks: both events occur on the last day of the week in question. In the case of the miracle at Cana, this is indicated by the phrase "on the third day" (2:1). Although this formula is not used in John's Gospel to indicate the day of Jesus's resurrection (but cf. 2:20: "in three days"), versions of it with such a reference are so common in New Testament literature (especially 1 Cor. 15:4; cf. Matt. 16:21; 17:23; 20:19; Luke 9:22; 18:33; 24:7, 46) that John's readers would be likely to recognize that usage.

There is also an important parallelism between 2:11 and 20:30–31:

> Jesus made this beginning [*tautēn epoiēsen archēn*] of the signs, in Cana of Galilee, and revealed his glory; and his disciples believed in him. (2:11 [my translation])

> Now Jesus did many other signs in the presence of his disciples, which are not written in this book. But these are written so that you may believe that Jesus is the Messiah, the Son of God, and that believing, you may have life in his name. (20:30–31 NRSV altered)

The latter passage, coming immediately after the story of Jesus's appearance to Thomas, must presuppose that Jesus's resurrection is the last of the signs. This text therefore indicates the end of the sequence of signs whose "beginning" is signaled in 2:11. The disciples are mentioned in both passages, both

---

113. This passage differs significantly in the LXX. Note that the words immediately following in Isa. 25:8, about the wiping away of tears, are cited with reference to the new creation in Rev. 7:17; 21:4.

recalling the claim in the prologue, "We have seen his glory" (1:14). "We" in that verse are the disciples in whose presence Jesus performed his signs and revealed his glory so that they came to believe in him. The sequence of signs[114] that John has selected from the many that he could have narrated has been chosen so that readers of the Gospel may, like the disciples, believe.

The phrase "beginning of the signs" is also recalled in 15:27: "You also are to testify because you have been with me from the beginning [*ap' archēs*]." The miracle at Cana is the first of the events to which the disciples can testify because it was through this that Jesus first revealed his glory.

Finally, we should note that Jesus performed this miracle before the beginning of his public ministry. Few people other than his disciples even knew that it had taken place. Shortly afterwards, in this Gospel's narrative, Jesus goes up to Jerusalem, where he inaugurates his public ministry to Israel at the heart of Israel, in Jerusalem and its temple (2:13–24). Now he begins to do signs in public, so that "many believed in his name because they saw the signs that he was doing" (2:23). None of the following signs that John narrates, up to and including the raising of Lazarus, are performed only "in the presence of his disciples" (20:30). But the seventh and climactic sign, his resurrection, is again, like the first, witnessed only by the disciples. The public ministry begins in 2:13 and ends in 12:50. The witness of the disciples covers this period but also extends beyond it in both directions. The first sign precedes the public ministry, the seventh follows it.

Conclusion

The Gospel's narrative of its first week (1:19–2:11) is full of beginnings. It contains the following:

the first witness to Jesus, John the Baptist

the first disciples of Jesus

the first occurrence of the Gospel's key christological titles

the first question about Jesus's origins

the first examples of irony

the first words of Jesus

the first "Amen, Amen, I say to you" saying

114. The fact that, after the first sign, only the second is explicitly numbered (4:54) does not indicate a "signs source." It is sufficient to show readers that they should be counting the signs. After the second, they can do so for themselves.

the first "Son of Man" saying
the first predictions of Jesus's death and exaltation
the first of the signs
the first revelation of Jesus's glory
the first reference to Jesus's "hour"
the first references to the Spirit
the first appearance of Jesus's mother

But not only is this a narrative of beginnings. As a result of the multiple ways in which the author has loaded it with more-than-literal meanings, this beginning of the Gospel's narrative also contains, in anticipation, its end.

8

The Johannine Jesus and the Synoptic Jesus

The Four Gospels and the "Real" Jesus

How do the four Gospels, in their respective distinctiveness, relate to "the real Jesus"?[1] It seems that the diversity of the Gospels was a problem virtually from the time when they began to be read as a collection. Arguably, it was already a problem to which Papias of Hierapolis, at the beginning of the second century, was responding, and certainly it was a perceived problem by the end of the second century. One solution to the problem, which remained popular until the modern period, also originated in the second century: the production of a Gospel harmony. Tatian's *Diatessaron* wove the four Gospels into a single continuous narrative. That it did not replace the Gospels in the emerging New Testament canon is significant, as is the fact that Marcion's attempt to canonize just one Gospel, Luke's, was not taken up by the church's canonizing process. The criterion of apostolicity—invoked both against Marcion's reduction of the canon to a single apostle and against the proliferation of Gnostic gospels, only spuriously apostolic—ensured a canon comprising a diversity of witnesses reliably received from the apostolic age. It was no doubt thought that, since the four Gospels were the form that the

1. My use of this term alludes to Luke Timothy Johnson, *The Real Jesus: The Misguided Quest for the Historical Jesus and the Truth of the Traditional Gospels* (San Francisco: Harper-SanFrancisco, 1996).

apostolic witness itself took, they should not be superseded by a secondary compilation, even if it preserved in some way the contents of all four. But the diversity of the Gospels seems to have remained more of a problem than a perceived advantage. Tatian's solution had many successors, especially in the early modern period, when harmonies were not envisaged as replacing the canonical Gospels as authoritative Scripture but must in fact have functioned to supersede the Gospels in the practice of those who used them.

In the patristic period the problem of the diversity of the Gospels seems to have taken the form of such historical discrepancies as differences in the order of events and differences in the parallel accounts of the same event. The most obvious of such problems were found in the differences between the Synoptics and John. The larger problem of diversity in the Gospels' portrayal of Jesus—again most obvious in the contrast between the Synoptics and John—emerged as a major issue only in the nineteenth century, when the anti-dogmatic stance of Liberal scholars made the Fourth Gospel's portrayal of Jesus the least palatable of the four. From the nineteenth-century Liberals to Ernst Käsemann and the Jesus Seminar, John came to be seen as historical fiction in the service of an alien interpretation imposed on the real Jesus. Developments in Gospels studies in the second half of the twentieth century increasingly stressed the diversity of the Gospels' portrayals of Jesus, in line with a relentless insistence on the theological diversity of the New Testament writings. While these developments stressed, more strongly than previously, the distinctiveness of each Gospel, the greatest gulf still looms between the Synoptics and John. It is widely accepted even by those whose evaluation of the Fourth Gospel is strongly positive.

Harmonization—once regarded as desirable, even necessary—has come to be regarded as a practice that critical scholarship should shun, associated as it is with dogmatic conservatism, even fundamentalism. Arguably, much contemporary New Testament scholarship has exaggerated the theological diversity of the New Testament by equating difference with incompatibility or even polemical opposition. The Gospels may be seen as competitive propaganda for versions of the Gospel story that validate the identity of different communities or interest groups. At the same time, overspecialization (such that, for example, Johannine studies seem often to be pursued in complete disregard of Synoptic studies, and vice versa) impedes the kind of competent comparative studies that could produce appropriately nuanced accounts of unity and diversity. Unharmonizable diversity has become a critical axiom that is constantly asserted without adequate study of the evidence.

Yet, while the recent scholarly emphasis on diversity may be exaggerated, few could now be happy with achieving harmony by Tatian's method.

Conflation of the four narratives into one denies each Gospel the integrity of its own distinctive portrayal of Jesus. It creates harmony too soon, before the diversity has even been noticed. Yet the problem remains: how do the four Gospels, in their respective distinctiveness, relate to "the real Jesus"? An alternative solution, of course, is the quest of the historical Jesus in any of its forms or phases. The real Jesus is sought in the historical facts behind the four (or more) Gospel versions of his story. This usually means that whatever is distinctive of each Gospel is stripped away (often along with much else). The process is inevitably reductive and results, just as much as Tatian's solution, in a replacement of the four Gospels. Where harmonization substitutes an artificial conflation for the diverse Gospels, the historical quest substitutes a historical reconstruction for the diverse Gospels. If this reconstruction has any theological interest, then it will be an interpretation of Jesus that parallels and competes with the Gospels' own portrayals of Jesus. (This is certainly not to disallow every kind of historical reconstruction. The fact that the Gospels are undoubtedly a kind of historiography, whatever kind that may be, warrants historical study of them. But their function as canonical Scripture cannot be reduced to that of historical sources.)

The more purely historical a historical reconstruction of "the real Jesus" is, the more obvious it becomes that such a Jesus is bound to be *less than* the Jesus of any of the Gospels. But if "the real Jesus" is the person that the Gospels, in their very diversity as well as their commonality, portray for us and enable us to know, then the real Jesus must be *more than* the Jesus of any of the Gospels. An important function of the plurality of the Gospels is to keep us constantly aware of this. If each of the four is in its own way a valid portrayal of Jesus, then we cannot evade the fact that none is complete, that the perspective of each is just one perspective among several. The "real Jesus" is not in, but beyond, the texts. From various perspectives they point to him, but they do not capture him. Of course, it is always the case that a person is more than any literary portrayal of him or her. Persons exceed and escape any portrayal and any number of complementary portrayals. This would be true of Jesus even if we had only one Gospel. But the plurality of the Gospels requires their readers to recognize this fact. By presenting us with four portrayals that are not harmonized already for us, the texts keep us seeking the Jesus to whom all four portrayals are reliable but not exhaustive witnesses. Seeking "the real Jesus" to whom all four Gospels point us, we cannot rest content with Jesus as a literary character in any of these texts but must seek the living Jesus, who transcends his literary portrayals.

Reading the Gospels in Canonical Relationship

That there should be four different accounts of Jesus, not incompatible but complementary, is in principle entirely possible, but are the character and content of the four Gospels in fact of this kind? In offering some approaches to this issue, I shall focus on the differences between John and the Synoptics, since the Gospel of John is undoubtedly the most distinctive of the four and raises problems that do not arise in the comparison of the Synoptics themselves.[2]

1. The Explicit Incompleteness of the Gospel of John

The extent to which John presupposes traditions about Jesus that he does not record is not often noticed. Whether the evangelist's intention was in some sense to complement one or more of the Synoptic Gospels is not important for our present purposes, though there is quite a strong case to be made for the view that he presupposes that his readers know Mark.[3] It is more important to notice that John's Gospel is explicitly incomplete in aspects that, in the canonical collection of the four Gospels, the Synoptic Gospels supply. Contrary to the assumption made by most contemporary Johannine scholars, this Gospel does not represent itself as the only and sufficient repository and interpretation of the traditions about Jesus. We cannot here appeal to the last verse of the Gospel (21:25), which does not necessarily imply the existence, still less the desirability of other records of Jesus's ministry, but there are several other features of the Gospel that suggest its explicit incompleteness and implicit complementarity.

A. *Other signs*. That Jesus performed many more miracles than the Gospel records is clearly asserted (2:23; 3:2; 4:45; 20:30). The small number of miracles that John narrates (eight, including the walking on the water and the miraculous catch of fish, neither of which the Gospel calls "signs" as it does the other six) contrasts with the much greater number in all of the Synoptics. They have evidently been carefully selected from those known in the traditions: they are the most impressive of their kind (a huge quantity of wine; healing at a distance and at the point of death; lameness that had persisted for thirty-eight years; blindness since birth; food for five thousand people; a man

---

2. On canonical readings of John, see D. Moody Smith, *Johannine Christianity: Essays on Its Setting, Sources, and Theology* (Edinburgh: T&T Clark, 1984), chap. 8; Smith, *The Fourth Gospel in Four Dimensions: Judaism and Jesus, the Gospels and Scripture* (Columbia: University of South Carolina Press, 2008), chaps. 15–16.

3. Richard Bauckham, "John for Readers of Mark," in *The Gospels for All Christians: Rethinking the Gospel Audiences*, ed. Richard Bauckham (Grand Rapids: Eerdmans; Edinburgh: T&T Clark, 1997), 147–71.

already dead three days) and in the variety of symbolic meaning that they offer (wine; healing on the Sabbath; blindness and sight; bread; life for the dead [see table 3.3]). But they are also representative. Most Synoptic miracles, with the exception of exorcisms,[4] could easily be classified as similar in kind to one or more of the Johannine "signs." Thus John's extreme selectivity, which allows him the scope to narrate each sign at greater length than most Synoptic miracle stories and to expound the meanings of the signs in discourses and dialogues attached to them, should not be understood as excluding other miracle stories that his readers know, but rather as representing them. Readers who learn from this Gospel the Johannine manner of understanding the meaning of Jesus's miracles will have no difficulty in reading other miracle stories in the same way.

B. *Teaching the crowds.* It is sometimes remarked that, unlike the Synoptic (and especially the Matthean and the Lukan) Jesus, the Johannine Jesus is not a teacher. He teaches his disciples at length in the Farewell Discourse, but in the chapters that describe his public ministry his words are largely debate, often with the Jewish authorities, sometimes with the crowds, about his mission and his identity, which are also the subject on the rather rare occasions on which he takes the initiative in speaking (e.g., 7:37–38; 8:12; 10:1–18)[5] rather than responding to questions and criticisms.[6] The kind of teaching to the crowds, as well as to the disciples, that is familiar from the Synoptics is largely lacking in John. Yet it is presupposed by references to Jesus as "Rabbi" (which John explains as meaning "Teacher" [1:38]) or "Teacher" (1:38; 3:2; 6:25; 9:2; 11:28; 20:16) and to Jesus teaching a general audience in both the temple and synagogues (7:14; 18:19–21). It is unlikely that the teaching that 7:14 represents Jesus as giving, which astounds the Jewish authorities with its learning (7:15) and which Jesus then defends as teaching from God (7:16–18),

4. A possible explanation of the lack of exorcisms in John is that all the signs are understood as events in the physical realm that symbolize salvation in the spiritual realm. Exorcisms would not easily fit this pattern. John reserves the language of exorcism for Jesus's definitive victory over the devil at Jesus's death-and-exaltation (12:31; 14:30; 16:11). See Ronald A. Piper, "Satan, Demons and the Absence of Exorcisms in the Fourth Gospel," in *Christology, Controversy, and Community: New Testament Essays in Honour of David R. Catchpole*, ed. David G. Horrell and Christopher M. Tuckett, NovTSup 99 (Leiden: Brill, 2000), 253–78; Graham H. Twelftree, "Exorcisms in the Fourth Gospel and the Synoptics," in *Jesus in Johannine Tradition*, ed. Robert T. Fortna and Tom Thatcher (Louisville: Westminster John Knox, 2001), 135–43; Tom Thatcher, *Greater than Caesar: Christology and Empire in the Fourth Gospel* (Minneapolis: Fortress, 2009), 116–22.

5. Note that this speech seems to be addressed to the Pharisees of 9:40.

6. The "discourse" of 6:32–58 has some characteristics of a sermon expounding scriptural texts, but it takes the form of a rather polemical dialogue. It is the crowd that proposes the principal text that Jesus expounds (6:31).

had the kind of content that the Johannine discourses and dialogues themselves attribute to Jesus. Their intense christological focus is the aspect of Jesus's ministry that John has selected for attention and exposition in line with his Gospel's purpose (20:31). But it does not in any way disallow or denigrate, rather it explicitly leaves space for, Gospels with other and broader purposes to recount the traditions of Jesus's teaching.

C. *Galilean ministry.* One of the most obvious differences between John and the Synoptics is that most of the former's account of Jesus's public ministry is located in Jerusalem and only a relatively small amount in Galilee (4:43–54; 6:1–7:1).[7] Yet John's own chronology (see 6:4; 7:2) makes it clear that about six months are covered by the uninformative statement "After this Jesus went about in Galilee" (7:1a).[8] This is as long as the period in which all the events narrated from 7:2 to the end of the Gospel take place. Clearly, John's narrative does not displace the rich traditions about Jesus's ministry in Galilee that his readers know from other sources; rather, it leaves an explicit place for them. (John's own concentration on Jerusalem is no doubt at least partly due to his focus on Jesus's debate with and escalating conflict with the Jewish authorities in Jerusalem.) Conversely, as has often been noted, Matthew and Luke imply visits to Jerusalem by Jesus prior to the only one they narrate (Matt. 23:37; Luke 13:34).

D. *Other Johannine omissions.* At least three other Synoptic events—all of key importance in the Synoptic narratives of Jesus—are not simply absent in John, but notable precisely by their absence. In the first place, the baptism of Jesus, not narrated, is presupposed as prior to the start of John's narrative by John the Baptist's reference to what he had seen (1:32). Second, the Twelve appear for the first time in the Gospel at 6:67, without explanation and with no account of their appointment as a group of twelve by Jesus. Third, a place for the trial before Caiaphas is left vacant in John's narrative, which contrives to say nothing at all of what happens to Jesus after he is taken to Caiaphas and before he is taken from Caiaphas to Pilate (18:24, 28).

E. *Ethical teaching.* In 14:15 and 15:10 Jesus refers to his "commandments" (plural) that the disciples must keep. Elsewhere in the Farewell Discourse he gives them "a new commandment" (singular) (13:34; 15:12; cf. 15:17): to love one another as he has loved them. It is not obvious to what the plural "commandments" refers. The only commandment, besides the "new" command to love one another, that Jesus in this Gospel gives the disciples is the

---

7. John 2:1–12 precedes the beginning of the public ministry.
8. No doubt some period of ministry in Galilee is implied between 4:54 and 5:1, but it is not possible to tell how long.

command to wash one another's feet (13:14–15), clearly an instance of loving one another as Jesus has loved them. But readers of John who know other Gospels or Gospel traditions will surely think, when they read of Jesus's commandments (14:15; 15:10), of the ethical teaching of Jesus in passages such as the Matthean Sermon on the Mount or the Lukan Sermon on the Plain. Such teaching is summed up by the Johannine Jesus in the one command to love one another as he has loved his own, just as it is by the Synoptic Jesus in the command to love one's neighbor as oneself. The Johannine summary in the "new commandment" gives a particular—christological and ecclesial—interpretation to the ethical teaching of Jesus, but it need not make the Synoptic sayings of this type redundant. The references to "commandments" (14:15; 15:10) provide, as it were, a Johannine rubric under which sayings of Jesus not recorded by John may be placed. (Admittedly, this does not illuminate the contrast between the universal love required by the Synoptic Jesus and the community love required by the Johannine Jesus.)

2. Exposition of Selected Motifs in the Fourth Gospel

We have already noticed that, in comparison with the Synoptics, the Gospel of John is highly selective in the events that it includes in its account of Jesus's ministry. The same can be said of themes in the teaching of Jesus. It is not really the case that what the Johannine Jesus says is completely different from what the Synoptic Jesus says. Rather, particular themes that may occur only briefly and without extensive development in the Synoptics are selected for fuller exposition in John. These are especially themes with christological implications, but not only those, as the following examples will show.

A. *Prayer.* The Synoptic saying "Ask and it will be given you" (Matt. 7:7a; Luke 11:9a) is the text that is interpreted by the Johannine Jesus's teaching on prayer (14:13–14; 15:7, 16; 16:23–24).

B. *The Paraclete.* The Paraclete sayings in John (14:16–17, 25; 15:26–27; 16:7–14), along with the context of persecution (15:18–16:4), are developments of the Synoptic Jesus's promise that when the disciples are persecuted and brought to trial, the Spirit will enable them to bear testimony (Matt. 10:17–20; Mark 13:9–11; Luke 21:12–15).[9] The latter is the only context in which the Synoptic Jesus speaks during his ministry of the role of the Spirit with his disciples after his resurrection. The term "Paraclete" itself most likely reflects the courtroom context of this Synoptic teaching, and so the intertextual connection between the Paraclete passages in John and these

---

9. Gary M. Burge, *The Anointed Community: The Holy Spirit in the Johannine Tradition* (Grand Rapids: Eerdmans, 1987), 205–8.

Synoptic passages explains the fact that this term for the Spirit is limited in John to these passages in chapters 14–16.

C. *Eternal life*. The explanation for the oft-remarked absence of the term "kingdom of God" from John (only in 3:3, 5), by comparison with its prominence as the central theme of Jesus's message in the Synoptics, is that "eternal life" or "life" is the Johannine substitute for it. The beginning of Jesus's conversation with Nicodemus is designed precisely to make this clear to the reader. By means of the saying "No one can see the kingdom of God without being born from above" (3:3 [with variation in v. 5]), the Johannine Jesus effects a transition from "the kingdom of God" to "eternal life" (3:15–16). Entry into the kingdom is by means of birth from above or from the Spirit, but the purpose and consequence of birth is life. Seeing the kingdom—or, at least, the aspect of it on which this Gospel focuses—is thus equivalent to eternal life. From now on, the Gospel thus indicates to its readers, the subject of "the kingdom of God" will be developed under the aspect of the "life" or "eternal life" that Jesus gives. Nor is this transposition in terminology without warrant in the Synoptic traditions themselves: in Mark 9:43–48, the phrase "enter into life" (vv. 43, 45) is used in parallel with "enter the kingdom" (v. 47). The Gospel of John can therefore be seen as selecting and developing this aspect of the kingdom of God. Thus, in John, all of Jesus's miracles signify, in different ways, the eternal life that Jesus will give, just as in the Synoptics the miracles are indications of the kingdom of God that is coming through Jesus. The contrast between the Synoptics and John at this point is not, as often supposed, between the significance of the miracles for the coming of the kingdom in the Synoptics and the christological significance of the miracles in John. In the Synoptics too the miracles raise the question of Jesus's own identity (Matt. 11:3–6; Mark 2:6–10; 4:41); John simply makes this more explicit and emphatic. The real difference is that in the Synoptics the miracles relate to the kingdom of God and to Jesus as the one who inaugurates the kingdom, while in John they relate to eternal life and to Jesus as the one who gives eternal life.

D. *Christological terms and titles*. It is often noticed that the Johannine Jesus talks much more about himself than the Synoptic Jesus does. It is less often noticed that the terms and titles that the Johannine Jesus uses correspond closely to those that the Synoptic Jesus uses. Like the Synoptic Jesus, the Johannine Jesus never calls himself "Messiah" (with the one exception: 17:3; comparable with the Synoptic exceptions: Matt. 23:10; Mark 9:41), although others and the narrator do, as they do in the Synoptics. Like the Synoptic Jesus, the Johannine Jesus uses the enigmatic term "the Son of Man" of himself, almost always in riddling references to his coming death and resurrection, which is one category of the Synoptic usage. Rarely does the Johannine Jesus call himself "the Son of God" (5:25; 10:36; 11:4; cf. 3:16), but he frequently speaks of himself as "the Son" in relation to "the Father." This too corresponds to Synoptic usage, though the latter is limited to two sayings (Matt. 11:27; 24:36; Mark 13:32; Luke 10:22; but cf. also Matt. 28:19). In other words, when the Johannine Jesus speaks of his unique relationship with the Father, as he does often, he does so in the same terms as the Synoptic Jesus does, on the rare occasions when he does. Like the Synoptic Jesus, the Johannine Jesus always addresses God as "Father."

E. *The Son sent by his Father*. John's "agency Christology" combines the idea that Jesus is the Son of his Father with the idea that he has come into the world as his Father's agent, commissioned and sent by the Father to represent the Father and to accomplish his Father's work. Both ideas—Jesus is the Son of his Father, and Jesus has been sent as God's agent—occur in the Synoptics, the latter rather more often than the former (see Matt. 10:40 [a saying that actually occurs in John: 13:20]; 15:24; Mark 9:37; Luke 4:18, 43; 9:48; 10:16).[10] The two ideas of sonship and agency come together in the Synoptics only in parabolic form in the parable of the vineyard (Matt. 21:37; Mark 12:6; Luke 20:13). But most of the Johannine Jesus's lengthy exposition of the meaning of his sonship to the Father can easily be read as exposition of these three Synoptic sayings: about the Son and the Father (Matt. 11:27; Luke 10:22), about Jesus as the one sent by God (Matt. 10:40; Luke 10:16), and about the son sent by the father to the tenants of his vineyard (Matt. 21:37; Mark 12:6; Luke 20:13). Once again it is in the selection and concentrated exposition of a theme, not in the theme itself, that John is different.

F. *"I have come" sayings*. Another way in which the Johannine Jesus characteristically expresses his mission from God is in sayings to the effect that he "has come" from God (8:42; 16:28), in his Father's name (5:43), "into the world" (9:39; 12:46; 16:28; cf. 3:19), and for specific purposes (9:39; 10:10; 12:27, 46, 47; 18:37). This way of speaking of his mission is characteristic also of the Synoptic Jesus (Mark 1:38; Mark 2:17//Matt. 9:13//Luke 5:32; Mark 10:45//Matt. 20:28; Matt. 5:17; Matt. 10:34//Luke 12:51; Matt. 10:35; Luke 12:49; 19:10).[11] In the Synoptics these are always statements of the purpose for which Jesus has come. But they are also alternative ways of saying that God sent him, and so the Johannine interpretation that he has come from

---

10. Note also Luke 14:17, where the messenger in the parable could be taken to represent Jesus. On these Synoptic sayings about Jesus's being sent, see Simon J. Gathercole, *The Preexistent Son: Recovering the Christologies of Matthew, Mark, and Luke* (Grand Rapids: Eerdmans, 2006), 177–89.

11. Note also the words of the demons in Matt. 8:29//Mark 1:24//Luke 4:34.

God his Father is not unnatural. Arguably, the Synoptic sayings also imply Jesus's preexistence,[12] and in that case John's characteristic expansion of "I have come" into "I have come into the world" makes explicit what is implicit in the Synoptic sayings. In any case, John is developing a Synoptic theme.

G. *"I am" sayings.* Most distinctive of the Christology expressed by the Johannine Jesus are the two sets of seven "I am" sayings (see table 8.1).[13] These are the "I am" sayings with predicates ("I am the bread of life," etc.), and the absolute "I am" sayings, which either by double entendre or less ambiguous reference echo the divine self-declaration ("I am he") in Deut. 32 and Isa. 40–55.[14] (They do not, as is sometimes argued, represent the divine Name itself.) The absolute "I am" sayings declare who Jesus is in his divine identity, while the "I am" sayings with predicates declare what he is in his salvific work as the one who gives eternal life. The absolute "I am" sayings correspond to and give a Johannine interpretation of the "I am" of Mark 6:50 (//Matt. 14:27), a saying that appears in John (6:20) as one of John's seven. It is arguable that in Mark 6:50 and 14:62 (cf. also 13:6) Mark himself presents Jesus's ambiguous "I am" sayings as implicit echoes of the divine self-declarations in Deuteronomy and Isaiah. John merely extends the category and, in some cases, eliminates the ambiguity.

All the "I am" sayings with predicates are christological interpretations of parabolic actions (6:48; 11:25) or parabolic sayings of Jesus (8:12; 10:7, 11; 14:6; 15:1), most of which occur in the Synoptics (for the parabolic sayings, see Mark 4:21; Matt. 5:14–16; Matt. 18:12–13//Luke 15:3–6; Matt. 7:13–14//Luke 13:23–24). At this point those who are used to studying the Synoptics without reference to John may well question the legitimacy of John's christological reading of these aspects of the Jesus traditions. It is perhaps the most remarkable aspect of the christological concentration common to the whole Gospel of John (which can be observed even in category 1 above). But for a canonical reading of the four Gospels, John can be read as making explicit—or bringing to light and to full expression—the Christology implicit in the Synoptics. That the salvation Jesus gives is inseparable from Jesus himself and his divine identity is implied in the whole of each Synoptic portrayal of Jesus.

H. *Anguish in the face of death.* It may seem surprising to treat Jesus's spiritual struggle in Gethsemane as a Synoptic motif on which John enlarges, since

12. Gathercole, *Preexistent Son*, 148–70.

13. For discussion, see Richard Bauckham, *The Testimony of the Beloved Disciple: Narrative, History, and Theology in the Gospel of John* (Grand Rapids: Baker Academic, 2007), 243–50.

14. The definitive study is Catrin H. Williams, *I Am He: The Interpretation of 'Anî Hû' in Jewish and Early Christian Literature*, WUNT 2/113 (Tübingen: Mohr Siebeck, 2000).

Table 8.1 The "I Am" Sayings

Seven "I Am" Sayings with Predicates in John

I am the bread of life (6:35, 41, 48)
I am the light of the world (8:12; cf. 9:5)
I am the gate for the sheep (10:7, 9)
I am the good shepherd (10:11, 14)
I am the resurrection and the life (11:25)
I am the way and the truth and the life (14:6)
I am the true vine (15:1)

Seven Absolute "I Am" Sayings

4:26
6:20
8:24
8:28
8:58
13:19
18:5 (repeated in vv. 6, 8)

"I Am He" in the Hebrew and Septuagint Greek Bible

Hebrew (MT)
'ănî 'ănî hû' (Deut. 32:39)
'ănî hû' (Isa. 41:4; 43:10, 13; 46:4; 48:12; 52:6)
'ānōkî 'ānōkî hû' (Isa. 43:25; 51:12)

Greek (LXX)
egō eimi (Deut. 32:39; Isa. 41:4; 43:10; 45:18)
egō eimi egō eimi (Isa. 43:25; 46:4; 51:12)

"I Am" Sayings in Mark

6:50 (= John 6:20)
14:62

the Gethsemane narrative itself is absent from John's passion narrative,[15] but John in fact depicts Jesus in deep distress at the prospect of his approaching passion at three earlier points: in the story of the raising of Lazarus (11:33, 35, 38), at the end of his public ministry (12:27), and at the Last Supper, before predicting his betrayal (13:21). In chapter 11, with its exceptional stress on Jesus's emotions, the point is that Jesus knows that his raising of Lazarus from death is going to provoke the course of events that will lead to his death. His sympathy with the bereaved is mixed with anguish on his own behalf. In order to help the family he loves by restoring their brother, he must initiate the process of his own suffering and death. (In this way, John depicts the raising of Lazarus as the event that prefigures Jesus's willingness to die for the sake of those he loves [cf. 10:11–18; 13:1–3].) In the case of 12:27, it is not legitimate to contrast the Synoptics with John, in the sense that the Synoptic Jesus asks the Father to save him, whereas the Johannine Jesus raises the possibility of such a prayer only to reject it. The latter's question, "What should I say— 'Father, save me from this hour'?" asked in great distress, really entertains the possibility that it raises. It is out of real struggle, depicted in this question, that Jesus submits to what he knows to be the divine purpose for him. Conversely, in the Synoptics, Jesus's prayer in Gethsemane is accompanied from the start by his acceptance of the Father's will ("not what I want, but what you want"). The impression that the Synoptic Jesus has to struggle long and hard with accepting the Father's will, whereas the Johannine Jesus resolves any struggle as soon as it comes into view, results from isolating 12:27 as John's equivalent to Gethsemane and ignoring the fact that the Johannine Jesus's anguish at the prospect of the passion begins in chapter 11 and continues through 13:21, where the anguish accompanies a further step in Jesus's active acceptance of God's will for him: his sending Judas away to do what he must.

I. *Voluntary death*. It is often said that in the Johannine passion narrative Jesus is depicted as in sovereign control of the situation, voluntarily and deliberately laying down his life, as though this were a contrast with the Synoptics.[16] In reality, it is a feature of the Synoptic passion narratives that receives especial emphasis in John. In Mark it is clear that Jesus knows of the fate to which he is traveling when he goes to Jerusalem (2:20; 8:31; 9:31; 10:33–34; 12:6–8; 14:8, 18–21, 24, 27). That Jesus voluntarily embraces this God-given destiny is displayed in Mark especially when, after struggling with and accepting God's will in Gethsemane, he wakes the disciples by announcing, "The hour has come. . . . Get up, let us

---

15. Thus Smith can write, "The tragic dimensions of Jesus' death, his own anguish and suffering in the face of it, are largely absent in John" (*Johannine Christianity*, 179).

16. See, for example, Smith, *Johannine Christianity*, 179.

be going. See, my betrayer is at hand" (14:41–42 [cf. Matt. 26:45–46]). Instead of fleeing, he goes deliberately to meet his betrayer. It is no accident that these seemingly insignificant words, "Get up, let us be going," occur also, word for word, in John 14:31, following Jesus's assertion that he goes to his death not because the devil has power over him, but because he obeys the Father's command. The words from the tradition are cited by John as an indication that Jesus went voluntarily to his death. By comparison with Mark, the theme is heightened, in different ways, by both Matthew and Luke. Matthew's Jesus meets Peter's attempt to save him from arrest by pointing out that, if he chose, in defiance of his scriptural destiny, he could ask the Father to send an army of angels to his aid (26:53–54). Luke's Jesus sets his face to go to Jerusalem (9:51) in deliberate fulfillment of the destiny that he knows he must accomplish (13:32–33). John's further development of the theme consists especially in placing before the whole passion narrative an emphatic declaration by Jesus that he is going to lay down his life for others in obedience to his Father (10:11–18). The sense in which his death is voluntary is that he chooses to go to Jerusalem, walking with open eyes into mortal danger, since he knows that the opposition of the authorities is now such as to ensure his death if they can. Then, whereas on previous occasions he has eluded arrest, he now goes to meet it (13:31; 18:1).

In summary, the foregoing sections on "The Explicit Incompleteness of the Gospel of John" and "Exposition of Selected Motifs in the Fourth Gospel" indicate, respectively, how John may be read in the light of the Synoptics and how the Synoptics may be read in the light of John. In neither process is the distinct integrity of each Gospel violated. The intertextual readings are additional to intratextual reading of each Gospel.

3. Incarnational-Revelatory Christology in the Gospel of John

In the preceding sections we have noticed many of the specific divergences between the Synoptics and John in their respective portrayals of Jesus. But is not the overall impression that the Gospel of John gives of Jesus irreconcilable with the Synoptics? Has not this Gospel's incarnational interpretation of Jesus robbed him of the human reality he has in the Synoptics? Does not this Gospel, the only one explicitly to use the word "God" of Jesus, allow his divinity to crowd out his humanity? In contrast to the Synoptics, is the Johannine Jesus, in Ernst Käsemann's oft-quoted phrase, "God walking the earth,"[17] his human features no more than a temporary costume that he has donned for the purpose?

17. Ernst Käsemann, *The Testament of Jesus: A Study of the Gospel of John in the Light of Chapter 17*, trans. Gerhard Krodel (London: SCM, 1968), 7.

The reply has often enough been made that the Gospel of John actually does lay some stress on both Jesus's human physicality (4:6–7; 19:28) and his human emotions (11:33, 35, 38; 12:27; 13:21). He has particular human affections for friends (11:5; 13:23), while his Farewell Discourse to the disciples, with its concern to console them for the suffering awaiting them, is a sustained expression of sympathy. In view of this, it is hard to see how his "emotional responses," "noticeably different from those ascribed to him in the other gospel narratives," convey "a sense of distance and aloofness."[18] If he acts and speaks with authority, so does the Synoptic Jesus. Jan du Rand maintains that "his emotions and conduct are motivated by his missionary"—or, as he also says, "professional"—"convictions."[19] This is an odd way of putting what is surely equally true of Jesus in all the Gospels: his whole life is given over to fulfilling the mission that he has from the Father. This is no less true of the "compassion" for the crowds and the sick that the Synoptic Gospels ascribe to Jesus than it is of the "love" that Jesus shows for his disciples in the Gospel of John. In both cases Jesus's emotional attitude stems from his relationship with the Father and belongs to his mission to enact God's love for the world. Within this overall perspective on Jesus's mission (cf. 1:14, 17; 3:16) it need not be significant that none of the five miracles of healing and provision that Jesus performs before the raising of Lazarus is said by John to be motivated by compassion. This motive would not be inconsistent with the Johannine angle on the purpose of the miracles: to reveal God's and Jesus's glory (2:11; 11:4, 40), since it is in Jesus as "full of grace and truth" that God's glory is seen (1:14) in the incarnation. Even in the Gospel of John Jesus does not perform mere conjuring tricks as proofs of his divinity; rather, his miracles meet human needs in order to show not only God's power but also God's love.

At the heart of the claim that John's Jesus is divine in a way that contradicts the Synoptic portrayal lies the peculiarly Johannine development of the idea of Jesus's "glory" and its relation to the passion narrative. The issue is very important because it is decisive for the way we understand what is doubtless the most distinctive aspect of John's Christology: the incarnation as revelation of God, Jesus as the one in whom we see God's glory. Käsemann takes glory to be the opposite of the suffering and humiliation that characterize the passion in the Synoptic Gospels.[20] Since the glory of Jesus is manifested from

18. Jan A. du Rand, "The Characterization of Jesus as Depicted in the Narrative of the Fourth Gospel," *Neot* 19 (1985): 18–36, here 29.

19. Du Rand, "Characterization," 29.

20. The influence of Martin Luther's contrast between a "theology of glory" and a "theology of the cross" should probably be surmised. Mark's Gospel is often, correctly, seen to embody a theology of the cross, while "glory" is obviously a dominant theme in John. If one works with

the beginning of John's story (rather than in the resurrection), the passion becomes a problem, which John is supposed to have solved by transforming it into glory. Instead of humiliation, the cross becomes a triumph for Jesus. However, more attentive reading of the Fourth Gospel[21] will find that only by turning Käsemann's view on its head can justice be done to John's passion narrative. What John has done is not to dissolve the passion in glory, but to redefine God's glory by seeing the suffering and the humiliation of the cross as the high point of its revelation.[22] It is remarkable that Käsemann can claim that the passion narrative, "apart from a few remarks that point ahead to it," appears only at the end of the Gospel, like "a mere postscript."[23] In fact, in no other Gospel is there so much reference to the cross throughout the story, for those who can penetrate the riddles in which Jesus refers to it (1:29, 36, 51; 2:17–22; 3:14; 6:51, 62; 7:33, 39; 8:21, 28; 10:11, 15, 17–18; 11:51; 12:7–8, 23–24, 32–33). If Jesus's glory begins to be manifested from the start, it is also true that the shadow of the cross falls across the narrative from the start. The issue of their paradoxical coincidence is in view from the start, though only resolved at the end.

That the Johannine passion narrative would have been read by its early readers as a narrative of triumph rather than as a narrative of abject humiliation is intrinsically very unlikely. Everyone in the ancient world knew that crucifixion was an excruciatingly painful way to die, and that—even more important for the social values of the time—the most shameful way to die, the fate of slaves, enemies of the state, and others who were treated as subhuman, deserving of this dehumanizing fate. This is why none of the Gospel narratives needs to say explicitly that Jesus suffered physical pain or to point out the humiliation of such a death. The mere telling of the familiar tale of events entailed in death by crucifixion—familiar to people from observation, though rarely recounted in ancient literature—was more than enough to convey the agony and the shame. There are in fact as many references to physical violence against Jesus in John as in the Synoptics (a little noticed fact[24] that betrays how easily a prejudice about the difference between John and the Synoptics can blind readers to what the texts themselves say). John depicts the mockery of Jesus before the

---

a contrast between a "theology of the cross" and a "theology of glory," it may be all too easy to polarize Mark and John in these terms.

21. See chap. 3, "Glory."

22. Cf. Rudolf Bultmann: "The δόξα becomes apparent precisely in the cross" (*The Gospel of John: A Commentary*, trans. G. R. Beasley-Murray, ed. R. W. N. Hoare and J. K. Riches [Oxford: Blackwell, 1971], 524).

23. Käsemann, *Testament*, 7.

24. I owe it to Helen C. Orchard, who provides the evidence (*Courting Betrayal: Jesus as Victim in the Gospel of John*, JSNTSup 161 [Sheffield: Sheffield Academic Press, 1998], 192–94).

crucifixion but not the mockery of Jesus on the cross that the Synoptics also have. However, he has a more powerful means of stressing the humiliation of the cross. His passion narrative begins with Jesus's washing of the disciples' feet. No action was more characteristically and exclusively that of a slave. Jesus adopts the role of a slave on the way to his death by the form of execution reserved for slaves. The footwashing signifies the voluntary self-abasement that took Jesus to the ultimate humiliation of the cross. Of course, John has Jesus ironically proclaimed king, in the title on the cross, at the same time as he dies like a slave, while after his death he receives a burial fit for a king. But the irony does not mean that the glory cancels the shame. Only through a reversal of values in which kingship acquires a different meaning from that assumed by Pilate and the chief priests can the paradox be resolved. God's glory and Christ's kingship embrace the pain and the humiliation of the cross in such a way that their true nature is thereby revealed as self-giving love—or "grace and truth" (1:14), John's version of the Old Testament's classic revelation of the character of God ("abounding in steadfast love and faithfulness").

Luke Timothy Johnson characterizes the difference between the Jesus of John and the Jesus of the Synoptics thus: Jesus "in John appears as more a symbolic than a literal figure. He bears the narrative burden of revealing God in the world."[25] He means that John's Jesus in his humanity signifies God in the world, and that John's Jesus, unlike the Jesus of the Synoptics, explicitly claims this. However, Jesus's "symbolic" function, as revelation of God, would be meaningless unless Jesus were also a "literal" figure. To the extent that the symbolic replaces the literal, it is self-defeating. For those who suppose that this happens in John's Gospel, Jesus reveals only that he is the revealer of God.[26] But then there is no revelation, only an empty tautology. Only if Jesus retains his human particularity and story—only in his miracles, his human emotions and relationships, his suffering and humiliation in his death, his resurrection: the story that John shares with the Synoptics—can Jesus be the revelation of God. The glory is revealed in the flesh, which could not occur were the glory to overwhelm the flesh or be merely disguised in the flesh. Thus, the integrity of John's portrayal of the human character and story of Jesus is essential to his christological project, and a sensitive reading will show that he does not dissolve the literal in the symbolic. The "metahistorical" aspect of John's story—Jesus comes from God and returns to God—does not deprive the historical of its reality, but interprets its meaning.

25. Luke Timothy Johnson, *Living Jesus: Learning the Heart of the Gospel* (San Francisco: HarperSanFrancisco, 1999), 183.

26. Rudolf Bultmann, *Theology of the New Testament*, trans. Kendrick Grobel (London: SCM, 1955), 2:66.

John is, however, as I have repeatedly stressed, very selective. Only by reducing the "literal" story to key moments and indispensable sequences—albeit told in relatively lavish detail—has John allowed himself space to expound the "symbolic" meaning of it all. Yet, if we take John's Christology seriously as exposition precisely of the "symbolic" meaning of it all, then there is no reason why we should not include the more plentiful stories that the Synoptics tell in this "all." In this way, which has been the predominant way the church has read the Gospels in the past, we may develop the complementarity of the Synoptics and John that I proposed above into a more comprehensive interrelatedness. The Synoptic abundance of "literal" human particularity will prevent us from taking the Johannine "symbolism" in a docetic direction (a danger not unknown in the tradition), while the incarnational-revelatory Christology of John provides the most all-encompassing theological framework for reading Jesus's story, in all the Gospels, as the story of God with us. (Compare Calvin's comment in the introduction to his commentary on John: "I am accustomed to say this Gospel is a key to open the door to the understanding of the others. For whoever grasps the power of Christ as it is here graphically displayed, will afterwards read with advantage what the others relate about the manifested Redeemer.")[27]

---

27. John Calvin, *The Gospel according to St. John 1–10*, trans. Thomas H. L. Parker (Grand Rapids: Eerdmans; Carlisle: Paternoster, 1995), 6.

Bibliography

Anderson, Paul N. *The Christology of the Fourth Gospel: Its Unity and Diversity in the Light of John 6*. WUNT 2/78. Tübingen: Mohr Siebeck, 1996. Repr., Valley Forge, PA: Trinity, 1997.

Applebaum, Shimon. *Judaea in Hellenistic and Roman Times: Historical and Archaeological Essays*. SJLA 40. Leiden: Brill, 1989.

Appold, Mark L. *The Oneness Motif in the Fourth Gospel: Motif Analysis and Exegetical Probe into the Theology of John*. WUNT 2/1. Tübingen: Mohr Siebeck, 1976.

Ashby, Godfrey W. "Body and Blood in John 6:41–65." *Neot* 36 (2002): 57–61.

Ashton, John. *Understanding the Fourth Gospel*. Oxford: Clarendon, 1991.

Aune, David E. "Dualism in the Fourth Gospel and the Dead Sea Scrolls: A Reassessment of the Problem." Pages 281–303 in *Neotestamentica et Philonica: Studies in Honor of Peder Borgen*. Edited by David E. Aune, Torrey Seland, and Jarl Henning Ulrichsen. NovTSup 106. Leiden: Brill, 2003.

Barnard, Leslie William. *St. Justin Martyr: The First and Second Apologies*. ACW 56. New York: Paulist Press, 1997.

Barnes, Julian. *Levels of Life*. 2nd ed. London: Vintage, 2014.

Barrett, C. Kingsley. *Essays on John*. London: SPCK, 1982.

———. *The Gospel according to St. John: An Introduction with Commentary and Notes on the Greek Text*. 2nd ed. Philadelphia: Westminster, 1978.

Barton, Stephen C. "The Unity of Humankind as a Theme in Biblical Theology." Pages 233–58 in *Out of Egypt: Biblical Theology and Biblical*

Interpretation. Edited by Craig Bartholomew et al. SHS 5. Milton Keynes: Paternoster; Grand Rapids: Zondervan, 2004.

Bauckham, Richard, ed. *The Gospels for All Christians: Rethinking the Gospel Audiences*. Grand Rapids: Eerdmans; Edinburgh: T&T Clark, 1997.

———. *Jesus and the Eyewitnesses: The Gospels as Eyewitness Testimony*. Grand Rapids: Eerdmans, 2006.

———. *Jesus and the God of Israel:* God Crucified *and Other Studies on the New Testament's Christology of Divine Identity*. Grand Rapids: Eerdmans, 2008.

———. "Qumran and the Gospel of John: Is There a Connection?" Pages 267–79 in *The Scrolls and the Scriptures: Qumran Fifty Years After*. Edited by Stanley E. Porter and Craig E. Evans. JSPSup 26. Sheffield: Sheffield Academic Press, 1997.

———. "The Qumran Community and the Gospel of John." Pages 105–15 in *The Dead Sea Scrolls Fifty Years after Their Discovery: Proceedings of the Jerusalem Congress, July 20–25, 1997*. Edited by Lawrence H. Schiffman, Emmanuel Tov, and James C. VanderKam. Jerusalem: Israel Exploration Society, 2000.

———. *The Testimony of the Beloved Disciple: Narrative, History, and Theology in the Gospel of John*. Grand Rapids: Baker Academic, 2007.

Bauckham, Richard, and Carl Mosser, eds. *The Gospel of John and Christian Theology*. Grand Rapids: Eerdmans, 2008.

Beasley-Murray, George R. *John*. WBC 36. Waco: Word, 1987.

Belleville, Linda. "'Born of Water and Spirit': John 3:5." *TJ* 1 (1980): 125–41.

Bennema, Cornelis. *Encountering Jesus: Character Studies in the Gospel of John*. Milton Keynes: Paternoster, 2009.

———. "A Theory of Character in the Fourth Gospel with Reference to Ancient and Modern Literature." *BibInt* 17 (2009): 375–421.

Bernard, John Henry. *A Critical and Exegetical Commentary on the Gospel according to St. John*. ICC. Edinburgh: T&T Clark, 1928.

Boismard, Marie-Émile. *Du baptême à Cana (Jean, 1,19—2,11)*. LD 18. Paris: Cerf, 1956.

Borgen, Peder. *Bread from Heaven: An Exegetical Study of the Concept of Manna in the Gospel of John and the Writings of Philo*. NovTSup 10. Leiden: Brill, 1965.

Brodie, Thomas L. *The Gospel according to John: A Literary and Theological Commentary*. New York: Oxford University Press, 1993.

Broer, Ingo. "Knowledge of Palestine in the Fourth Gospel?" Pages 83–90 in *Jesus in Johannine Tradition*. Edited by Robert T. Fortna and Tom Thatcher. Louisville: Westminster John Knox, 2001.

Brown, Raymond E. *The Churches the Apostles Left Behind*. London: Chapman, 1984.

———. *The Epistles of John*. AB 30. Garden City, NY: Doubleday, 1982.

———. *The Gospel according to John*. 2 vols. AB 29, 29A. New York: Doubleday, 1966.

———. *An Introduction to the Gospel of John*. Edited by Francis J. Moloney. New York: Doubleday, 2003.

———. "John, Gospel and Letters of." Pages 414–17 in vol. 1 of *Encyclopedia of the Dead Sea Scrolls*. Edited by Lawrence H. Schiffman and James C. VanderKam. Oxford: Oxford University Press, 2000.

———. *New Testament Essays*. New York: Paulist Press, 1965.

———. "The Qumran Scrolls and the Johannine Gospel and Epistles." *CBQ* 17 (1955): 403–19, 559–74.

Bultmann, Rudolf. *The Gospel of John*. Translated by George R. Beasley-Murray. Oxford: Blackwell, 1971.

———. *Theology of the New Testament*. 2 vols. Translated by Kendrick Grobel. London: SCM, 1955.

Burge, Gary M. *The Anointed Community: The Holy Spirit in the Johannine Tradition*. Grand Rapids: Eerdmans, 1987.

Burnett, Gary W. *Paul and the Salvation of the Individual*. BIS 57. Leiden: Brill, 2001.

Caird, George B. *New Testament Theology*. Edited by L. D. Hurst. Oxford: Clarendon, 1994.

Calvin, John. *The Gospel according to St. John 1–10*. Translated by Thomas H. L. Parker. Grand Rapids: Eerdmans, 1961.

Carson, Donald A. *The Gospel according to John*. Leicester: Inter-Varsity; Grand Rapids: Eerdmans, 1991.

Casey, Maurice. *Is John's Gospel True?* London: Routledge, 1996.

Charlesworth, James H. (ed.). *John and Qumran*. London: Geoffrey Chapman, 1972.

Cohen, Anthony P. *Self Consciousness: An Alternative Anthropology of Identity*. London: Routledge, 1994.

Collins, Raymond F. *These Things Have Been Written: Studies on the Fourth Gospel*. LTPM 2. Louvain: Peeters; Grand Rapids: Eerdmans, 1990.

Coloe, Mary L. *God Dwells with Us: Temple Symbolism in the Fourth Gospel*. Collegeville, MN: Liturgical Press, 2001.

Coloe, Mary L., and Tom Thatcher, eds. *John, Qumran, and the Dead Sea Scrolls: Sixty Years of Discovery and Debate*. SBLEJL 32. Atlanta: Society of Biblical Literature, 2011.

Crossan, John Dominic, and Jonathan L. Reed. *Excavating Jesus: Beneath the Stones, behind the Texts*. London: SPCK 2001.

Cullmann, Oscar. *Early Christian Worship*. Translated by A. Stewart Todd and James B. Torrance. SBT 10. London: SCM, 1953.

Culpepper, R. Alan. *Anatomy of the Fourth Gospel: A Study in Literary Design*. Philadelphia: Fortress, 1983.

Dennis, John A. *Jesus' Death and the Gathering of True Israel: The Johannine Appropriation of Restoration Theology in the Light of John 11.47–52*. WUNT 2/217. Tübingen: Mohr Siebeck, 2006.

Dodd, Charles H. *The Interpretation of the Fourth Gospel*. Cambridge: Cambridge University Press, 1953.

Downing, F. Gerald. *Making Sense in (and of) the First Christian Century*. JSNTSup 197. Sheffield: Sheffield Academic Press, 2000.

Duke, Paul D. *Irony in the Fourth Gospel*. Atlanta: John Knox, 1985.

Dunn, James D. G. *Baptism in the Holy Spirit: A Re-examination of the New Testament Teaching on the Gift of the Spirit in Relation to Pentecostalism Today*. SBT 2/15. London: SCM, 1970.

———. *Jesus and the Spirit: A Study of the Religious and Charismatic Experience of the First Christians as Reflected in the New Testament*. London: SCM, 1975.

———. "John VI—A Eucharistic Discourse?" *NTS* 17 (1970–71): 328–38.

Du Rand, Jan A. "The Characterization of Jesus as Depicted in the Narrative of the Fourth Gospel." *Neot* 19 (1985): 18–36.

Earl, Douglas S. "'(Bethany) beyond the Jordan': The Significance of a Johannine Motif." *NTS* 55 (2009): 279–94.

Edwards, Ruth. *Discovering John*. London: SPCK, 1993.

Elliott, Mark Adam. *The Survivors of Israel: A Reconsideration of the Theology of Pre-Christian Judaism*. Grand Rapids: Eerdmans, 2000.

Elowsky, Joel C., ed. *John 1–10*. ACCS 4a. Downers Grove, IL: InterVarsity, 2007.

Ferguson, Everett. *Baptism in the Early Church: History, Theology, and Liturgy in the First Five Centuries*. Grand Rapids: Eerdmans, 2009.

Ferreira, Johan. *Johannine Ecclesiology*. JSNTSup 160. Sheffield: Sheffield Academic Press, 1998.

Feuillet, André. *Johannine Studies*. Translated by Thomas E. Crane. Staten Island, NY: Alba House, 1964.

Fitzmyer, Joseph A. "Qumran Literature and the Johannine Writings." Pages 117–33 in *Life in Abundance: Studies in Tribute to Raymond E. Brown*. Edited by John R. Donahue. Collegeville, MN: Liturgical Press, 2005.

Forestell, J. Terence. *The Word of the Cross: Salvation as Revelation in the Fourth Gospel*. AnBib 57. Rome: Biblical Institute Press, 1974.

Fowler, Russell. "Born of Water and the Spirit (John 3[5])." *ExpTim* 82 (1971): 159.

Franzmann, M., and M. Klinger. "The Call Stories of John 1 and John 21." *SVTQ* 36 (1992): 7–15.

Frey, Jörg. "Different Patterns of Dualistic Thought in the Qumran Library: Reflections on Their Background and History." Pages 275–335 in *Legal Texts and Legal Issues: Proceedings of the Second Meeting of the International Organization for Qumran Studies, Cambridge, 1995; Published in Honour of Joseph M. Baumgarten*. Edited by Moshe Bernstein, Florentino García Martínez, and John Kampen. STDJ 23. Leiden: Brill, 1997.

———. "Recent Perspectives on Johannine Dualism and Its Background." Pages 127–57 in *Text, Thought, and Practice in Qumran and Early Christianity: Proceedings of the Ninth International Symposium of the Orion Center for the Study of the Dead Sea Scrolls and Associated Literature*. Edited by Ruth A. Clements and Daniel R. Schwartz. STDJ 84. Leiden: Brill, 2009.

Frey, Jörg, and Udo Schnelle, eds. *Kontexte des Johannesevangeliums: Das vierte Evangelium in religions- und traditionsgeschichtlicher Perspektive*. WUNT 175. Tübingen: Mohr Siebeck, 2004.

Gammie, John G. "Spatial and Ethical Dualism in Jewish Wisdom and Apocalyptic Literature." *JBL* 93 (1974): 356–85.

Gathercole, Simon J. *The Preexistent Son: Recovering the Christologies of Matthew, Mark, and Luke*. Grand Rapids: Eerdmans, 2006.

Gergen, Kenneth J. *Relational Being: Beyond Self and Community*. Oxford: Oxford University Press, 2009.

Grenz, Stanley J. *The Social God and the Relational Self: A Trinitarian Theology of the* Imago Dei. Louisville: Westminster John Knox, 2001.

Grundmann, Walter. "The Decision of the Supreme Court to Put Jesus to Death (John 11:47–57) in Its Context: Tradition and Redaction in the Gospel of John." Pages 295–318 in *Jesus and the Politics of His Day*. Edited by Ernst Bammel and Charles F. D. Moule. Cambridge: Cambridge University Press, 1984.

Guilding, Aileen. *The Fourth Gospel and Jewish Worship: A Study of the Relations of St. John's Gospel to the Ancient Jewish Lectionary System*. Oxford: Clarendon, 1960.

Hanson, Anthony Tyrrell. *The Prophetic Gospel: A Study of John and the Old Testament*. Edinburgh: T&T Clark, 1991.

Hill, Charles E. *The Johannine Corpus in the Early Church*. Oxford: Oxford University Press, 2004.

Hill, David. *Greek Words and Hebrew Meanings: Studies in the Semantics of Soteriological Terms*. SNTSMS 5. Cambridge: Cambridge University Press, 1967.

Hoek, Annewies van den, and Claude Mondésert. *Clément d'Alexandrie: Les Stromates; Stromate IV*. SC 463. Paris: Cerf, 2001.

Holmes, Stephen R. *The Quest for the Trinity: The Doctrine of God in Scripture, History, and Modernity*. Downers Grove, IL: IVP Academic, 2012.

Hoskyns, Edwyn Clement. *The Fourth Gospel*. Edited by Francis Noel Davy. London: Faber & Faber, 1947.

Hurtado, Larry W. "Summing Up and Concluding Observations." Pages 159–77 in *Who Is This Son of Man? Latest Scholarship on a Puzzling Expression of the Historical Jesus*. Edited by Larry W. Hurtado and Paul L. Owen. LNTS 390. London: T&T Clark, 2011.

Instone-Brewer, David. *Prayer and Agriculture*. Vol. 1 of *Traditions of the Rabbis from the Era of the New Testament*. Grand Rapids: Eerdmans, 2004.

Jensen, Matthew D. *Affirming the Resurrection of the Incarnate Christ: A Reading of 1 John*. SNTSMS 153. Cambridge: Cambridge University Press, 2012.

Jeremias, Joachim. *The Eucharistic Words of Jesus*. Translated by Norman Perrin. NTL. London: SCM, 1966.

Johnson, Luke Timothy. *Living Jesus: Learning the Heart of the Gospel*. San Francisco: HarperSanFrancisco, 1999.

———. *The Real Jesus: The Misguided Quest for the Historical Jesus and the Truth of the Traditional Gospels*. San Francisco: HarperSanFrancisco, 1996.

Jones, Larry Paul. *The Symbol of Water in the Gospel of John*. JSNTSup 145. Sheffield: Sheffield Academic Press, 1997.

Käsemann, Ernst. *The Testament of Jesus: A Study of the Gospel of John in the Light of Chapter 17*. Translated by Gerhard Krodel. London: SCM, 1968.

Keener, Craig S. *The Gospel of John: A Commentary*. 2 vols. Peabody, MA: Hendrickson, 2003.

Kilby, Karen. "Perichoresis and Projection: Problems with Social Doctrines of the Trinity." *NBf* 81 (2000): 432–45.

Klink, Edward W. *The Sheep of the Fold: The Audience and Origin of the Gospel of John*. SNTSMS 141. Cambridge: Cambridge University Press, 2007.

Knight, George W. *The Pastoral Epistles: A Commentary on the Greek Text*. NIGTC. Grand Rapids: Eerdmans, 1992.

Koch, Klaus. "History as a Battlefield of Two Antagonistic Powers in the Apocalypse of Weeks and in the Rule of the Community." Pages 185–99 in *Enoch and Qumran Origins: New Light on a Forgotten Connection*. Edited by Gabriele Boccaccini. Grand Rapids: Eerdmans, 2005.

Koester, Craig R. "John Six and the Lord's Supper." *LQ* 40 (1990): 418–37.

———. *Symbolism in the Fourth Gospel: Meaning, Mystery, Community*. Minneapolis: Fortress, 1995.

———. "Topography and Theology in the Gospel of John." Pages 436–45 in *Fortunate the Eyes That See: Essays in Honor of David Noel Freedman in Celebration of His Seventieth Birthday*. Edited by Astrid B. Beck et al. Grand Rapids: Eerdmans, 1995.

Kooij, Arie van der. "The Yaḥad—What's in a Name?" *DSD* 18 (2011): 109–28.

Köstenberger, Andreas J. *John*. BECNT. Grand Rapids: Baker Academic, 2004.

Köstenberger, Andreas J., and Scott R. Swain. *Father, Son, and Spirit: The Trinity and John's Gospel*. NSBT 24. Nottingham: Apollos; Downers Grove, IL: InterVarsity, 2008.

Kruse, Colin G. *The Gospel according to John*. TNTC. Leicester: Inter-Varsity, 2003.

Kysar, Robert. *John, the Maverick Gospel*. Atlanta: John Knox, 1976.

La Potterie, Ignace de, and Stanislaus Lyonnet. *The Christian Lives by the Spirit*. Translated by John Morriss. New York: Alba House, 1971.

Larsson, Tord. *God in the Fourth Gospel: A Hermeneutical Study of the History of Interpretations*. ConBNT 35. Stockholm: Almqvist & Wiksell, 2001.

Lee, Dorothy A. *Flesh and Glory: Symbol, Gender, and Theology in the Gospel of John*. New York: Crossroad, 2002.

———. *The Symbolic Narratives of the Fourth Gospel: The Interplay of Form and Meaning*. JSNTSup 95. Sheffield: Sheffield Academic Press, 1994.

Léon-Dufour, Xavier. "Le mystère du pain de vie (*Jean VI*)." *RSR* 46 (1958): 481–523.

———. *Sharing the Eucharistic Bread: The Witness of the New Testament.* Translated by Matthew J. O'Connell. New York: Paulist Press, 1987.

———. "Towards a Symbolic Reading of the Fourth Gospel." *NTS* 27 (1981): 439–56.

Lieu, Judith M. "The Mother of the Son in the Fourth Gospel." *JBL* 117 (1998): 61–77.

———. "Scripture and the Feminine in John." Pages 225–40 in *A Feminist Companion to the Hebrew Bible in the New Testament.* Edited by Athalya Brenner. FCB 10. Sheffield: Sheffield Academic Press, 1996.

Lincoln, Andrew T. *The Gospel according to Saint John.* BNTC. Peabody, MA: Hendrickson; London: Continuum, 2005.

———. *Truth on Trial: The Lawsuit Motif in the Fourth Gospel.* Peabody, MA: Hendrickson, 2000.

Lindars, Barnabas. *Essays on John.* Edited by Christopher M. Tuckett. SNTA 17. Louvain: Leuven University Press; Peeters, 1992.

———. *The Gospel of John.* NCB. London: Marshall, Morgan & Scott, 1972.

Longenecker, Bruce W. *Art at the Boundaries: The Art and Theology of New Testament Chain-Link Transitions.* Waco: Baylor University Press, 2005.

Malina, Bruce J. *The New Testament World: Insights from Cultural Anthropology.* 2nd ed. Louisville: Westminster John Knox, 1993.

———. *The Social World of Jesus and the Gospels.* London: Routledge, 1996.

Malina, Bruce J., and Richard L. Rohrbaugh. *Social-Science Commentary on the Gospel of John.* Minneapolis: Fortress, 1998.

Manns, Frédéric. *L'Évangile de Jean à la lumière du Judaïsme.* ASBF 33. Jerusalem: Franciscan Printing Press, 1991.

———. "Les mots à double entente: Antécédents et fonction herméneutique d'un procédé johannique." *Liber Annuus* 38 (1988): 39–57.

Marshall, I. Howard, and Philip H. Towner. *A Critical and Exegetical Commentary on the Pastoral Epistles.* ICC. Edinburgh: T&T Clark, 1999.

Martyn, J. Louis. *History and Theology in the Fourth Gospel.* Rev. ed. Nashville: Abingdon, 1979.

McCollough, C. Thomas. "City and Village in Lower Galilee: The Import of the Archeological Excavations at Sepphoris and Khirbet Qana (Cana) for Framing the Economic Context of Jesus." Pages 49–74 in *The Galilean*

Economy in the Time of Jesus. Edited by David A. Fiensy and Ralph K. Hawkins. SBLECL 11. Atlanta: Society of Biblical Literature, 2013.

McHugh, John F. *A Critical and Exegetical Commentary on John 1–4.* ICC. London: T&T Clark, 2009.

McNamara, Martin. *Targum and Testament: Aramaic Paraphrases of the Hebrew Bible: A Light on the New Testament.* Shannon: Irish University Press, 1968.

Mealand, David L. "The Language of Mystical Union in the Johannine Writings." *DRev* 95 (1977): 19–34.

Menken, Maarten J. J. "John 6,51c–58: Eucharist or Christology?" *Bib* 74 (1993): 1–26.

———. "The Translation of Psalm 41:10 in John 13:18." *JSNT* 40 (1990): 61–79.

Meyers, Eric M. "From Myth to Apocalyptic: Dualism in the Hebrew Bible." Pages 92–106 in *Light against Darkness: Dualism in Ancient Mediterranean Religion and the Contemporary World.* Edited by Armin Lange et al. JAJS 2. Göttingen: Vandenhoeck & Ruprecht, 2011.

Michaels, J. Ramsey. *The Gospel of John.* NICNT. Grand Rapids: Eerdmans, 2010.

Moloney, Francis J. *Belief in the Word: Reading the Fourth Gospel, John 1–4.* Minneapolis: Fortress, 1993.

———. *The Gospel of John.* SP 4. Collegeville, MN: Liturgical Press, 1998.

———. *"A Hard Saying": The Gospel and Culture.* Collegeville, MN: Liturgical Press, 2001.

———. "A Sacramental Reading of John 13:1–38." *CBQ* 53 (1991): 237–56.

———. *Signs and Shadows: Reading John 5–12.* Minneapolis: Fortress, 1996.

Moltmann, Jürgen. *The Trinity and the Kingdom of God: The Doctrine of God.* Translated by Margaret Kohl. London: SCM, 1981.

Moreau, Jean-Claude. "Rabbouni." *RB* 199 (2012): 403–20.

Morgen, Michèle. "La promesse de Jésus à Nathanaël (Jn 1,51) éclairée par la haggadah de Jacob-Israël." *RevScRel* 67 (1993): 3–21.

Morris, Leon. *The Gospel according to John.* NICNT. Grand Rapids: Eerdmans, 1971.

Moule, Charles F. D. "The Individualism of the Fourth Gospel." *NovT* 5 (1962): 171–90. Reprinted in Charles F. D. Moule, *Essays in New Testament Interpretation* (Cambridge: Cambridge University Press, 1982), 91–109; and in *The Composition of John's Gospel: Selected Studies from*

Novum Testamentum, ed. David E. Orton, BRBS 2 (Leiden: Brill, 1999), 21–40.

———. "A Neglected Factor in the Interpretation of Johannine Eschatology." Pages 155–60 in *Studies in John: Presented to Professor Dr. J. N. Sevenster on the Occasion of His Seventieth Birthday*. Edited by M. C. Rientsma. NovTSup 24. Leiden: Brill, 1970.

Murphy-O'Connor, Jerome. "Place-Names in the Fourth Gospel (II): Bethany (John 1:28; 11:18) and Ephraim (John 11:54)." *RB* 120 (2013): 85–98.

Neyrey, Jerome H. *An Ideology of Revolt: John's Christology in Social-Science Perspective*. Philadelphia: Fortress, 1988.

———. "The Jacob Allusions in John 1:51." *CBQ* 44 (1982): 586–605.

Niewalda, Paul. *Sakramentssymbolik im Johannesevangelium? Eine exegetisch-historische Studie*. Limburg: Lahn-Verlag, 1958.

O'Day, Gail R. *Revelation in the Fourth Gospel: Narrative Mode and Theological Claim*. Philadelphia: Fortress, 1986.

Odeberg, Hugo. *The Fourth Gospel Interpreted in Its Relation to Contemporaneous Religious Currents in Palestine and the Hellenistic-Oriental World*. Amsterdam: Grüner, 1968.

O'Grady, John F. "Individualism and the Johannine Ecclesiology." *BTB* 5 (1975): 235–45.

Orchard, Helen C. *Courting Betrayal: Jesus as Victim in the Gospel of John*. JSNTSup 161. Sheffield: Sheffield Academic Press, 1998.

Pamment, Margaret. "John 3:5: 'Unless One Is Born of Water and the Spirit, He Cannot Enter the Kingdom of God.'" *NovT* 25 (1983): 189–90.

Paschal, R. Wade. "Sacramental Symbolism and Physical Imagery in the Gospel of John." *TynBul* 32 (1981): 151–76.

Petochowski, Jakob J., and Michael Brocke, eds. *The Lord's Prayer and Jewish Liturgy*. London: Burns & Oates, 1978.

Piper, Ronald A. "Satan, Demons and the Absence of Exorcisms in the Fourth Gospel." Pages 253–78 in *Christology, Controversy, and Community: New Testament Essays in Honour of David R. Catchpole*. Edited by David G. Horrell and Christopher M. Tuckett. NovTSup 99. Leiden: Brill, 2000.

Pollard, T. E. *Johannine Christology and the Early Church*. SNTSMS 13. Cambridge: Cambridge University Press, 1970.

Quinn, Jerome D. *The Letter to Titus*. AB 35. New York: Doubleday, 1990.

Rapport, Nigel. *Transcendent Individual: Towards a Literary and Liberal Anthropology*. London: Routledge, 1997.

Reed, Jonathan L. *Archaeology and the Galilean Jesus: A Re-examination of the Evidence.* Harrisburg, PA: Trinity, 2000.

Rensberger, David. *Overcoming the World: Politics and Community in the Gospel of John.* London: SPCK, 1989.

Ridderbos, Herman N. *The Gospel according to John: A Theological Commentary.* Translated by John Vriend. Grand Rapids: Eerdmans, 1997.

Riesner, Rainer. *Bethanien jenseits des Jordan: Topographie und Theologie in Johannes-Evangelium.* SBAZ 12. Giessen: Brunnen, 2002.

———. "Bethany beyond the Jordan (John 1:28): Topography, Theology and History in the Fourth Gospel." *TynBul* 38 (1987): 29–64.

Roberge, Michel. "Le discours sur le pain de vie (Jean 6,22–59): Problèmes d'interprétation." *LTP* 38 (1982): 265–99.

Rowland, Christopher. "John 1.51, Jewish Apocalyptic and Targumic Tradition." *NTS* 30 (1984): 498–507.

Schnackenburg, Rudolf. *The Gospel according to St. John.* Vol. 1. Translated by Kevin Smyth. London: Burns & Oates, 1968.

Schneiders, Sandra M. "Born Anew." *ThTo* 44 (1987): 189–96.

Schnelle, Udo. *Antidocetic Christology in the Gospel of John: An Investigation of the Place of the Fourth Gospel in the Johannine School.* Translated by Linda M. Maloney. Minneapolis: Fortress, 1992.

Schuchard, Bruce G. *1–3 John.* ConC. Saint Louis: Concordia, 2012.

Segovia, Fernando F. "Inclusion and Exclusion in John 17: An Intercultural Reading." Pages 183–209 in *Literary and Social Readings of the Fourth Gospel*, vol. 2 of *What Is John?* Edited by Fernando F. Segovia. SBLSymS 7. Atlanta: Scholars Press, 1998.

Shanahan, Daniel. *Toward a Genealogy of Individualism.* Amherst: University of Massachusetts Press, 1992.

Smith, D. Moody. *The Fourth Gospel in Four Dimensions: Judaism and Jesus, the Gospels and Scripture.* Columbia: University of South Carolina Press, 2008.

———. *Johannine Christianity: Essays on Its Setting, Sources, and Theology.* Edinburgh: T&T Clark, 1984.

———. *John.* ANTC. Nashville: Abingdon, 1999.

———. *The Theology of the Gospel of John.* NTT. Cambridge: Cambridge University Press, 1995.

Snodgrass, Klyne R. "That Which Is Born from ΠΝΕΥΜΑ Is ΠΝΕΥΜΑ: Rebirth and Spirit in John 3:5–6." Pages 181–205 in *Perspectives on John: Method and Interpretation in the Fourth Gospel.* Edited by Robert B. Sloan and Mikeal C. Parsons. Lewiston, NY: Edwin Mellen, 1993.

Spicq, Ceslas. "ΤΡΩΓΕΙΝ: Est-il synonyme de ΦΑΓΕΙΝ et d'ΕΣΘΙΕΙΝ dans le Nouveau Testament?" *NTS* 26 (1979–80): 414–19.

Spriggs, D. G. "Meaning of 'Water' in John 3⁵." *ExpTim* 85 (1974): 149–50.

Stuckenbruck, Loren T. "The Interiorization of Dualism within the Human Being in Second Temple Judaism: The Treatise of the Two Spirits (1QS III:13–IV:26) in Its Tradition-Historical Context." Pages 145–68 in *Light against Darkness: Dualism in Ancient Mediterranean Religion and the Contemporary World.* Edited by Armin Lange et al. JAJS 2. Göttingen: Vandenhoeck & Ruprecht, 2011.

Talbert, Charles H. *Reading John: A Literary and Theological Commentary on the Fourth Gospel and the Johannine Epistles.* London: SPCK, 1992.

Teeple, Howard M. "Qumran and the Origin of the Fourth Gospel." *NovT* 4 (1960–61): 6–25. Reprinted in *The Composition of John's Gospel: Selected Studies from Novum Testamentum,* ed. David E. Orton, BRBS 2 (Leiden: Brill, 1999), 1–20.

Thatcher, Tom. *Greater than Caesar: Christology and Empire in the Fourth Gospel.* Minneapolis: Fortress, 2009.

———. *The Riddles of Jesus in John: A Study in Tradition and Folklore.* SBLMS 53. Atlanta: Society of Biblical Literature, 2000.

Thompson, Marianne Meye. *The Humanity of Jesus in the Fourth Gospel.* Philadelphia: Fortress, 1988.

Tilborg, Sjef van. *Imaginative Love in John.* BIS 2. Leiden: Brill, 1993.

Tsutserov, Alexander. *Glory, Grace, and Truth: Ratification of the Sinaitic Covenant according to the Gospel of John.* Eugene, OR: Pickwick, 2009.

Twelftree, Graham H. "Exorcisms in the Fourth Gospel and the Synoptics." Pages 135–43 in *Jesus in Johannine Tradition.* Edited by Robert T. Fortna and Tom Thatcher. Louisville: Westminster John Knox, 2001.

Van der Watt, Jan G. "Knowledge of Earthly Things? The Use of ἐπίγειος in John 3:12." *Neot* 43 (2009): 289–310.

Vawter, Bruce. "The Johannine Sacramentary." *TS* 17 (1956): 151–66.

Volf, Miroslav. *After Our Likeness: The Church as the Image of the Trinity.* Grand Rapids: Eerdmans, 1998.

Von Wahlde, Urban C. *The Gospel and Letters of John.* ECC. Grand Rapids: Eerdmans, 2010.

Waaler, Erik. *The Shema and The First Commandment in First Corinthians: An Intertextual Approach to Paul's Re-reading of Deuteronomy.* WUNT 2/253. Tübingen: Mohr Siebeck, 2008.

Webster, Jane S. *Ingesting Jesus: Eating and Drinking in the Gospel of John.* SBLAB 6. Atlanta: Society of Biblical Literature, 2003.

Westcott, Brooke Foss. *The Gospel according to St. John.* London: John Murray, 1889.

Wiles, Maurice. *The Spiritual Gospel: The Interpretation of the Fourth Gospel in the Early Church.* Cambridge: Cambridge University Press, 1960.

Williams, Catrin H. *I Am He: The Interpretation of 'Anî Hû' in Jewish and Early Christian Literature.* WUNT 2/113. Tübingen: Mohr Siebeck, 2000.

Witherington, Ben, III. *John's Wisdom: A Commentary on the Fourth Gospel.* Louisville: Westminster John Knox, 1995.

———. *A Socio-Rhetorical Commentary on Titus, 1–2 Timothy and 1–3 John.* Vol. 1 of *Letters and Homilies for Hellenized Christians.* Downers Grove, IL: InterVarsity, 2006.

———. "The Waters of Birth: John 3:5 and 1 John 5:6–8." *NTS* 35 (1989): 155–60.

Xeravits, Géza G., ed. *Dualism in Qumran.* LSTS 76. London: T&T Clark, 2010.

Index of Scripture and Other Ancient Sources

Index of Modern Authors

Index of Subjects